The
New
Father

—

A Dad's Guide
to the First Year

The
New
Father

—

A Dad's Guide
to the First Year

SECOND EDITION

Armin A. Brott

Abbeville Press · Publishers
New York · London

For Zoë, Talya, and Tirzah, who teach me every day
what fatherhood is all about

EDITORS: Jackie Decter and Susan Costello
DESIGNERS: Celia Fuller and Misha Beletsky
PRODUCTION EDITOR: Amber Reed
COPYEDITOR: Miranda Ottewell
PRODUCTION MANAGER: Louise Kurtz

Second paperback edition
15   14   13   12

Cover photograph by Milton Heiberg. For cartoon credits, see page 316.

Library of Congress Cataloging-in-Publication Data
Brott, Armin A.
    The new father : a dad's guide to the first year / Armin A. Brott.
        p.   cm.
    Includes bibliographical references and index.
    ISBN 978-0-7892-0806-4   ISBN 978-0-7892-0815-6 (pbk.)
    1. Infants.   2. Infants—Care.   3. Father and infant.   I. Title.
HQ774.B777 2004
6498'.122—dc21   04-47489

For bulk and premium sales and for text adoption procedures, write to Customer
Service Manager, Abbeville Press, 137 Varick Street, New York, NY 10013, or
call 1-800-ARTBOOK.

Visit Abbeville Press online at www.abbeville.com.

Contents

Introduction

Nobody really knows how or when it started, but one of the most widespread—and most cherished—myths about child-rearing is that women are naturally more nurturing than men, that they are instinctively better at the parenting thing, and that men are nearly incompetent.

The facts, however, tell a very different story. A significant amount of research has proven that men are inherently just as nurturing and responsive to their children's needs as women. What too many men (and women) don't realize is that to the extent that women are "better" parents, it's simply because they've had more practice. In fact, the single most important factor in determining the depth of long-term father-child relationships is opportunity.

Basically, it comes down to this: "Having children makes you no more a parent than having a piano makes you a pianist," writes author Michael Levine in *Lessons at the Halfway Point*.

Men and women parent differently in a wide variety of ways:

♦ Dads tend to play more with their children than mothers do, and that play tends to be more rough-and-tumble and more unpredictable than mothers'. In other words, dads are more likely than moms to become human jungle gyms.

♦ Dads tend to emphasize independence more than moms and give children more freedom to explore. If a baby is struggling to grab a toy that's just out of reach, mothers are more likely to move the toy closer, while dads are more likely to wait a little longer, seeing whether the baby will be able to get it. Moms are more likely to pick up a toddler who's fallen, while dads are more likely to see whether the child can get up on his own.

♦ Dads tend to use more complex speech patterns than mothers, who tend to simplify what they're saying and slow it down.

♦ Dads tend to think more about how a child will fare in the world as he or she grows; moms tend to think more about the child's emotional development. When reacting to a test score, for example, a dad might be concerned about how the score will affect the child's future plans, while a mom is more likely to be concerned about how the score makes the child feel.

♦ Dads tend to represent the outside world while mothers represent the home. You can see this almost anyplace where parents are out with their babies: dads tend to hold their children face out, while mothers hold them face in.

Please keep in mind here that I'm talking about general *tendencies*. Many moms wrestle with their kids and use big words, and many dads rush to pick up fallen toddlers and hold their babies facing inward. The point is that they parent differently—not better or worse, just differently. And children benefit greatly from having plenty of exposure to both styles.

It shouldn't come as any surprise, then, that fathers have very different needs from mothers when it comes to parenting information and resources. But nearly every book, video, seminar, and magazine article on raising kids has been geared specifically to women and to helping them acquire the skills they need to be better parents. Fathers have been essentially ignored—until now.

How This Book Is Different

Because babies develop so quickly, most books aimed at parents of infants (babies from birth through twelve months) are broken down by month. The same goes here. But while the majority of parenting books focus on how babies develop during this period, the primary focus of *The New Father: A Dad's Guide to the First Year* is on how *fathers* develop. This is an approach that has rarely, if ever, been tried.

Going from *man* to *father* is one of the most dramatic changes you'll ever experience. It'll force you to rethink who you are, what you do, and what it means to be a man. Your relationships—with your partner, your parents, your friends, your coworkers—will change forever as you begin to reevaluate what's important to you and reorder your priorities. Some parts of the man-to-father transition are sudden: one day it's just you and your partner, the next day you've got a baby. Most fathers develop and change along fairly predictable lines, although the progression is different for everyone. But for everyone, it's a gradual, ever-changing process that will last your entire lifetime.

The first year may be the most important one in your development as a father. It's the time when the initial parent-child bonds and the foundation of your lifelong relationship with each other are formed. It's also especially interesting because the growth and development you experience during these first twelve months is kind of a condensed version of what you'll go through over the rest of your life as a parent.

Each of the chapters is divided into several major sections:

What's Going On with the Baby

This section is designed to give you an overview of the four major areas of your baby's development: physical, intellectual, verbal, and emotional/social. A lot of what you're going to experience as a father is directly related to, or in response to, your children. So knowing the basics of your baby's growth will help put your own growth into better perspective. Please remember, however, that all babies develop at different rates, and that the range of "normal" behavior is very wide. If your baby isn't doing the things covered in the predicted month, don't worry. But if he is six months behind, check with your pediatrician.

What You're Going Through

Because the experience of fatherhood has largely been ignored in parenting books, many men think the feelings they have are abnormal. In this section we examine at length what new fathers go through and the ways they grow and develop—emotionally and psychologically—over the course of their fatherhood. You're a lot more normal than you think.

What's Going On with Your Partner

An important part of being a good dad is being a good spouse. For that reason I'm including special sections in the first several chapters that deal with your partner's physical, emotional, and psychological recovery and specific ways you can help.

You and Your Baby

This section gives you all the tools you need to understand and create the deepest, closest possible relationship with your child—even if you have only half an hour a day to spend with her. In this section we cover topics as diverse as play, music, reading, discipline, and temperament.

Family Matters

A number of the chapters feature a "Family Matters" section in which we discuss a variety of issues that will have a major impact not only on you but also on your family as a whole. Topics include dealing with crying, postpartum depression (which men get too!), childproofing, family finances, and finding appropriate child care. Many chapters also include a special "You and Your Partner" section that focuses on specific topics that affect your relationship with the mother of your children.

Why Get Involved?

First, because it's good for your kids, your partner, and even yourself:

 ♦ **For your baby**. Numerous studies have shown that the more involved dads are with their infants, the better they perform on all sorts of intelligence tests. Babies who are deprived of quality time with their fathers in the first year of life often have problems forming stable relationships later in life. Apparently, not having a dad around makes it hard for children to develop the kinds of behavior that other children value. In addition, the more actively involved dads are with their babies, the more physically coordinated they are. They also feel more comfortable around strangers and handle stressful situations better.

 ♦ **For your partner and your marriage**. Division-of-labor issues cause the most marital stress. The more involved you are and the more emotionally supportive, the happier your partner will be and the better she'll perform her parenting duties. Men whose partners are happy in their marriages tend to be happier themselves. And men who are happy in their marriages are generally more involved in their fathering role. It just never ends; and there's no reason why it should.

 ♦ **For you**. As we'll discuss throughout this book, being an involved father will affect you in a number of ways. You'll learn to feel and express emotions you never knew you had. You'll be more empathetic and better able to see things from others' perspective. Plus, dads who are actively involved with their children tend to be healthier, more happily married, and more likely to advance in their careers. It can also change the way you think about yourself. "Fathering often helps men to clarify their values and to set priorities," writes my colleague Ross Parke, who is one of the pioneers in fatherhood research. "It may enhance their self-esteem if they manage its demands and responsibilities well, or alternatively, it may be unsettling and depressing by revealing their limitations and weaknesses. Fathers can learn from their children and be matured by them."

A Note on Terminology

He, She, It

In the not-so-distant past (and the present, too, really) parenting books, in which
the parent is assumed to be the mother, almost always referred to the baby as
"he." While there's an argument to be made that in English the male pronoun is
sort of a generic term, as the father of three girls, I wanted to see at least an
occasional "she," just to let me know that what was being said might actually
apply to my children. But as a writer, I find that phrases like "his or her," "he or
she," and especially "s/he" make for cumbersome reading and awkward sentences. The solution? Since I don't like using "they" as a singular, I decided
simply to alternate between "he" and "she" one chapter at a time. Except in a
few specific cases (circumcision, for example), the terms are interchangeable.

Your Partner in Parenting

In the same way that calling all babies "he" discounts the experience of all the
"shes" out there, calling all mothers "wives" essentially denies the existence
of the many, many other women who have children: girlfriends, lovers, live-in
companions, fiancées, and so on. So, to keep from making any kind of
statement about the importance (or lack of importance, depending on how you
feel) of marriage, I refer to the mother of your child as your partner, as in
The Expectant Father: Facts, Tips, and Advice for Dads-to-Be.

If Some of This Sounds a Little Familiar . . .

If you read *The Expectant Father* (and if you didn't, it's not too late), you may
notice that there's some overlap between the end of that book and the early
part of this book. I assure you that this repetition of material is less the result
of laziness on my part than of the necessity born of having to cover several of
the same important topics in both books.

What This Book Isn't

While there's no doubt that this book is filled with information you can't get
anywhere else, it is not intended to take the place of your pediatrician, financial planner, or lawyer. Naturally, I wouldn't suggest that you do anything I
wouldn't do (or haven't done already). Still, before blindly following my advice,
please check with an appropriate professional.

Congratulations, You're a Dad!

What's Going On with the Baby

Physically

♦ Although most of your newborn's physical capabilities are run by a series of reflexes (see pages 62–65), she does have some control over her tiny body.

♦ She can focus her eyes—for a few seconds, at least—on an object held 8 to 10 inches from her face, and she may be able to move her head from side to side.

♦ She probably won't eat much for the first 24 hours, but after that, she'll want 7 to 8 feedings each day. In between all those meals, she'll try to suck on anything that comes near her mouth.

♦ At 33 breaths and 120 heartbeats/minute, her metabolism is moving about twice as fast as yours.

♦ Her intestines are moving even faster: she'll urinate as many as 18 times and move those brand-new bowels 4 to 7 times every 24 hours.

♦ To help her recover from all that activity, she'll spend 80 to 90 percent of her time asleep, taking as many as 8 naps a day. Some babies, though, sleep as few as 8 hours.

Intellectually

♦ Right from birth, your baby is capable of making a number of intellectual decisions.

♦ If she hears a sound, she can tell whether it's coming from the right, left, straight ahead, or even behind.

- She can distinguish between sweet and sour (preferring sweet, like most of us).
- She also has a highly developed sense of smell. At seven days, she'll be able to tell the difference between a pad sprinkled with her own mother's milk and one from another nursing mother.
- Although her eyes may seem to work independently of each other, she likes looking at things, preferring simple patterns to complex ones and the borders of objects (such as your jaw or hairline) to the inner details (mouth and nose).
- She can't, however, differentiate herself from the other objects in her world. If she grasps your hand, for example, her little brain doesn't know whether she's holding her own hand or yours—or, for that matter, that those things on the ends of her arms even belong to her.

Verbally

- At this point, most of the vocal sounds your baby produces will be cries or animal-like grunts, snorts, and squeaks.

Emotionally/Socially

- Although she's alert and comfortable for only 30 or so minutes out of every 4 hours, your baby is already trying to make contact with you.
- When she hears a voice or other noise—especially your partner's or yours—she'll become quiet and try to focus.
- She's capable of showing excitement and distress, and will probably quiet down when you pick her up.

What's Going On with Your Partner

Physically

- Vaginal discharge (called *lochia*) that will gradually change from bloody to pink to brown to yellow over the next six weeks or so.
- Major discomfort if there is an episiotomy or C-section incision (the pain will disappear over the next six weeks).
- Constipation.
- Breast discomfort—starting on about the third day after the birth (when her breasts become engorged with milk), and as soon as she starts breast-feeding, her nipples will probably be sore for about two weeks.
- Gradual weight loss.

♦ Exhaustion—especially if her labor was long and difficult.
♦ Continued contractions, especially while breast-feeding, but disappearing gradually over the next several days.
♦ Hair loss. Most women stop losing hair while they're pregnant, but when the pregnancy's over, so are all those great-hair days.

Emotionally
♦ Relief that it's finally over.
♦ Excitement, depression, or both (see page 61).
♦ Worry about how she'll perform as a mother, and whether she'll be able to breast-feed. But as her confidence builds over the next few weeks, those worries should disappear.
♦ A deep need to get to know the baby.
♦ Impatience at her lack of mobility.
♦ Decreased sex drive, assuming she had any left before the baby came.

What You're Going Through

Congratulations, You're a Dad!

Well, the pregnancy you and your partner have shared for the past nine months is over, and although it may not have hit you yet, you've got a *family* now, which means all sorts of new responsibilities, pressures, and expectations to live up to. For some new fathers, this seemingly basic epiphany comes early, before they leave the hospital. For others, reality may not sink in for a few days. But whenever it hits, you'll always remember being there for the birth of your baby as one of the great moments of your life.

Right now, though, you may be feeling a little helpless. But if you're like most guys I've spoken with over the years, you'll also experience at least some of the following feelings immediately after the birth:

♦ love
♦ excitement, almost like being intoxicated
♦ the desire to hold and touch and rock and kiss the baby
♦ an even stronger desire to simply stare dumbfounded at the baby
♦ accomplishment, pride, and disbelief
♦ virility and self-worth
♦ a powerful connection to your baby and partner
♦ the need to count toes and fingers to make sure everything's where it's supposed to be
♦ curiosity about whether the baby's features are more like yours or your partner's

Back in the 1970s, Dr. Martin Greenberg did a study of fathers who were present for their child's delivery (which was a lot less common then than it is now). The men in his study had many of the above feelings, and Greenberg coined a term, *engrossment*, to describe "a father's sense of absorption, preoccupation, and interest in his baby."

So what triggers engrossment in men? Exactly the same thing that prompts similar nurturing feelings in women: early contact with their infants. Take a deep breath and do what feels most natural to you—chances are it'll be exactly the right thing.

The truth is that from the instant their children are born, fathers are just as caring, interested, and involved with their infants as mothers are, and they hold, touch, kiss, rock, and coo at their new babies at least as frequently as mothers do.

Comparing How You Imagined the Birth Would Go with How It Went

Let's face it: every expecting couple secretly (or not so secretly) hopes for a pain-free, twenty-minute labor, and nobody ever really plans for a horrible birth experience. Even in childbirth education classes, if the instructor talks at all about the unpleasant things that can happen, she usually refers to them as "contingencies"—a word that makes it seem as though everything is still under control.

If your partner's labor and delivery went according to plan, chances are you're delighted with the way things turned out and you're oohing and ahhing over your baby. But if there were any problems—induced labor, an emergency C-section, a threat to your partner's or your baby's life—your whole impression of the birth process may have changed. It's not unusual in these cases to blame the baby for causing your partner so much physical pain and you so much psychological agony. It can happen easily, without your really being aware of it.

So pay close attention during the first few weeks to how you're feeling about your baby. And if you find yourself being angry or resentful of her, or thinking or saying things—even in jest—such as "All the pain is the baby's fault," or (as I did) "The baby had jammed herself in there sideways and refused to come out," try to remember that no matter how brilliant and talented you think your baby is, she was a completely passive player in the entire process. Giving in to the temptation to blame your baby for *anything* at this point can seriously interfere with your future relationship together.

The Brief "Is This Really My Baby?" Phase

The first thing I did after each of my daughters was born was to count their arms, legs, fingers, and toes. Once all limbs and extremities were accounted for, I quickly looked them over to see whether they had "my" nose or chin.

Later on, I felt a little guilty about that—after all, shouldn't I have been hugging and kissing my daughters instead of giving them a full-body inspection? Maybe, but as it turns out, that's what almost all new dads do within the first few minutes after the birth of their babies: immediately look for physical similarities—as if to prove to themselves that the baby is truly theirs. This happens for a reason: for most of us—regardless of how many prenatal doctor appointments we went to, how many times we heard the baby's heartbeat or saw her squirm around on an ultrasound, and how many times we felt her kick—the baby isn't completely "real" until after the birth, when we finally have a chance to meet each other face to face. "Seeing the infant emerge from his mate's body through vaginal or cesarean birth is a powerful experience for each father," writes researcher Pamela Jordan. "Birth proved that this infant had been the growth within the mother's abdomen."

As it turns out, only one of my daughters has "my" chin, and it's looking like none of them will have to suffer through life with my nose (and the accompanying sinus problems). When the first two were born, I remember being very disappointed that neither of them had the Brott family webbed toes (it isn't all that noticeable, but it helps my swimming immeasurably). But you can't imagine my delight when I found a little webbing between the youngest one's toes.

Now, Wait a Minute— This Isn't What I Was Expecting at All

Babies hardly ever look exactly as you imagined they would before they were born. And being disappointed about a nose, a chin, or even some toes is something you'll get over soon enough—especially when you discover in a few weeks that the baby does have something of yours (they always do).

But what if the baby has a penis or a vagina when you were expecting the opposite? Getting a boy when you expected a girl, or vice versa, can be a real shock. A team of Swedish researchers recently found that fathers are generally more satisfied with their roles when their babies—boys or girls—are the gender they'd hoped for. But if the fantasy doesn't materialize, regret can settle in and interfere with your accepting and loving your baby. In fact, children who aren't the gender their parents wanted have worse relationships with their parents in childhood than preferred-gender kids. That seems to be especially true for kids whose parents had wanted a boy but got a girl.

You and Your Partner

Her Emotional and Physical Recovery After a C-Section

Having an unplanned C-section can trigger a whole host of conflicting emotions in your partner. She, like you, may feel greatly relieved that the pain is over and the baby is safe. At the same time, it's very natural for her to second-guess herself and the decision she made, to start wondering whether there was anything she could have done to avoid the operation, or to believe she's failed because she didn't deliver vaginally. These feelings are especially common when the C-section was performed because labor "failed to progress" (meaning that the cervix wasn't dilating as quickly as the doctors may have thought it should).

If you sense that your partner is experiencing any of these negative

Coping with a Handicapped Child

We all expect a perfect baby, but unfortunately not everyone gets one.
In recent years, technology has made it easier for expectant parents
to avoid having—or at least prepare themselves for—a disabled child.

But prepared or not, parents of disabled children still have plenty
of adjusting to do. For some fathers, having a disabled child is similar to
having a miscarriage—there's a mourning for the child who might have
been. Some feel shock, anger, disbelief, or denial. They may blame themselves and see the child as a kind of punishment, or they may blame
their wife. Others feel ambivalent and may even secretly wish that the
child had died.

Having a handicapped child can be particularly tough for highly
educated or intellectual couples who had great expectations for their
baby, expectations the baby will never be able to live up to. Interestingly,
moms and dads react somewhat differently. Moms tend to be more
concerned about the emotional strain of having to care for the child,
while dads are more concerned with the costs of providing care and with
the baby's ability to be a leader and her potential for academic success.
Having a disabled child can undermine a father's feelings of masculinity
and his confidence in himself.

According to researcher Michael Lamb, couples who are in better
marriages and who have more social support have an easier time coming
to terms with their disabled child. He also found that acceptance of the
disabled child by the father's parents has a big influence on the father's
acceptance of the child. Oddly, boys who are mentally retarded seem
to have a more negative impact on marriages than girls. This may reflect
fathers' and mothers' greater expectations for their sons (and lower ones
for their daughters).

emotions, it's important for you to counter them immediately. She really needs
to know that no one could have done more, or been stronger or braver than
she was; that she didn't give in to the pain too soon; that she tried everything
she could have to jump-start a stalled labor; that another few hours of labor
wouldn't have done anyone any good; and that the decision she made (or at
least agreed to) was the best one—both for the baby and for herself.

Some of these thoughts might seem obvious—so obvious that you might
think they don't need to be said at all. But they do—especially by you. You

were there with her, and you know better than anyone else exactly what she went through. So being comforted and praised by you will mean a lot more to her than hearing the same words from a well-meaning relative.

Having a baby isn't some kind of competition, although some people make it into one. (Hearing a bunch of new moms talk about their labor redefines the concept of macho. "I had a 17-hour labor." "Well, mine was 22 hours—and I did it without any drugs." "Oh, yeah, mine was. . . .")

As far as her physical recovery goes, keep the following in mind while you're at the hospital. We'll talk more about at-home recovery a little later in this chapter.

♦ Your partner's incision will be tender or downright painful for at least several days. Fortunately, she'll undoubtedly be receiving some intravenous pain medication.

♦ The nursing staff will visit quite frequently to make sure that your partner's uterus is getting firm and returning to its proper place, to see whether she's producing enough urine, and to check her bandages.

♦ Your partner will have an IV until her bowels start functioning again (usually one to three days after delivery). After the IV is removed, she'll start on a liquid diet, then add a few soft foods, and finally return to her normal diet.

♦ Your partner will need to get up and move around. Despite the fact that a C-section is major abdominal surgery, less than twenty-four hours after the delivery the nurses will probably encourage—and help—your partner to get out of bed and take a couple of rather painful-looking steps.

♦ Before your partner leaves the hospital, the sutures or staples will be removed. Yes, staples. Until I heard the clink as the doctor dropped them into a jar, I'd just assumed that my wife had been sewn up after her C-section.

You and Your Baby

First Impressions

Before I became a father, I'm quite sure that I believed that my children—even right after their birth—would be stunningly gorgeous. Well, chalk up another victory for the ad execs. The fact is that in most cases, babies look a little strange. If your baby was born vaginally, the trip through the birth canal may have made her look like she just got beat up—cone-headed, mushed, and bruised. She came out covered in white cheesy-looking stuff, her eyes may be swollen and cross-eyed, and her hairy back and shoulders might have you worrying about what'll happen when the moon is full.

Take it easy. Within a few weeks her nose will pop out, and her head will get rounder (C-section babies usually look a little better). The cheesy stuff is called *vernix*, and it's a natural moisturizer that protects the baby's skin while she's in the womb. The puffy eyes are most likely the result of the antibiotic ointment the medical staff put in her eyes after birth to prevent infection; all you need to do is wash them gently with warm water. As soon as her eye muscles get a bit more developed and coordinated, she'll be able to look you straight in the eye. And that fuzz on her back is called lanugo, and it'll fall out pretty soon.

But for a lot of new dads, the biggest shock is the condition of their babies' skin—all those splotches (especially on the neck and the eyelids), strange-looking birth marks, and tiny zits can be a little disconcerting. But before you grab your cell phone and call a dermatologist, take a minute and read about some of the more common, and perfectly normal, conditions:

- **Acne.** These cute little pimples are usually confined to the baby's face and are either the result of your partner's hormones continuing to swim through the baby's system or of her underdeveloped pores. Either way, don't squeeze, poke, pick at, or scrub these pimples. Just wash them with water a few times a day, pat them dry, and they'll go away in a few months.
- **Blisters.** Pictures taken of babies in utero have shown that long before birth, they frequently suck their thumbs—or any other part of their body they can reach. Sometimes they suck so hard, they raise blisters.
- **Jaundice.** If your baby's skin and/or the whites of her eyes seem a little yellow, she may have jaundice. This condition is the result of the baby's liver being unable to adequately process bilirubin, a yellowish by-product of red blood cells. It affects about 25 percent of newborns (and a higher percentage of preemies), appears within the first five days of life, and is usually gone a few days later.
- **Splotches, blotches, and birthmarks.** They can be white, purple, brown, or even yellow with white bumps in the center, and they can appear on the face, legs, arms, and back. In most cases, they'll go away on their own if you just leave them alone. But if you're really worried, check with your pediatrician.
- **Cradle cap** (or, more informally, "cradle crap"). Also called *seborrheic dermatitis*, cradle cap looks like flaky, yellowish, sometimes greasy dandruff. It usually shows up on the head, but it can also work its way into baby's eyebrows. It's not a serious condition and will bother you much more

than it does the baby. It's also not contagious, and regular shampooing with a baby shampoo may help it go away.

Let the Tests Begin

Your baby's first few minutes outside the womb are going to be a time of intense physical and emotional release for you and your partner. She may want to try nursing the baby (although it's going to be mostly for bonding purposes; most newborns aren't hungry for at least the first twelve hours or so), and you'll probably want to stroke her brand-new skin and marvel at her tiny fingernails. But depending on the hospital and the conditions of the birth, your baby's first few minutes could be spent being poked and prodded by doctors and nurses instead of being held and cuddled by you.

One minute after she's born, your baby will be examined to give the medical staff a quick take on her overall condition. (You may have thought that the first test your child would really have to worry about passing would be the SAT, or maybe the test they give kids before they get accepted into exclusive preschools. But oh, no—it starts waaaay sooner than that.) The Apgar test (named after anesthesiologist Virginia Apgar, who first started using the test in the early 1950s) measures your baby's Appearance (skin color), Pulse, Grimace (reflexes), Activity, and Respiration. The nurse or midwife will chart your baby's Apgar score at one minute and five minutes after birth. The score sheet looks something like the chart below.

Keep in mind that the scores are used by the medical staff to help them determine how much intervention (if any) the baby needs. Although the scores have absolutely nothing to do with IQ or future earning power, and college

	2 POINTS
A—Appearance and color	♦ The entire body is pink from head to toe
P—Pulse and heart rate	♦ Above 100 beats per minute
G—Grimace (reflexes)	♦ Loud cry when reflexes are stimulated
A—Activity	♦ Lots of movement of the arms and legs
R—Respiration	♦ Big breaths and lots of crying means lungs are working well

admissions committees never ask for them, they do give new parents a handy (but completely useless) way of comparing their children.

The theoretical maximum score is 10, but anything between 7 and 10 at one minute is a sign of good health. Almost no baby gets a 10 because most of them are born with slightly blue toes and fingers. This means that the baby needs only routine care. A baby who scores 4 to 6 may require some medical intervention such as oxygen or suction to remove mucus from the throat or lungs. A score of less than 4 may indicate the need for resuscitation. However, a low score could be the result of pain medication given to the mother or of the baby being born prematurely. The test will be done again at five minutes after birth to assess the effectiveness of the interventions. If the score is still low, the test will be repeated at five-minute intervals.

At the same time as the tests are going on, your baby will be weighed, measured, given ID and security bracelets, bathed, diapered, footprinted, have some antibiotic ointment applied to her eyes, and be wrapped in a blanket. She may even get her first picture taken. (If your baby was delivered by C-section, or if there were any other complications, she'll have her little lungs suctioned before returning for the rest of the cleanup routine.)

Quality Time Starts Now

A lot of hospitals have surprisingly rigid rules about parent/infant contact. Feeding, for example, may be highly regulated, and the hours you can visit your child may be limited. The nursing staff may also bottle-feed your baby—either sugar water or formula—in the nursery. If this isn't what you want, you'll need to let them know.

1 POINT	0 POINTS
♦ Body is pink but arms and legs may be bluish	♦ Body is all blue, pale, or gray
♦ Fewer than 100 beats per minute	♦ Not detectible
♦ Moderate cry or whimpering when reflexes are stimulated	♦ No response
♦ Some movement of the arms and legs	♦ No movement at all
♦ Slow, weak, or irregular breaths	♦ No breathing

The Placenta

For some reason, before my first child was born I'd never really thought very much about the placenta, which had been my daughter's life-support system for a lot of the pregnancy. But whether you think about it or not, it's still there—and it has to come out.

After the baby is born, your partner will continue to have mild contractions for anywhere from five minutes to about an hour until the placenta is delivered. The strange thing about this stage of the delivery is that neither you nor your partner will probably even know it's happening—you'll be much too involved with your new baby and with each other.

Once the placenta is out, however, you need to decide what to do with it. In this country most people never even see it, and those who do just leave it at the hospital (where it will either be destroyed or, more likely, sold to a cosmetics company—honest). But in many other cultures, the placenta is considered to have a permanent, almost magical bond with the child it nourished in the womb, and disposal is handled with a great deal more reverence. Some have special rituals and believe that if the placenta isn't properly buried, the child—or the parents, or even the entire village—will suffer some terrible consequences.

In rural Peru, for example, the father is required to go to a far-off location and bury the placenta deep enough so that no animals or people will accidentally discover it. Otherwise, it might become "jealous" of the attention paid to the baby and take revenge by causing an epidemic.

An increasing number of hospitals, however, are becoming more flexible. Some don't have nurseries at all, except for babies with serious health problems, and healthy babies are expected to stay in the mother's room for their entire hospital stay. Others still have nurseries but offer unlimited access for the parents.

If your hospital does have a nursery, take advantage of it. You may be tempted to have the baby room with your partner, but believe me, she needs to rest. Ask the nursing staff to bring the baby to your partner at feeding times. You, on the other hand, can spend as much time as you want with the baby.

And while we're on the subject of rest, you may have to get tough with the staff to make sure your partner gets enough. The nurses will tell her that she needs to sleep as much as possible, but if you don't ask them to give her a break, they'll be in every hour or two to check her vital signs.

In some South American Indian cultures, they believe that a child's life can be influenced by objects that are buried with its placenta. Boys' placentas are frequently buried with a shovel or a pick, and girls' are buried with a loom or a hoe. In the Philippines, some bury the placenta with books as a way of ensuring intelligence.

But placentas are not always buried. In ancient Egypt, pharaohs' placentas were wrapped in special containers to keep them from harm. Traditional Vietnamese medicine uses placentas to combat sterility and senility, and in India, touching a placenta is supposed to help a childless woman conceive a healthy baby of her own. And in China, some believe that breast-feeding mothers can improve the quality of their milk by drinking a broth made of boiled placenta.

This sort of placenta usage isn't limited to non-Western cultures. Even today, in France and other countries, placentas are found in a variety of products, including cosmetics and medicines.

Whatever you and your partner decide to do, it's probably best to keep it a secret—at least from the hospital staff. Some states try to regulate what you can do with a placenta and may even prohibit you from taking it home (although if you really want to, you can probably find a sympathetic nurse who will pack it in a Tupperware container for you). My oldest's placenta stayed at the hospital, but we stored the younger ones' in the freezer for a year before burying them and planting trees on top.

Newborn Screenings

If you thought the testing was over with the Apgar test, think again. Even the healthiest-looking babies sometimes have invisible disorders that, if undetected, could stunt their physical and intellectual growth and even cause death. Caught early, most of these disorders can be controlled or even cured. For that reason, your baby will be tested for several conditions before you're allowed to take her home. The March of Dimes suggests that all newborns be screened for nine separate conditions, plus have a hearing exam. Sounds like a lot of tests, but the good news is that almost all of them (except the hearing test, of course) can be done from the same sample, a few drops of blood taken from the baby's heel.

Unfortunately, the screenings your baby gets depend on the state you live in—that could be as few as 3 or as many as 40 (Savebabies.org

has a complete listing of the screenings required by your state at
http://www.savebabies.org/NBS/statenbsprogramreport.htm). If by some chance
your baby was born at home, have these screenings done before she's a week
old. If you want to have more screenings done, you'll probably have to pay for
them yourself. Contact your local March of Dimes chapter for information.
Here are descriptions of the tests the March of Dimes suggests. The first two
are required by all states. Most states do the next two. The rest are done relatively rarely.

DISEASE AND WHAT IT IS	WHAT IT DOES
Phenylketonuria (PKU) ♦ Hereditary: affects the way the baby's body processes certain proteins	Can cause brain damage or mental retardation if not treated
Hypothyroidism ♦ Hereditary: babies don't produce enough thyroid hormone to keep up normal bodily functions	Retards physical and mental growth
Galactosemia ♦ Hereditary: baby doesn't process galactose, a sugar in breast milk	Damages eyes, brain, and liver. Leads to slowed physical and mental development and can cause death
Sickle Cell and Other Blood Diseases ♦ Affects baby's red blood cells	Babies can't fight off common infections. Can cause death
Biotinidase Deficiency ♦ Recycles a B vitamin, biotin	Deficiency of biotinidase causes frequent infections, hearing problems, blood and organ malfunction, mental retardation, and death
Maple Syrup Urine Disease ♦ Inability to process certain amino acids	Vomiting, dehydration, seizures and brain swelling

Hearing Tests

About 1 in 1,000 healthy babies and 2 in 100 in intensive care units have hearing loss. If the loss is caught during newborn screenings, babies can be fitted with hearing aids that can help prevent speech and language problems. If it's not caught early, it might not be evident until age two or three and will be far harder to deal with. The tests are safe, quick, and painless; in fact, babies usually sleep right through them.

HOW COMMON IT IS	TREATMENT
1 in 10,000 to 25,000 births	If PKU is caught within the first 3–4 weeks, a special diet will help the baby grow and develop normally
1 in 4,000 births	Daily thyroid medication can help ensure a normal life
1 in 50,000 births	Galactose-free diet can prevent serious problems
1 in 400 births for African Americans, less for other ethnic groups	Treatment with antibiotics
1 in 70,000 to 125,000 births	Extra biotin
Fewer than one in 100,000 births. However, 1 in about 750 births for Mennonites in Lancaster, Pa.	Special diet containing specific fats, vitamins, and amino acids

DISEASE AND WHAT IT IS	WHAT IT DOES
Homocystinuria ♦ Deficiency of enzyme necessary to digest methionine	Causes mental retardation, bone disease
Tyrosinemia ♦ Hereditary.	Causes severe liver disease and kidney problems. Death can occur within 6–9 months.
Congenital Adrenal Hyperplasia (CAH) ♦ Deficiency in the ability to create cortisol	Early appearance of body hair, short stature in adulthood, no female puberty characteristics
Medium-Chain Acyl-CoA Dehydrogenase (MCAD) Deficiency ♦ Can't convert fat into energy	Vomiting, lethargy, respiratory arrest. May be related to Sudden Infant Death Syndrome (SIDS)

Getting to Know You

"Most people make babies out to be very complicated," says comedian Dave Barry, "but the truth is they have only three moods: Mood One: Just about to cry. Mood Two: Crying. Mood Three: Just finished crying. Your job, as a parent, is to keep the baby in Mood Three as much as possible." With just a few days of fatherhood under your belt, you may be inclined to go along with Barry's summary. But the real truth is that babies' moods are a bit more subtle.

In the previous book in this series, *The Expectant Father: Facts, Tips, and Advice for Dads-to-Be,* I discussed the six clearly defined behavioral states evident within moments of every baby's birth.

In my first few weeks of fatherhood, I found that learning about these six states—which were explained to me by Dr. Marshall Klaus, author of *The Amazing Newborn*—was absolutely critical to my getting to know my babies. So I thought it would be worthwhile to go over them again.

QUIET ALERT

Within the first hour of life, most healthy infants have a period of quiet alertness that lasts an average of forty minutes, and during her first week, she'll spend about 10 percent of any twenty-four-hour period in this state. Babies in quiet alert mode rarely move—all their energy is channeled into seeing, hearing, and absorbing information about their new world. They can (and do) follow

HOW COMMON IT IS	TREATMENT
Fewer than one in 200,000 births in the U.S. Twice as frequent in Britain	Non-methionine diet, lots of B vitamins
Fewer than one in 100,000 births	Specialized diet until child is able to receive liver transplant
1 in 10,000 births	Cortisol therapy
1 in 10,000 births	Avoiding fasting, give frequent meals

objects with their eyes and may even imitate your facial expressions. That's when it'll first hit you that there's a real person inside that tiny body.

ACTIVE ALERT

In the active alert state, the baby will make small sounds and move her arms, head, body, face, and eyes frequently and actively.

Her movements usually come in short bursts—a few seconds of thrashing around every minute or two. Some researchers say these movements are designed to give parents subtle clues about what the baby wants and needs. Others say these movements are just interesting to watch, and therefore promote parent-infant interaction. Either way, the active alert state is a great time to put your baby on her stomach for a while, which will help strengthen her neck and back muscles.

CRYING

Crying is a perfectly natural—and for some, frequent—state (for more on this, see pages 69–70). Your infant's eyes may be open or closed, her face red, and her arms and legs moving vigorously. (Don't be surprised if you don't see any tears: newborns' tear ducts often don't function for the first week or two after delivery. When the tears finally do kick in, though, they'll break your heart.)

Often just picking her up and walking around with her will stop the crying.

Interestingly, researchers used to think that babies were soothed by being held or rocked in the upright position. It turns out, though, that what makes them stop crying is not *being* upright, but the movement that gets them there.

Keep in mind, too, that crying is not a bad thing—it not only allows the baby to communicate but also provides valuable exercise. So if your efforts to calm aren't immediately successful (and the baby isn't hungry or stewing in a dirty diaper), don't worry; chances are she'll settle down by herself in a few minutes.

DROWSINESS

Drowsiness is a transition state that occurs as the baby is waking up or falling asleep. There may still be some movement, and the eyes will often look dull or unfocused. Leave her alone to drift off to sleep or move into one of the alert stages.

QUIET SLEEP

During quiet sleep the baby's face is relaxed and her eyelids are closed and still. Her body is almost completely still, with only tiny, almost imperceptible mouth movements.

When your baby is in this state, you may be alarmed at the lack of movement and be afraid she has stopped breathing. If so, lean as close as you can and listen for her breath. Otherwise, gently put a hand on her stomach (she should be sleeping on her back—for information on why this is so important, see page 104) and feel it rise and fall. Try to resist the urge to wake the baby up—most newborns spend up to 90 percent of their first week asleep.

ACTIVE SLEEP

Eyes are usually closed, but may occasionally flicker open. The baby may also smile or frown, make sucking or chewing movements, and even whimper or twitch—just as adults do in their active sleep state.

Half of a baby's sleep time is spent in quiet sleep, the other half in active sleep, with the two states alternating in thirty-minute shifts. So if your sleeping baby starts to stir, whimper, or seems to be waking up unhappy, wait a few seconds before you pick her up to feed, change, or hold. Left alone, she may well slip back into the quiet sleep state.

Newborn babies are capable of a lot more than crying, sleeping, filling their diapers, and looking around. Just a few hours out of the womb, they are already trying to communicate with those around them.

Marshall Klaus told me about playing a game with an eight-hour-old girl in which he asked one colleague (who was a stranger to the baby) to stick out her tongue slowly while holding the baby. After a few seconds the baby imitated the woman. Then Dr. Klaus took the baby and passed her around to twelve other doctors and nurses who were participating in the game, all of whom were told not to stick their tongues out. When the baby finally came back to the first doctor, the baby—without any prompting—immediately stuck out her tongue again. Even at just a few hours old, she had apparently remembered her "friend."

Interacting with Your Baby

Although it may be tempting just to sit and stare at your baby, marveling at every little thing she does, you'll need to do a lot more than that if you're really going to develop a relationship with her. Here are some of the best ways to get to know your baby:

- ♦ **Hold her.** Newborns love to be held and carried around. If you can, take off your shirt—skin-to-skin contact helps warm the baby, and you'll love it too. It's perfectly fine for you to lie down on your back and let the baby nap facedown on your chest. But remember, this is the only time that she should sleep on her tummy.
- ♦ **Talk to her.** No, she can't understand a word you're saying. In fact, she barely even knows you exist. But talk to her anyway—explain everything you're doing as you're doing it, tell her what's happening in the news, and so forth—it will help her get to know the rhythm of the language.
- ♦ **Change her.** It doesn't sound like much fun, but it's a great time to interact with the baby one-on-one, to rub her soft belly, tickle her knees, kiss her tiny fingers. For at least the first month or so, she needs to be changed every two hours—a baby's supersensitive skin shouldn't soak in human waste—so there are plenty of opportunities. See "Diaper Changing 101" on pages 32–33.
- ♦ **Keep her clean—but not too clean.** You may take a shower every day, but until your baby starts crawling, she's unlikely to do anything that would get her terribly dirty, so there's no real need to bathe her any more than three times a week—any more than that could unnecessarily dry her skin. Two small exceptions: it's okay to wash the baby's face every day using plain water, and carefully clean everything covered up by her diapers every time you change her.

When you're cleaning your baby's head, pay close attention to the soft spots on the top; sometimes you can see them beat in time with the baby's pulse. These soft spots (called fontanels) are there for a purpose—to allow

Diaper Changing 101

By the time your baby gets potty-trained, you'll have changed about 10,000 diapers (more for boys than for girls, and way, way more for twins), so the faster and more efficiently you learn to get the job done, the less time you'll spend doing it. Here's the short course:

1. Get everything you need ready *before* you start: fresh diaper, water, towels, and a new outfit (mostly for the baby, but you might need one too if things get messy enough). Stay away from commercial baby wipes for the first few weeks. Even the ones that are alcohol-free contain too many chemicals for brand-new skin. Use warm, wet wash- cloths or cotton balls instead. If you're planning to be away from the house at any point during this period, bring along some moistened disposable washcloths in a resealable plastic bag.

2. Find yourself a nice, flat place to do the job. Changing tables— or any other sturdy table—are great. Some changing tables come with straps for holding the baby secure, but don't rely on them—make sure you keep at least one hand on your baby at all times. Newborns are surprisingly strong—and clever too—and she'll pick the precise sec- ond you choose to turn around to propel herself over the edge. The floor is probably the safest spot, since there's no possibility of the baby falling, but it can be hard on the back.

3. Undress the baby enough to slip the legs out. Be sure to take the baby's socks, if any, off. Babies love to kick their legs around while they're being changed and have an uncanny ability to drag their feet through their own poop.

4. Lay the baby face-up on the changing surface. Some babies absolutely love having their diapers changed and are perfectly calm throughout the whole process. Others will kick and squirm and bounce and scream. If your baby is less than thrilled to be there, hanging a mobile right above the changing surface might provide enough distraction for you to do what you need to do.

5. Open a clean diaper and place it underneath the baby. Then unfasten the old one, gently lift the baby up by her ankles, and pull the dirty

diaper out. Be sure to immediately cover the baby's genitals with a towel or cloth diaper. This isn't for modesty purposes; it's to keep you dry when the sudden rush of fresh air on your baby's crotch causes him or her to spray you.

6. Clean the bottom and genitals well—if there's a clean spot on the old diaper, use that to make a first pass. For girls, wipe from front to back to minimize the possibility of infection-causing bacteria getting into the vagina. For boys, clean under the scrotum. Keep a gentle but firm grip on your baby's ankles until you're through with step 8. With your free hand move the soiled diaper out of the way.

7. Apply diaper rash cream, but only if you really need to. Skip the lotions for the first few weeks (again, too harsh), and never, ever use talcum powder. Besides being a carcinogen, it can damage the lungs if inhaled. If you happen to have been raised in a family that doesn't think a baby is properly changed unless her bottom is covered in white powder, try using cornstarch, which doesn't have the same health hazards as traditional baby powder. Some people find that cornstarch absorbs moisture and reduces diaper rash. However, cornstarch has recently been linked with yeast growth, which is the last thing you want on your baby's bottom.

8. Fasten the diaper—snug but still loose enough so it doesn't pinch the skin. And fold down the front edge so it doesn't rub against the cord stump. If the baby pees or poops into the new, clean diaper, repeat steps 4, 5, and 6.

9. Wash up—your hands and the baby's feet, if necessary. I've found that keeping a bottle of Purell or other cleanser is great if you aren't near running water.

10. Get the baby dressed.

Changing diapers is an acquired skill; in just a few days you'll be able to do it with your eyes closed (although you probably shouldn't). In the meantime, even if you don't do it right, baby stool washes right off your hands—but not off your clothes, so quickly rinse off anything that gets hit.

the baby's skull to make it through the birth canal without breaking—and the skin covering them is pretty sturdy, so there's no reason to worry about harming the baby when washing the area.

A Note on Diapers

It seems as though you can hardly do anything anymore without having to make choices—do you want the Tastes Great kind of beer or the Less Filling kind? Do you want toothpaste with tartar control or with peroxide and baking soda? Fortunately, most of the choices we make are pretty easy. But some come with their very own built-in political controversy: Death penalty or life in prison? Paper or

---

What's *Really* Going on Inside Those Diapers?

♦ **Meconium.** That's the word for those greenish black, sticky, tarry bowel movements that may have you worrying that there's something wrong with your baby's intestines. By about the fourth day of age, as your baby starts breast- or bottle-feeding, the meconium will be replaced with a much more pleasant-looking concoction. Breast-fed babies usually fill their diapers with seedy, Dijon-mustard-colored stool that doesn't smell all that bad. Formula-fed babies produce a more pasty substance that can smell like milk gone bad. Occasional changes in color and consistency are normal for both.

♦ **Early puberty?** It's not uncommon for boys' and girls' genitals and nipples to be swollen for the first few days after birth. There may even be a few drops of milk. Girls sometimes also have a whitish discharge and even some tiny streaks of blood from the vagina. Again, nothing to worry about. This has to do with the high levels of hormones the baby got from your partner, and all these symptoms will clear up within a week or two after delivery.

♦ **The umbilical cord stump.** Your baby's umbilical cord stump will drop off anywhere from one to three weeks after she's born. Folding down the front of the diaper exposes the stump to more air and speeds up the falling-off process. Until then, limit your baby-washing efforts to sponge baths. Other than keeping the stump clean and dry, there's no need to do anything special to take care of it. You can clean any drainage on or around the cord by gently wiping it off with a cotton swab or wet washcloth. When it does fall off, a small amount of bleeding is normal.

---

plastic? Well, now that you're a parent, you can add "Disposable diapers or cloth?" to your list. Let's take a quick look at the pros and cons of each kind:

♦ **Disposable Diapers**. Americans throw away something like eighteen billion disposable diapers a year, enough to constitute more than 1 percent of the nation's landfills. They're made of plastic and will stay in their present form for about five hundred years. "Biodegradable" disposables are available in some places, but since these diapers are buried under tons of other garbage, they're deprived of the oxygen and sun they need to decompose. As a result, they may take just as long to break down.

On the other hand, disposables are a lot more convenient. If you're traveling, you can just toss the dirty ones away instead of having to carry them around with you. And even if you're not traveling, they're very easy to use, which is probably why about 90 percent of parents (and about 100 percent of hospitals) use disposables.

Disposable diapers for newborns are inexpensive. However, as your baby and her diapers get bigger, the number per package goes down while the cost per package stays about the same. Since you'll be using 5 to 8 diapers a day, this option can get pretty pricey. But if you keep your eyes out for coupons (most parenting magazines have a bunch of them in every issue) or shop at warehouse stores, you can save a lot. In addition, places like Toys "Я" Us, Walgreens, and other drugstore chains have generic or house brands that are a lot cheaper and usually just as good.

On the downside, disposables are so effective in absorbing moisture that kids who wear them stay comfortable longer and tend to be potty-trained later. (The average child who wears disposables is in them for 36–40 months, compared to 24–30 months for kids in cloth diapers.) Disposable-wearing kids are also more likely to get diaper rash because even though the moisture gets absorbed, the bacteria and ammonia that cause the rash stay inside.

♦ **Cloth Diapers**. These diapers are a lot easier on babies' brand-new, sensitive skin—no harsh chemicals or plastics. One of the traditional arguments against cloth diapers is that they aren't as convenient as disposables, and to some extent that is still true. You'll go through more cloth diapers in a day than you would with disposables, plus, if you're out of the house you'll have to schlep dirty ones with you until you get home, and if you run out, you'll have a tougher time finding extras. Still, there have been some important changes in the past few years. Today, for example, cloth diapers come in all sorts of styles: hourglass-shaped diapers, ones with elastic around the legs for better seal, Velcro closures instead of pins, rubber pants, special liners to make cleanup easier, and more. That means fewer leaks for you, but all those extras add to the cost.

At the same time, although they're all natural, cloth diapers are made of cotton, which is taxing on farmland. And in order to sterilize cloth diapers properly, diaper services wash them seven times in near-boiling water, consuming huge amounts of power, water, and detergents. The diapers are then delivered all over town in trucks that fill the air with toxic pollutants. The pro-disposable lobby says that using diaper services consumes more fuel and causes as much air pollution as disposable diapers do. Seems like a bit of a stretch to me.

If you're buying them yourself, cloth diapers cost about $10 for a package of six plain ones, and can go as high as $10 each for the form-fitted, all-in-one kind. However, most people who use cloth go with a diaper service. Costs vary greatly around the country. If you sign up with a diaper service, you'll probably start with about eighty diapers per week. If you're doing your own laundry, you should buy about forty.

Even if you decide against using cloth diapers for the baby, buy a dozen anyway—they're great for drying baby bottoms on changing tables and for draping over your shoulder to protect your clothes when your baby spits up.

Overall it's a tough choice, and it's all yours. But I suggest that you do a combination of the two: use cloth diapers during the day and when you're at home, disposables at night and whenever you go out. Alternatively, if you're not worried about spending a little extra money, there are a few eco-friendly disposables out there. Tushies use cotton and wood pulp to absorb liquid instead of gels, and Nature Boy & Girl uses a cornstarch film instead of plastic. They're available at health-food stores and on the Internet.

Dads in the NICU

If your baby was born before about 32 weeks, had a very low birth weight, or you have multiples, she (or they) will have to spend some time in the neo-natal (or newborn) intensive care unit (NICU, sometimes pronounced "*Nick-U*"). In the case of healthy-but-small babies, there's not a lot to worry about—they're called "growers and feeders" and just have to bulk up to 4 or 5 pounds before you can take them home. But not all babies in the NICU are healthy.

Watching your child struggle to hold on to life can be a frightening and humbling experience. A lot of dads I talked to told me that the feeling of helplessness was overwhelming. Not only were they powerless to help their child, but they often felt left out or ignored by the medical staff, who focused almost exclusively on the mother. For that reason, most new dads who have children in the NICU are generally left to come up with coping strategies on their own. Here are some that worked for many of the dads in my research:

+ **Try not to take it personally**. The truth is that although it might feel like you're being left out, the staff's primary concern is to save your baby's life—and it should be yours too. And if the staff is focusing on your partner more than on you, that's because it's important that the baby eat, and her mother's milk is the best medicine.

+ **Don't be afraid to ask questions**. You have a right to know exactly what's going on with your child every step of the way. A lot of men find that knowing what's going on—the procedures, the reasons, the odds of success—is incredibly helpful.

+ **Ask about kangaroo care**. In Colombia, the mortality rate for premature infants was as high as 70 percent as recently as the 1980s. But a few doctors decided to try something different: they placed the tiny babies, wearing only a cap and a diaper, on a parent's bare chest, skin to skin, for several hours a day. The results were amazing. To start with, the mortality rate dropped to 30 percent. In studies in the United States and other countries, human kangaroo babies slept better, were taken off respirators sooner, cried less and were alert more, were better able to regulate their body temperature, gained more weight, and came home earlier. There were benefits for the parents as well: dads and moms who held their babies like this felt more confident in their parenting abilities and better able to do something productive for their babies. And breast-feeding moms who did kangaroo care were able to produce more milk. Unfortunately, not all hospitals allow kangaroo care (sometimes also called skin-to-skin care). If yours doesn't, ask the nursing staff whether you and your partner can do it anyway. If they need any convincing, show them this section.

+ **Be a little bit selfish**. Sounds horrible, but it's not as bad as you think. The point is that you're not going to be much use to anyone—baby or partner—if you're walking around like a zombie because you haven't slept in 48 hours. Mom and baby need you to be there and to be strong. So if you need to find a couch and take a nap, do it. And if you need to go for a run or play basketball or do something else to blow off steam, do it. Your whole family will be better off in the long run.

+ **Be emotionally strong too**. You and your partner may have very different ways of coping with your baby's illness. A lot of men, for example, are fascinated by the technology and find that focusing on that helps them cope. Other men only feel safe expressing anger. Women, though, tend to just go straight to the emotions—particularly sadness and sorrow. Some women get upset at what they interpret as their partner's insensitivity. If this happens, talk to her about what you're feeling. She needs to know you care.

Once it's okay for you to touch your baby, don't waste a second. Babies who had daily ten-minute sessions of neck, shoulder, back, and leg massage and five minutes a day of gentle limb flexing grew almost 50 percent more than those who didn't get the massage—even though calorie intake for the two groups was the same, according to Dr. Tiffany Field, the director of the Touch Research Institute at the University of Miami School of Medicine. Hospital stays were shortened almost a week, and the bills were correspondingly lower as well. On their first birthdays, formerly premature babies who'd been massaged were bigger and better developed than similarly premature kids who didn't get massaged. Pretty neat, eh? If you're interested in trying this, take a look at the instructions on pages 87–89.

Family Matters

Coming Home

Boy, has your life changed. You're still your partner's lover and friend, just as you were a few weeks ago, but now, of course, you're also a father. You may be worried about how you're going to juggle all your various roles, but for the next few days the most important thing you can do is be a solid support person to your partner. Besides her physical recovery (which we'll talk more about below), she's going to need time to get to know the baby and to learn (if she chooses to) how to breast-feed. Your first days as a father will be awfully busy—mine sure were: cooking, shopping, doing laundry, fixing up the baby's room, getting the word out, screening phone calls and visitors, and making sure my wife got plenty of rest.

Recovery

As far as the baby is concerned, there's not much to do in the beginning besides feed, change, and admire. But your partner is a different story. Despite whatever you've heard about women giving birth in the fields and returning to work a few minutes later, that's not the way things usually happen. Having a baby is a major shock—physically and emotionally—to a woman's system. And, contrary to popular belief, the recovery period after a vaginal birth is not necessarily any shorter or easier than the recovery period after a C-section. In fact, a lot of women I've spoken with who've delivered both ways say that recovering from the C-section is actually easier.

Physically, whatever kind of delivery your partner has, she'll need some time—probably more than either of you think—to recover fully. Fatigue, breast soreness, and lingering uterine contractions may not disappear for months, and vaginal discomfort, bleeding, hemorrhoids, poor appetite, constipation, increased perspiration, acne, hand numbness or tingling, dizziness, and hot flashes may continue for weeks after delivery. In addition, between 10 and 40 percent of women feel pain during sexual intercourse (which they won't get around to for a few months anyway, so don't even bother thinking about it), have respiratory infections, and lose hair for three to six months.

Emotionally, your partner isn't much better off. She's likely to be a little impatient at her lack of mobility, and while she's undoubtedly excited to be a mother and relieved that the pregnancy is finally over, she'll probably experience the "baby blues" and may even suffer from postpartum depression (see pages 61, 64–66). Now that the baby is really here, she may feel a lot of pressure to assume her new role as mother and to breast-feed properly. That's an awful lot to ask. Fortunately, as she and the baby get to know each other, her confidence will grow, and a lot of her anxieties should disappear. Here are some things you can do to help your partner through the recovery process and to start parenting for both of you off on the right foot:

♦ **Help your partner resist the urge to do too much too soon.**
♦ **Take over the household chores, or ask someone else to help.** And if the house is a mess, don't blame each other.
♦ **Be flexible.** Expecting to maintain your normal, prefatherhood schedule is a complete fantasy, especially for the first six weeks after the birth.
♦ **Be patient with yourself, your partner, and the baby.** You're all new at this.
♦ **Be sensitive to your partner's emotions.** Her emotional recovery can take just as long as her physical one; maybe longer.
♦ **Get some time alone with the baby.** You can do this while your partner is sleeping or, if you have to, while you send her out for a walk.
♦ **Control the visiting hours and the number of people who can come at any given time.** Dealing with visitors takes a lot more energy than you might think. And being poked, prodded, and passed around won't make the baby very happy. Also, for the first month or so, ask anyone who wants to touch the baby to wash his or her hands first. Babies' immune systems aren't ready to handle the day-to-day germs we deal with.
♦ **Keep your sense of humor.**

You and Your Baby

Within a few minutes after we'd brought our first daughter home from the hospital, my wife and I looked at each other and almost simultaneously asked, "Well, now what are we supposed to do with her?

The things I mentioned back on page 31—holding, talking, changing, bathing—are even more important now that you're home than they were back at the hospital. In addition, there are a few things you need to know about at this stage:

♦ **Dressing your newborn**. This isn't going to be easy: her head seems too big to go through the appropriate openings in her shirts, and her arms are so bunched up that they may refuse to come out of the sleeves. Doing the following should make getting dressed a little easier for everyone involved:

  ♦ Roll up the sleeves, then reach through and gently pull your baby's hands through—it's a lot easier than trying to shove from the other side.

  ♦ Buy pants or overalls whose legs snap open. Some manufacturers make baby clothes that are absolutely beautiful but impossible to put on or take off. The snap-open legs also make diaper changing much easier—you don't have to remove the whole outfit to access the diaper.

  ♦ Forget the clothes and keep her in nightgowns, but make sure you get the kind with elastic at the bottom and *not* string, which can be a choking hazard. You'll have to go back to real clothes with separate legs if you're putting the baby into a car seat or stroller.

  ♦ If she can't walk, she doesn't need shoes. It's not only a waste of money, but confining your baby's feet in a hard pair of shoes all day long can actually damage her bones.

♦ **Manicures and pedicures**. Your baby's flailing arms and amazingly sharp fingernails are a bad combination, particularly around her eyes and face. Some clothes come with extra long sleeves that can be folded over to keep the baby from scratching her face too badly. But you should still learn how to do manicures.

  ♦ First, collect all your supplies: blunt-tipped scissors and a nail file (regular nail clippers are too big).

  ♦ Make sure your baby is fast asleep—trimming grain-of-rice-sized nails when she's awake is going to be nearly impossible.

  ♦ Then, take one finger and gently pry it away from the fist. Push back on the pad of the finger so the nail sticks out a little bit more.

  ♦ Trim the nail by cutting straight across.

♦ File the entire edge of the nail, especially the corners.

♦ Repeat with all ten fingers.

When you get more comfortable with this process, you'll probably come up with a routine of your own. I've found, for example, that cuticle scissors work a lot better than ordinary baby-nail-trimming scissors. And I like to trim all the nails on one hand and then go back and do the filing. A few of the new dads I've interviewed have admitted that they actually bite their baby's nails. Hey, if it's not dangerous and it works, knock yourself out.

Pets

Don't expect your pet to be as excited as you are about the birth of your baby; many dogs and cats do not appreciate their new (lower) status in your house. To minimize the trauma for your pet (and to minimize the chance your pet will do something to harm the baby), try to get your pet used to the baby as early as possible.

You can do this even before the baby comes home by putting a blanket in the baby's bassinet in the hospital, then rushing it home to your pet. It'll give Rover or Fluffy a few days (or hours, at least) to get used to the little interloper's smell.

"Homewrecker!"

Different Isn't Bad, It's Just Different

From the moment their children are born, men and women have very different ways of handling them. Men tend to stress the physical and high-energy, women the social and emotional. Your baby will catch on to these differences within days, and she'll start reacting to you and your partner very differently. When she's hungry, she'll be more easily soothed by your partner (if she's breast-feeding), but she'll be happier to see you if she wants some physical stimulation. Don't let anyone tell you that the "guy things" you do are somehow not as important as the "girl things" your partner may do (or want *you* to do). Ultimately your baby needs both kinds of interactions, and it's a waste of time to try to compare or rate them. Just be gentle.

Because your baby's fingernails grow so quickly, you'll be doing this every two or three days. Toenails are a different story—you won't need to trim them any more than once or twice a month.

Have Some Fun

During the first few weeks, forget about football and chess. But try to spend at least twenty minutes a day (in five-minute installments) doing something with the baby one-on-one. Chatting, reading aloud, rocking, making faces, experimenting with the baby's reflexes (see pages 62–65), or even simply catching her gaze and looking into her eyes are great activities. Here are a couple of things to remember:

♦ **Take your cues from the baby**. If she cries or seems bored, stop what you're doing. Too much playing can overstimulate your child and make her fussy or irritable, so limit play sessions to five minutes or so.

♦ **Schedule your fun**. The best time for physical play is when the baby is in the active alert state; playing with toys or books is fine during the quiet alert state (see page 28). Also, choose a time when your full attention can be devoted to the baby—no phone calls or other distractions.

♦ **Be encouraging**. Use lots of smiles and laughter as well as verbal encouragement. Although the baby can't understand the words, she definitely understands the feelings. Even at only a few days old, she'll want to please you, and lots of reinforcement will help build her self-confidence.

- **Be gentle.** Sudden movements, bright lights, and loud noises (especially sneezes, slamming doors, and car alarms) can scare her.
- **Watch her head.** Because babies' heads are relatively enormous (one-quarter of their body size at birth versus one-seventh by the time they're adults), and their neck muscles are not yet well developed, their heads tend to be pretty floppy for the first few months. Be sure to support the head from behind at all times, and avoid sudden or jerky motions. Never shake your child. This can make her little brain rattle around inside her skull, causing bruises or permanent injuries. Never throw the baby up in the air. Yes, your father may have done it to you, but he shouldn't have. It looks like fun but can be extremely dangerous.

Feeding Your Baby: Breast versus Bottle

At the time most of the people reading this book were born, breast-feeding was out of style and most women our mothers' age were given a wide variety of reasons (by their doctors, of course) not to. But today you'd be hard-pressed to find anyone in the medical community who doesn't agree that breastfeeding is just about the best thing you can do for your child. Here's why:

FOR THE BABY

- Breast milk provides exactly the right balance of nutrients needed by your newborn. In addition, breast milk contains several essential fatty acids that are not found in baby formula.
- Breast milk adapts, as if by magic, to your baby's changing nutritional needs. None of my children had a single sip of anything but breast milk for at least the first six months of life, and they're all wonderfully healthy kids.
- Breast-feeding greatly reduces the chance that your baby will develop food allergies. If either of your families has a history of food allergies, you should withhold solid foods for *at least* six months.
- Breast-fed babies are less prone to obesity in adulthood than formula-fed babies. This may be because with the breast it's the baby—not the parent—who decides when to quit eating.
- Breast-fed babies have a greatly reduced risk of developing respiratory and gastrointestinal illness, ear infections, asthma, and some childhood cancers, and it may lower the risk of SIDS.
- Breast-feeding is thought to transmit to the infant the mother's immunity to certain diseases.

Just Because You Don't Have Breasts Doesn't Mean You Can't Help Breast-feed

Sounds strange, but you play a critical role in determining whether, how long, and how well your partner will breast-feed. Several studies have shown that women nurse longer when their partners learn about breast-feeding (which you'll do as you read these pages), support them, and have confidence in their ability. Here are a few ways you can stay involved:

- ♦ Help your partner find the most comfortable position and position the baby. In the early days of breast-feeding, she may need to try three or four positions at every meal.
- ♦ Make sure she's got a big glass of water nearby—and that she actually drinks it.
- ♦ Encourage her every chance you get. Tell her what a great job she's doing, and be sympathetic but supportive when she gets frustrated.
- ♦ Sit next to your partner while she nurses and read her interesting articles from the newspaper.
- ♦ Bring the baby to your partner for those night feedings.
- ♦ Do as much of the burping and diaper changing as you can.
- ♦ Gently stroke the baby's skin while she's feeding. But keep your hands off her head. Stroking the back of the head can sometimes trigger a pull-back reflex, and if the baby has a mouth full of breast and nipple at the time, your wife won't enjoy the experience.
- ♦ Let her set the tone outside. Some women are perfectly fine about lifting their shirts in public; others are incredibly shy. Don't put any pressure on her either way, regardless of how you feel.

Just Because Your Partner Has Breasts Doesn't Mean She Knows How to Use Them

As natural as breast-feeding appears to be, your partner and the baby may need anywhere from a few days to a few weeks to get the hang of it. The baby won't immediately know how to latch on to the breast properly, and your partner—especially if she's never done this before—won't know exactly what to do either. This initial period, in which cracked and even bloody nipples are not uncommon, may be quite painful for your partner. And with the baby feeding six or seven times a day for 10–15 minutes on each breast, it may take as long as two weeks for your partner's nipples to get sufficiently toughened up.

Surprisingly, she won't begin producing any real milk until two to five days after the baby is born. But there's no need to worry that the baby isn't getting enough food. Babies don't eat much the first 24–48 hours, and any sucking they do is almost purely for practice. Whatever nutritional needs your baby has will be fully satisfied by the tiny amounts of colostrum your partner produces. (Colostrum is a kind of premilk that helps the baby's immature digestive system get warmed up for the task of digesting real milk later.)

Overall, the first few weeks of breast-feeding can be stressful and often frustrating for your partner—so much so that she may be tempted to throw in the towel. Even if this happens, don't give in to the temptation to suggest switching to bottles. Instead, try some of the things on page 68 and encourage her to keep trying. She may find it hard to believe right now, but there's an excellent chance that in a week or two she and the baby will have settled into a comfortable rhythm, and she'll hardly remember all the troubles she had. At the same time, you also might ask your pediatrician for the name of a local lactation consultant (what a job!). We'll talk more about breast-feeding-related issues in the next chapter.

FOR YOU AND YOUR PARTNER

♦ It's convenient—no preparation, no heating, no bottles or dishes to wash. Plus, breast-fed babies are a lot easier to travel with—no need to find clean water for mixing powder, nothing to refrigerate.

♦ It's free. Formula can cost a lot of money.

♦ It gives your partner a wonderful opportunity to bond with the baby. In addition, breast-feeding will help get her lose weight and get her uterus

Parents, In-Laws, Siblings, and Other "Helpers"

One of the most common questions you'll hear from people is whether they can help out in any way. Some people are serious; others are just being polite. You can tell one group from the other by keeping a list of chores that need to be done and asking them to take their pick.

Be particularly careful about accepting offers of help from people—especially parents (yours or hers)—who arrive on your doorstep with suitcases and open-ended travel arrangements. New grandparents may have more traditional attitudes toward parenting and may not be supportive of your involvement with your child. They may also have very different ideas about how babies should be fed, dressed, carried, played with, and so on. It's important, then, to be very clear that although you appreciate the help and advice, you and your partner are the baby's parents, and what the two of you say ultimately goes.

Much the same can be said for just about anyone else who offers to move in with you for a few days, weeks, or months to "help out," especially people who have their own kids. With all your other responsibilities, the last thing you want to do is play host to a bunch of relatives. If someone does stay with you to help out after the birth, great—my sister-in-law spent a week with us after the birth of my youngest and ended up filling our freezer with months' worth of incredible food. But it's important that everyone understands that you and your partner are going to spend most of your free time sleeping and not socializing.

back into shape and may reduce her risk of both ovarian and breast cancer.

♦ In most cases, there's always as much as you need, and never any waste.

♦ Your baby's diapers won't stink. It's true. Breast-fed babies produce stools that—especially when compared to formula stools—doesn't smell half bad.

♦ You may end up getting more rest. If your partner is nursing, you won't have to get up in the middle of the night to prepare formula (although you still may need to get up to bring the baby to your partner).

What If Your Partner Doesn't Breast-feed?

FORMULA

Prices vary. You can use powdered, full-strength liquid, or liquid concentrate (which you have to add water to). But when you start checking formula prices, your partner may decide to keep breast-feeding a while longer.
All three options are basically the same in terms of their nutritional value.
The only issues are price (powder is usually the cheapest, since you can whip up a pitcher in the morning and keep it in the fridge for the day) and convenience (full-strength liquid is the easiest—and most expensive).

If you're going the formula route, you'll probably be wondering how much to feed the baby. The easy answer is, "As much as she wants." If she's hungry, food will be the only thing that will soothe her. When she's had enough, she'll stop sucking or clamp her mouth shut. As a general guideline, though, you'll want to give your baby 2–3 ounces of formula per pound of body-weight every day. Then divide that into 6–8 feedings. Remember, every baby is different, so you'll have to do a little experimenting before you find the right amount.

Despite what your mother may have told you, there's no need to sterilize bottles or nipples. Just wash them thoroughly with warm, soapy water and rinse carefully. If a nipple is torn, hard, stiff, cracked, or deformed in any way, replace it right away.

JUICE

If you and your partner decide not to breast-feed or feel that you want to supplement breast-feeding with a bottle, don't fill it with juice. Children who drink large quantities of fruit juice—especially apple juice—suffer from frequent diarrhea, and in the worst cases may fail to grow and develop normally. The problem is that babies love juice so much that, if you give them all they want, they'll fill up their tiny stomachs with it, leaving no room for the more nutritious foods they need. Even worse, if your baby gets too used to juice, there's a chance that she may flat-out refuse formula or milk. The American Dietetic Association recommends that parents refrain from giving their babies juice until they're at least six months old, and then restrict juice intake until age two.

WATER, SUGAR WATER, ELECTROLYTE DRINKS, COW'S MILK, AND GOAT'S MILK

The short answer is that unless your doctor specifically tells you that your baby need any of these, stay away from them.

Burping 101

When babies drink, especially from bottles, they almost always swallow some air. And because they tend to do most of their drinking on their side, that air tends to get trapped in their stomach. Sometimes babies burp on their own, but most of the time they need a little help.

You should burp your baby at the middle and the end of every feeding, more often if you feel it's necessary. There are three basic ways to bring up a belch. Pick the one that works best for you or alternate them.

♦ Hold the baby facing you, upright, her head above your shoulder. Pat or rub her back gently.
♦ Lay the baby facedown across your knees, head carefully supported. Pat or rub her back gently.
♦ Hold the baby on your knee in a sitting position, leaning forward slightly. Pat or rub her back gently.

Whichever option(s) you choose, remember this: always support the baby's head, and gently patting or rubbing is just as effective—and less dangerous—as thumping hard. What brings the air up is the pressure against the stomach, not the decibel level of your hand against the baby's back. Since burps sometimes bring some liquid with them, be sure to protect yourself and your clothing before you start.

And finally, keep in mind that there's a difference between spitting up and vomiting. Spitting up is essentially a wet burp—a little dribble coming out of the corner of the baby's mouth. Vomiting involves a lot more fluid. Spitting up is nothing to worry about, and vomiting rarely is. But if your baby vomits a lot, or if what comes out seems to be as much as what just went in, ask the pediatrician.

For Boys Only

I'm assuming that by now, you and your partner have already made your decision about whether or not to circumcise your son. Whatever your choice, your son's penis requires some special care.

THE CIRCUMCISED PENIS

The penis will be red and sore for a few days after the circumcision. Until it's fully healed, you'll need to protect the newly exposed tip and keep it from sticking to the inside of his diaper (a few tiny spots of blood on his diapers for a few days, however, is perfectly normal). Ordinarily, you'll need to keep the penis dry and the tip lubricated with petroleum jelly or antibiotic ointment and wrapped in gauze to protect it from urine, which is very irritating. The exception to this is if your baby received a plastibell (a plastic ring that goes between the foreskin and the head of the penis). In this case you'll want to stay away from any kind of ointment or dressings until the plastibell drops off (usually 5–10 days after it was put on). If you have any questions or worries, the person who performed the circumcision or the hospital nursing staff should be able to give you more specific and detailed care instructions.

THE UNCIRCUMCISED PENIS

Even if you elect not to circumcise your son, you'll still have to spend some time taking care of his penis. The standard way to clean an uncircumcised penis is to retract the foreskin and gently wash the head of the penis with mild soap and water. However, 85 percent of boys under six months have a foreskin that doesn't retract, according to the American Academy of Pediatrics. If this is the case with your son, don't force it. Check with your pediatrician immediately and follow his or her hygiene instructions carefully. Fortunately, as boys get older, their foreskins retract on their own; by age one, 50 percent retract, and by age three, 80 to 90 percent.

Knowing When to Get Help

If you have older kids, you already know that most of the stuff first-time parents panic about turns out to be perfectly normal. But if you're a first-time parent, you're going to worry about everything, no matter what anyone tells you. Your pediatrician will probably give you a list of what's normal and what's not for the first few weeks of life. But here are some things that warrant a call:

♦ If your baby seems unusually floppy and/or nonresponsive.
♦ If your baby cries for a very long time or sounds strange—whooping, gasping, high-pitched crying for a long time—or is completely inconsolable.
♦ Infection at the circumcision or umbilical cord site. Swelling, red streaks on the penis or near the cord, continued bleeding, or puslike discharge could indicate a problem.
♦ Excessive sleep. It can be a little hard to determine this in the early days, but generally speaking, your baby should wake up every 2–3 hours and be ravenous.

♦ Yellow skin. This could be jaundice, which is very common, but requires medical attention to keep it from becoming dangerous.
♦ Not enough pee and poop. If, after the third or fourth day of life, your baby isn't filling at least 2 diapers and soaking at least 4 (there can be some overlap) every 24 hours, she could be dehydrated. Other signs include dark-colored or strong-smelling urine, a sunken soft spot on the baby's head, dry mouth and tongue, sunken eyes, and listlessness.

Notes:

Getting to Know You

What's Going On with the Baby

Physically

♦ Most of your baby's physical movements are still reflexive, but the leg and arm thrashing should be fairly symmetrical. Sometime this month, while flailing his arms around, your baby will accidentally stick his hand into his mouth. After getting over the initial shock, he'll realize that sucking—even when there's no milk involved—is downright fun. By the end of the month, he'll probably be able to get his hand in his mouth—on purpose—fairly regularly, and if he had any hair to start with, he'll have worn away a nice bald spot on the back of his head.

♦ Lying on his tummy, he's now able to lift his head just enough to turn it so his nose won't be smashed into the mattress. Lying on his back, he should be able to lift his head up 45 degrees and hold it there for a few seconds.

♦ If you put him in a sitting position, he'll try to keep his head in line with his back, but he won't be able to hold it steady for more than a second or two without support.

♦ He wants to eat every two to four hours, but waste production is way down: 2 to 3 bowel movements and 5 to 6 wet diapers per day.

♦ Although his 3-D vision hasn't fully developed, his eyesight is improving, and he can now see and focus on objects a foot away or more.

Intellectually

♦ Your baby is alert for 30–60 minutes every 10–12 hours or so. He's already beginning to express an interest in finding out what's going on in his world. He'll stare at a new object for much longer than a familiar one, and his favorite things to look at are high-contrast black-and-white patterns and faces. By the end of this month he'll probably follow an object moving slowly by in front of him.

♦ According to psychiatrist Peter Wolff, an object exists for a baby only as "something to suck, or something to see, or something to grasp, but not as something to grasp and to see at the same time."

Verbally

♦ As his vocal chords mature, your baby will expand his collection of animal sounds to include some small, throaty, and incredibly cute cooing noises.
♦ He is already beginning to differentiate between language and the other kinds of noise he hears all day. He may respond to voices—especially your partner's and yours—by turning toward them. And he really enjoys being spoken to.
♦ Still, his main form of using his vocal chords will be to cry—something he'll do for as much as three hours a day.

Emotionally/Socially

♦ Don't expect many hints from your baby about what he's thinking—most of the time his expression is pretty blank. However, he loves being held, rocked, and making eye contact and may stare intently at you for 15–20 seconds or so before being distracted by an insect flying by or a light being turned on or off.
♦ Not quite ready for the cocktail circuit, your baby is probably sleeping 16 to 20 hours a day. In fact, he may use sleep as a kind of self-defense mechanism, shutting down his systems when he gets overstimulated.
♦ He's starting to form an emotional attachment to and feelings of trust for the people who care for him.
♦ He may cry as a way of demanding more attention or in protest at being overloaded with attention.

What's Going On with Your Partner

Physically

♦ Reduction in *lochia* (the normal, bloody vaginal discharge that happens after birth). Color will change from red to pink to brown to clear.

♦ Reduced pain around the C-section incision or episiotomy.

♦ Breasts may become engorged with milk. This may make them feel (and actually be) enormous.

♦ Lots of sweating and frequent urination as her body continues to eliminate excess fluids any way it can. Fortunately, her bladder control is improving, and any incontinence will probably be gone within another few weeks. A few hundred daily Kegels (tightening of the muscles used to hold back urination) will help the process along.

♦ Some continued hair loss.

♦ Stretch marks, if she had them at all, will start fading, as will the darker pigmentation around her nipples and that odd dark line that starts at her belly button and goes south.

Emotionally

♦ Continued irritability and moodiness. Some of this is hormonal, some brought on by sleep deprivation and/or pain.

♦ She may experience all sorts of conflicting emotions. Some are the same as the ones you may have been feeling (things like joy, possible disappointment about the way the birth went, and worries about what kind of a mother she's going to be). Others will be her very own (such as emptiness or sadness that the pregnancy is over, guilt if she doesn't love the baby as much as she thought she would or thought she was supposed to).

♦ She may feel confused, absentminded, forgetful, and generally like she's losing her mind.

♦ Depression or the blues (see page 61 for more)

What You're Going Through

Bonding with the Baby

In one of the earliest studies of father-infant interaction, my colleague Ross Parke made a discovery that shocked a lot of traditionalists: fathers were just as caring, interested, and involved with their infants as mothers were, and they held, touched, kissed, rocked, and cooed at their new babies with at least the same frequency as mothers did. The sooner and more frequently dads have a chance to spend time with their babies, the more quickly the bonding process will start. Generally speaking, men who attend their babies' birth bond slightly faster than those who don't. But if you weren't able to be there for the birth, don't worry—being there doesn't guarantee attachment, and not being there doesn't automatically interfere with it.

But What If I Don't Bond Right Away?

If you haven't established an instant bond with your baby, there's absolutely nothing wrong with you. In fact, it turns out that 25 to 40 percent of new parents—mothers and fathers—say that their first response to the baby is "indifference." Putting it in slightly stronger terms, researcher Katharyn May says, "This bonding business is nonsense. We've sold parents a bill of goods. They believe that if they don't have skin-to-skin contact within the first fifteen minutes, they won't bond. Science just doesn't show that."

This really makes more sense to me than the love-at-first-sight kind of bonding you hear so much about. And anyway, there's no evidence whatsoever that

---

Attachment and Bonding Are *Not* the Same Thing

While there's no question that bonding with your baby is an important goal, it's essentially a one-way street: you establish a relationship with the infant and don't get much back. But *attachment* is more of a two-way street: you and the baby establish a relationship with each other.

This relationship isn't even close to being equal, the way it is between adults. It is, however, balanced in some very interesting and delicate ways. Basically, it works like this: as you learn to read your baby's signals and satisfy his needs in an appropriate way, he learns to view you as a reliable and responsive person—someone he can count on in times of trouble. And he'll find some way (babies always do) to get you the message that you're needed and wanted.

This exchange of information is what psychologist Bertrand Cramer and pediatrician T. Berry Brazelton call *synchronous communication.* And according to them, even the most insecure parents who achieve it feel a sense of control, over their baby's vulnerabilities—and their own.

Meanwhile, babies who have synchronous "chats" with their parents come to prefer them over any of the other adults around who might be able to satisfy a need or two. Over time, this kind of preference (based on feelings of security and the parents' reliability) develops into self-confidence and becomes the foundation for all of the growing baby's future relationships.

Bonding, Attachment, and Adoptive Dads

Plenty of adoptive parents—particularly those who adopted because of infertility—feel a little insecure or inadequate. They often believe that the process of bonding and forming an attachment with a baby comes more naturally to birth parents than to them, and that since they weren't with the baby from the beginning, they'll never be as close to their child as a biological parent would. The good news is that this isn't true.

Studies of adoptive parents have shown that a majority feel some kind of love for their children right from the very first contact; it doesn't matter whether it's when they go to pick up the baby, when they first looked at a picture that arrived months before, or right at the birth, if they're lucky enough to be there. At the same time "most infants, if adopted before the age of nine months will take to their new parents as if they were born to them, developing an attachment to them as they would have done to their birth parents," according to adoption psychotherapists Judith Schaffer and Christina Lindstrom.

There are things, of course, that can interfere with adoptive parent-child attachment. Among the most common are the feelings of inadequacy discussed above, and the age and physical health of the child at adoption. If you're adopting a complete newborn, it's going to be a little easier to establish a bond. But a lot of adoptions aren't finalized until the babies are a few months older. Realistically, this makes the bonding process a little tougher for all concerned, as babies and parents take a little time to get used to each other. It's by no means an impossible task.

And remember, in all but the rarest cases, the desire for attachment to a child can overcome even the most formidable obstacles. (If you aren't consumed with paternal feelings right away, start by taking a look at the "But What If I Don't Bond Right Away?" section above.) So if you're worried for any reason about your abilities as a parent or about anything else that might get in the way of your relationship with your adopted child, call the National Adoption Information Clearinghouse at (703) 352-3488 or (888) 251-0075, or visit their website at www.calib.com/naic/. If you're adopting a child with special needs, contact the National Adoption Center, at (800) TO-ADOPT. Either of these organizations can refer you to resources—including support groups and counseling services—in your area. You'll find more adoption-related resources listed in the Resources appendix of this book.

your relationship with or feelings for your child will be any less loving than if you'd fallen head over heels in love in the first second. So, just take your time. Don't pressure yourself, and don't think for a second that you've failed as a father.

If your baby is very sick, the situation may be a little different. Some dads whose babies were born very prematurely or who are in intensive care, deliberately (though subconsciously) try to keep some psychological distance between themselves and the babies. They feel that they have to be strong for their partner and that not bonding with the baby will somehow protect them from the pain they'll experience if something bad happens. It won't. In fact, your establishing a close physical and psychological bond with your baby can actually improve his chances for survival. So jump in. The sooner dads hold their babies, the sooner those feelings of love work their way to the surface.

My Baby Doesn't Love Me

For about the first six to eight weeks of life, your baby probably won't give you much feedback about how you're doing as a father: he won't smile, laugh, or react to you in any noticeable way. In fact, just about all he will do is cry. This can result in your feeling unloved and, surprisingly often, feeling a need to "get even" with the baby by deliberately withholding your own love.

As the grown-up, it's your job to nip this destructive cycle in the bud before it gets out of hand. So if you find yourself feeling unloved or unappreciated by your newborn, here are a few things you can do:

♦ **Change your perspective**. Although your baby can express preferences for sounds, tastes, or patterns, he is not yet capable of expressing love. However, the fact that your baby often stops crying when you pick him up and that he loves to fall asleep on your chest are signs that he feels close to you and trusts you—critical steps on the way to the love you want him to feel. Allow yourself the pleasure of stroking his incredibly soft skin, of admiring his tiny fingers, and of filling your lungs with his clean, new-baby smell. If that doesn't hook you, nothing will.

♦ **Pay attention**. Your baby's needs and wants are fairly limited at this stage—feed me, change me, hold me, put me to bed—and he has a different way of letting you know which one he wants. If you pay close attention, you'll soon be able to figure out what he's "telling" you. Getting to know your baby in this way will make you feel less anxious and more confident as a parent, which will make the baby more comfortable with you, which in turn will make your mutual attachment more secure.

♦ **Read**. Another important way to get to know your baby is to carefully read the "What's Going On with the Baby" sections of this book. Knowing what

your baby is capable of—and what he isn't—at various stages can go a long
way toward helping you understand your baby's behavior and establish
reasonable expectations.

♦ **Get closer**. There's a lot of evidence that parent-child bonding comes as a
result of physical closeness. So if you'd like to speed up the process, try
carrying the baby every chance you get, taking him with you whenever you
can, and taking care of as many of his basic needs as possible.

The Incredible Shrinking Baby

In their first week or so of life, most babies lose some weight—often as much as
10 percent of their birth weight. This can be pretty scary, especially since
babies are generally supposed to get bigger over time, not smaller. This shrink-
ing baby thing is perfectly normal (in the first few days the baby isn't eating
much) and your baby will probably regain his birth weight by the time he's two
weeks old. After that, the rate of growth—for the next few months, at least—is
phenomenal: about an ounce a day and an inch per month. Doesn't sound like
much, but if he continued growing at this rate, by his eighteenth birthday your
baby would be nearly twenty feet tall and weigh in at about 420 pounds.

During every visit to the pediatrician your baby will be weighed, his overall
length and head circumference will be measured, and the results will be given
not only in inches (or centimeters) but in percentile. (If your baby is in the
75th percentile for weight, that means that he's heavier than 75 percent of
babies the same age.) Newer growth charts also include your child's BMI (body
mass index), which is a ratio of weight to height and has been very successful
in predicting obesity.

Try not to get too caught up in these numbers. As with most things, bigger
isn't necessarily better, plus it's normal for different parts of a baby's body to
grow at different rates. My two older daughters, for example, were built like
nails—90th percentile for both height and head size, but 40th percentile for
weight. The youngest was more of a pyramid: 50th percentile head, 90th in
length and weight.

Keep in mind that these charts, which are created by the National Center for
Health Statistics (and included in the Appendix of this book), are guidelines,
and can't possibly account for every situation. For the first few months, for
example, breast-fed babies tend to bulk up a little more quickly than their formula-fed agemates. But after that, formula-fed babies tend to be a bit heavier.
Unless your child is in an extreme part of the range (5th percentile and lower or
95th percentile and higher), what's significant is that he grow steadily over
time, not that he's achieved some kind of milestone.

"You have the right to remain silent . . ."

You and Your Baby

The most important thing you can do for your baby is to make him feel loved and cared for. And the best way to do this is to continue to do the activities listed on page 31, only more so.

Reading and Language

At this age, you can read just about anything to your baby—even *War and Peace* or those *New Yorker* profiles you're so behind on. The goal at this stage isn't to actually teach your baby anything; it's simply to get him used to the sounds and rhythms of language and to have him start associating reading with calm, quiet, and security. So try to read to him every day and set up a regular time and place. And as with most baby-related things, your baby will let you know whether he's interested or not, so don't force him to sit through the end of a chapter. If he lasts over five minutes, that's a lot.

If you feel like taking a break from reading, try a little singing instead. Infants love their dad's deeper voice.

If you and your partner are fluent in different languages, and you want your baby to grow up speaking both, this is the time to start compartmentalizing

them. What I mean is that you should establish some clear boundaries—
English only with Daddy, Russian with Mommy, French with the babysitter—
and stick with them. We'll talk more about this throughout the book.

Toys and Games

Giving your baby a rattle, stuffed animal, or anything else that needs to be
grasped is a total waste of time at this stage. He simply isn't interested in toys
right now. That doesn't mean, however, that he doesn't want to play. In fact, if
you pay close attention, he'll actually "tell" you when he's ready for some fun
and games. It'll probably happen during the active alert stage (page 29): your
baby will catch and hold your eye and make some kind of non-crying noise—
possibly a coo or a squeal.

It's even more important that you learn to recognize the clues your baby
gives you when he wants to quit. He'll start by turning his head or body away,
and if you ignore the message, he'll escalate to squirming, minor fussiness, and
eventually, crying or screaming.

Visual Stimulation

Since your baby still isn't capable of grabbing or holding onto much of anything, he's doing most of his learning with his eyes. Here are a few ways to
stimulate your baby visually:

- Fasten an unbreakable mirror securely to the inside of the baby's crib.
- Make sure the baby has a lot of different things to look at. For the first few
  months, infants are particularly responsive to high contrast, so black-and-
  white toys and patterns are often a big hit.
- Have your baby show you what he prefers. Hold up different patterns 12 to
  18 inches from his face for a few seconds. Which ones does he stare at
  intently? Which ones does he turn away from?
- Play some visual tracking games. With the baby on his back, hold a small
  object 12 to 18 inches from his nose. Move the object slowly to one side.
  Does the baby follow the object with his eyes? Does he move his head? Do
  the same thing for the other side.

Whatever you're doing, pay attention to the baby's mood and don't play
any longer than 5 minutes unless he really wants to. Your baby is not a trained
seal, and these activities are games, not college entrance exams.

Mobiles

Mobiles are among the most popular furnishings in almost any baby's room.

And this is the perfect time to put some up: one over the bed and perhaps another, smaller one over the changing table. When considering mobiles, keep these ideas in mind:

- Get the kind of mobiles that allow you to change the figures. As your baby gets older his taste will become more sophisticated and you'll need to keep up. My wife and I found that mobile characters were quite expensive; we could have bought a year's worth of clothes for the baby with what it would have cost us to buy five or six sets of mobile characters. The solution? Unleash the artist inside you and make your own.

- When buying or making mobile characters, keep in mind that the baby will be looking at them from underneath. Quite a number of manufacturers produce mobiles that are gorgeous when viewed from the parents' perspective, but from the baby's perspective they're essentially blank.

- At this point, your baby is still interested in simple lines: stripes, large squares, and the outlines of things. Intricate patterns or complicated designs are not appropriate now.

- Keep the mobile 6 to 18 inches above the baby's face and put it slightly to the side; babies don't like to look straight up for long.

Fun with Reflexes

"The newborn is faced with two fundamental and simultaneous challenges during the first weeks of life," writes child psychiatrist Stanley I. Greenspan. "The first is self-regulation—the ability to feel calm and relaxed, not overwhelmed by his new environment. The second is to become interested in the world about him."

Unfortunately, babies can't do much to accomplish either of these goals on their own. That's your job. And you'll do it by caring for and responding to your baby, and by providing him with a stimulating environment. But because your baby can't be expected to sit around waiting for you, he came fully equipped with a wide range of reflexes (pages 62–65) to get him started. Yes, all that wild, seemingly random arm and leg flailing really has a purpose.

Understanding these reflexes can give you greater insight into your baby's behavior. And by keeping track of when they disappear, you'll be able to monitor his development. Best of all, they're a lot of fun—for you as well as the baby.

In addition to these reflexes, there are a few more that the experts haven't yet figured out what to do with. For example, babies seem able to determine the path of an oncoming object; they will take defensive action (leaning back hard, turning away, closing eyes, bringing arms up in front of the face) if the object is going to hit them. But if the object isn't on a path that will hit the baby, he'll ignore it.

If you want to try this, strap your baby into his car seat and, from a few feet away, move a ball or other fairly large object straight at his head and again past him.

If you want to experiment with any of these reflexes, the best time is during your baby's active alert stage (see page 29). Remember to be extra careful of the baby's head and respect his desire to quit.

Family Matters: You and Your Partner

Dealing with Postpartum Blues and Depression

Somewhere between 50 and 80 percent of new mothers experience periods of mild sadness, weepiness, stress, moodiness, sleep deprivation, loss of appetite, inability to make decisions, anger, or anxiety after the baby is born. These postpartum blues, which many believe are caused by hormonal shifts in a new mother's body, can last for hours or days, but in most cases they disappear within a few weeks. One researcher, Edward Hagen, claims that postpartum blues has little, if anything, to do with hormones. Instead, he says, it's connected to low levels of social support—especially from the father. And it could be the new mother's way of "negotiating" for more involvement. Either way, if you notice that your partner is experiencing any of these symptoms, there's not much you can do except be supportive. Encourage her to get out of the house for a while and see to it that she's eating healthily.

For about 10 to 20 percent of new moms, postpartum blues can develop into *postpartum depression*, which is far more serious. Symptoms include:

♦ Postpartum blues that don't go away after two weeks, or feelings of depression or anger that surface a month or two after the birth.
♦ Feelings of sadness, doubt, guilt, helplessness, or hopelessness that begin to disrupt your partner's normal functioning.
♦ Inability to sleep when tired, or sleeping most of the time, even when the baby is awake.
♦ Marked changes in appetite.
♦ Extreme concern and worry about the baby—or lack of interest in the baby and/or other members of the family.
♦ Worries that she'll harm the baby or herself, or threats of doing either one.

Sadly, a lot of moms who have postpartum depression don't get the assistance they need—often because they feel too embarrassed to admit to anyone else what they're feeling. Untreated, the depression can last for years. Here are some other important things you can do to help your partner through this difficult time:

Exploring Your Baby's Reflexes

Your baby's reflexes are normal, involuntary actions. Some happen by themselves; some are triggered by outside events or stimuli. Because they come and go in a fairly predictable pattern, your pediatrician will track their

IF YOU	THE BABY WILL
◆ Tap the bridge of your baby's nose (gently, please), turn on a bright light, or clap your hands close to his head	◆ Close his eyes tightly
◆ Make a sudden, loud noise or give the baby the sensation of falling	◆ Fling legs and arms out and back, throw head back, open eyes wide, and cry, then bring arms back to the body and clench fingers
◆ Straighten the baby's arms and legs	◆ Flex arms and legs
◆ Pull baby up to a sitting position (be sure to support baby's head while doing this)	◆ Snap eyes open, tense shoulders, try (usually unsuccessfully) to right head
◆ Stand baby up (while holding him under the arms) on a solid surface; works just as well holding baby against a wall (but be sure to support his head)	◆ Lift one leg, then the other, as if marching
◆ Put baby on tummy on flat surface or support baby's chest on a water surface (if trying in water, *do not let go*—baby can't really swim); *never do this on a beanbag or other soft surface—baby can suffocate*	◆ Turn head to side and lift it slightly; wiggle arms around as if swimming
◆ Stroke back of hand or top of foot; gently poke sole	◆ Withdraw hand or foot and arch it
◆ Stroke leg or upper body	◆ Cross opposite leg or hand to push hand away

presence and strength as a way to assess your baby's growth and development. For you and your partner, though, they're another fun way of playing with and getting to know your baby.

WHAT IT MEANS	HOW LONG UNTIL IT'S GONE
♦ Protects baby's eyes from being injured by an object or a harsh light	♦ 1–2 months
♦ Called the Moro or startle reflex; a fairly primitive way for the newborn to call for help	♦ 3 or 4 months
♦ Probably the body's attempt to resist being held down	♦ 3 months
♦ Called the China Doll reflex; an attempt to get self upright	♦ 1–2 months
♦ Baby can protect himself by kicking away potentially dangerous things; has absolutely nothing to do with real walking	♦ About 2 months
♦ Called the Swimming reflex; a way for the baby to protect himself against smothering	♦ 2–4 months
♦ Protection against pain	♦ 2–4 months
♦ Protection against pain	♦ 3–4 months

(continued on next page)

Exploring Your Baby's Reflexes *(continued from pages 62–63)*

IF YOU	THE BABY WILL
♦ Stroke palm	♦ Tightly grasp with enough strength to allow you to pull baby to sitting position (be sure to support head)
♦ Stroke the sole of the foot from heel to toe	♦ Raise the big toe, spread the small ones, and flex the foot as if grasping
♦ Stroke cheek or mouth	♦ Turn head toward side being stroked, open mouth, and start sucking
♦ Place an object over baby's face (be *very careful* while doing this)	♦ Open and close mouth vigorously, twist head, flail arms
♦ Place baby on his back and turn his head to one side (don't force anything)	♦ Straighten arm on the side he is looking, bend arm and leg on other side

♦ Remind her that the depression is not her fault, you love her, the baby loves her, she's doing a great job, and that the two of you will get through this together.

♦ Spend more time with the baby and do as much of the housework as you can so she won't have to worry about not being able to get everything done herself.

♦ Encourage her to take breaks—regularly and frequently.

♦ Take over enough of the nighttime baby duties so your wife can get at least 5 hours of uninterrupted sleep. This means that you'll probably do a feeding or two, which is a great way to get in some extra dad-baby bonding.

♦ Help her snack on protein throughout the day instead of carbohydrates. This will help keep her blood sugar levels as even as possible, which will help smooth out her moods. If she doesn't have much of an appetite, make her a protein-rich shake.

♦ If you see that she's feeling anxious or obsessive, keep her as far away as possible from caffeine and make sure she drinks a lot of water (dehydration has been linked to anxiety).

♦ Turn off the TV news, and don't let her read the news section of the newspaper.

WHAT IT MEANS	HOW LONG UNTIL IT'S GONE
♦ Called the Palmar reflex; encourages baby to start understanding the shape, texture, and weight of whatever he's grasping	♦ 2–4 months
♦ A throwback to our monkey days, called the Babinski reflex	♦ The end of the first year
♦ Helps baby get ready to eat; called the Rooting reflex	♦ 3–4 months
♦ Attempt to keep from suffocating	♦ 5–7 months
♦ Called the Tonic Neck reflex or fencer's pose; encourages baby to use each side of body and to notice own hands	♦ 1–3 months

♦ Find a support group for her that's specifically geared for people with postpartum depression. You'll probably feel safer sharing what's going on in your house and in your head with others who are going through the same thing.

♦ Get regular breaks to relieve your own stress. Yes, she's relying on you to help her, but if you're falling apart yourself, you're not going to do her or anyone else any good.

One or two out of every thousand new mothers will develop *postpartum psychosis*. The symptoms usually start right after the birth and are usually immediately recognizable by anyone. They include wild mood swings, hallucinations, being out of touch with reality, doing something to harm herself or the baby, and making crazy or delirious statements. Postpartum psychosis is treatable—often with powerful antipsychotic drugs—but women who have it need help, and they need it fast. So if you see that your partner has any of these symptoms, put down this book and call her doctor immediately. Fortunately, despite the extensive media coverage of mothers who drown five of their children, the majority of women with postpartum psychosis don't hurt their babies or anyone else.

Even Guys Get the Blues

Although postpartum blues or depression are almost always associated with women, the fact is that many men also get the blues after their babies are born. Men's blues, however, are not usually hormonally based like their partner's. (Canadian researcher Anne Storey found that new fathers' testosterone levels often drop by as much as a third right after the birth of their children. Since testosterone is involved in energy and mood, lower levels could explain why some men feel a little down.) More likely, the feelings of sadness, the mood swings, and the anxiety you may be experiencing are the result of facing the stress, the responsibilities, the bills, and the reality of your changing life.

Here's how author S. Adams Sullivan put it: "The hearty congratulations at work last a few days, but then your status as a celebrity wears off and you begin to notice that you're coming home every night to a demanding baby and a distraught wife .... You look at your wife and . . . the healthy, radiant glow that made her beautiful while she was pregnant has disappeared, and you're tempted to agree with her when she gripes about her looks . . . you're getting maybe four and a half hours of sleep, total, and that's broken up into hour-and-a-half naps, so that you're nodding off every day at work and falling behind."

Fortunately, most men (and women, for that matter) don't suffer from any kind of postpartum depression. But if you do, you can take some comfort in knowing that it will eventually pass: you'll get caught up at work, the baby will settle into a routine, you'll get more sleep, and your wife's body will somehow get back to looking pretty much the way it did before she got pregnant.

Breast-feeding Problems

As natural as breast-feeding is, a large percentage of women have some kind of difficulty, ranging from stress and frustration to pain and infection. Researchers at the University of Utah recently discovered that a specific gene called *xanthine oxidoreductase* (XOR) may actually put some women at risk of developing breast-feeding problems. Most of the time, though, the difficulties are usually the result of not having been given proper instruction on how to breast-feed. But whether it's genetic or operator error, the fact remains that women who have problems are far more likely to give up breast-feeding than those who don't.

Because breast-feeding is so important to both your baby and your partner, it's important that you learn about the potential problems and ways of dealing with them. Here are the possibilities:

♦ **Leaky breasts**. It's exactly what it sounds like. Some women's breasts never leak; others' do during every feeding or every time they hear their baby cry. It's usually most common in the morning when the breasts are at their fullest. Breast leaking peaks during the first few weeks and tapers off over the next few months.

♦ **Sore nipples**. Breast-feeding usually takes some getting used to—for the mom and the baby—and a little discomfort is normal. Sore nipples aren't the result of frequent nursing; instead they're usually caused when the baby doesn't latch on to the breast properly. Untreated, the nipples can go from simply being sore to cracking and bleeding, which can make the entire experience miserable for your partner.

♦ **Engorged breasts**. Within a week after giving birth, your partner's milk will "come in," and her breasts may become painfully full, swollen, enormous, or hard. She may also develop a low fever. Oddly, this is actually a good thing, because it means that she's producing milk. Although engorgement is most common during the first few days of breast-feeding, it can happen any time. Painful engorgement can, for example, wake up your partner in the middle of the night. The easy solution to the problem is to empty the breast, either by having the baby eat or by pumping. Unfortunately, it's sometimes hard for babies to latch on to an engorged breast.

Medications and Mothers' Milk

During the entire time that your partner is breast-feeding, there's a risk that almost any drug she takes—whether it's for pain or for some kind of chronic or acute medical condition—could get passed into her milk and affect the baby. Most of the time the risk is very small, but sometimes it's not. Unfortunately, a lot of doctors aren't familiar with the potential risks medications pose to lactating mothers and nursing infants. As a result they may either prescribe something that's potentially dangerous or may suggest that the woman stop breast-feeding. There is an easier solution.

My wife gets migraines, and she has an entire medicine cabinet full of all sorts of powerful drugs with unpronounceable names consisting mostly of Z's and X's. After her doctors couldn't give her a definitive answer as to whether it was safe for her to take any of those drugs, we were lucky enough to stumble upon a fantastic book called *Medications and Mothers' Milk* by Thomas W. Hale. It's a comprehensive listing of prescription and nonprescription drugs, herbal remedies, and even illegal drugs, each evaluated for safety to both mother and baby during breast-feeding. If you can't order it through your local bookstore, you can get it from the publisher at 800-378-1317 or www.iBreast-feeding.com.

♦ **Clogged ducts.** This happens when milk flow within the breast is interrupted and backs up. It can cause uncomfortable lumps inside the breast and hardness, redness, and heat on the skin above the blocked duct. Clogged ducts can be caused by wearing tight bras or from not fully emptying the breast at each feeding. They usually clear up by themselves within a day or two.

♦ **Mastitis.** Mastitis is a bacterial infection. It can feel a lot like a clogged duct but is more painful and is often accompanied by fever and/or other flu-like symptoms. It can be caused by not completely emptying the breast, but the number-one reason is lowered resistance to illness, which is the result of exhaustion, stress, and poor diet. Mastitis can develop any time, but is most common during the first month of breast-feeding. Diagnosed early, it's easy to treat, usually with antibiotics. Untreated, though, it can become an abscess which has to be drained surgically.

If your partner experiences these or any other problems breast-feeding, she's going to need as much support from you as possible. In addition to the suggestions on page 45, here's how you can help:

♦ **Make sure she's comfortable.** A lot of women love breast-feeding pillows, which keep the baby high enough so they don't have to lean over, and free up their arms. Two very good ones are Boppie and My Brest Friend (I have no idea why they spell it that way).

♦ **Encourage her to nurse the baby frequently.** She should also change the baby's position every feeding and have the baby empty the breast.

♦ **Cover the breasts with warm, wet compresses for a few minutes before every feeding.** If the breasts are engorged, she should try to express some milk out before letting the baby latch on. After feedings, try cool compresses. Some women swear that putting cabbage leaves on their breasts after feeding works wonders. Hey, it's worth a try.

♦ **Buy Lansinoh cream.** It helps soothe sore, cracked, and bloody nipples and doesn't contain any ingredients that could be harmful to the baby.

♦ **Have her check her bras.** Underwire or poor fit (especially too tight) can sometimes cause or aggravate problems.

♦ **Help the baby latch on.** The baby should have a great big mouthful of breast, including as much of the areola (the dark part around the nipple) as will fit. Sucking on just the tip of the nipple will hurt.

♦ **To unclog ducts during feedings, massage the area of the clog gently and toward the nipple.**

♦ **Call her doctor if she has a fever of 100 degrees or more.** She should check with her doctor if she has pain or other symptoms that persist for more than 24 hours. She may need antibiotics.

♦ **Encourage her to continue**. The pain can be intense, and she may be tempted to quit, but in many cases, nursing through the problem can help resolve it, while stopping can make things worse.

♦ **Call in the pros**. If none of these steps helps your partner's pain or discomfort within a few days, get in touch with one of the following groups:

> ♦ La Leche League, a nonprofit organization that provides support and education to women. Phone (847) 519-7730 or (800) 525-3243, or visit their Web site, www.lalecheleague.org.
>
> ♦ International Lactation Consultant Association. Phone (919) 861-5577, or visit the Web site, www.ilca.org.

You and Your Baby

Crying

Since the moment your baby was born, he's been trying to communicate with you. That's the good news. The bad news is that he settled on crying as the way to do it. It will take you a while to teach him that there are more effective, and less annoying, ways of getting your attention. In the meantime, though, if he's like most babies, he's a real chatterbox: 80 to 90 percent of all infants have crying spells that last from twenty minutes to an hour every day. Of course, not all of your baby's tears mean that he is sad, uncomfortable, or dissatisfied with something you've done. Nevertheless, holding an inconsolably crying baby can bring out a range of emotions, even in the most seasoned parent, running from pity and frustration to fury and inadequacy.

Fathers are likely to experience these feelings—especially inadequacy—more acutely than mothers. As with so many mother/father differences, the culprit is socialization: most men come into fatherhood feeling less than completely confident in their own parenting abilities, and a baby's cries are too easily seen as confirmation that Daddy is doing a less-than-adequate job.

As difficult as crying can be to deal with, you obviously don't want your baby to be completely silent (in fact, if your baby *doesn't* cry at least several times a day, have a talk with your pediatrician). Fortunately, there are a few things you can do to make your baby's crying a less unpleasant experience for both of you:

♦ **When (not if) your child starts to cry, resist the urge to hand him to your partner**. She knows nothing more about crying babies than you do

"See what Daddy has for you, if you stop crying?"

(or will soon enough). Since each of you instinctively has a different way of interacting with the baby, your hanging in there through a crying spell will double the chances that you'll find new ways to soothe the baby.

♦ **Learn to speak your baby's language.** By now, you can almost always tell your baby's cry from any other baby's, and you can probably recognize his "I'm tired," "Feed me now," and "Change my diaper" cries. And while the language he speaks isn't as sexy or as vocabulary-rich as French, your baby has added a few more "phrases" to his repertoire, including "I'm as uncomfortable as hell," "I'm bored out of my mind," and "I'm crying because I'm mad and I'm not going to stop no matter what you do." Responding promptly when your baby cries will help you learn to recognize which cry is which. You'll then be able to tailor your response and keep your baby happy.

♦ **Carry your baby more.** The more you hold him (even when he's not crying), the less likely he is to cry. In one study, researchers found that a two-hour increase in carrying time per day resulted in a 42 percent decrease in crying time.

♦ **Get to know your baby's routine.** Keeping a diary of when your baby cries, how long the crying spells last, and what (if anything) works to slow him down can really help. Some babies like to thrash around and cry a little (or a lot) before going to sleep; others don't.

♦ **If your partner is breast-feeding, watch what she eats**. This is especially important if the baby suddenly and inexplicably deviates from his normal crying routine. Broccoli, cauliflower, brussels sprouts, and milk, when consumed by nursing mothers, may result in gastrically distressed (and weepy) babies.

After you've tried soothing, feeding, changing the diaper, checking for uncomfortable clothing, and rocking, the baby may still continue to howl. Sometimes there's really nothing you can do about it (see the next section, "Coping with Crying"), but sometimes all it takes is a new approach. Here are a few alternatives you might want to try:

♦ **Hold the baby differently**. Not all babies like to be held facing you; some want to face out so they can see the world. One of the most successful ways I've learned to soothe a crying baby—and I've tried this on many kids besides my own—is the Magic Baby Hold. (I used to call this Dave's Magic Hold because I was sure that Dave, the father of a close friend, had told me that he invented the Hold to calm his own three children. But after the first edition of this book came out, Dave denied the whole thing!) Quite simply, have the baby "sit" facing you in the palm of your hand—thumb in front, the other fingers on the baby's bottom. Then have the baby lie face down on the inside of your forearm, with his head resting on the inside of your elbow. Use your other hand to stroke or pat his back.

♦ **Distraction**. Offer a toy, a story, a song. If the baby is diverted by a story or song, you'd better be prepared to repeat it over and over and over. And don't be surprised if whatever stops the crying today seems to make it worse tomorrow. Babies are just like that.

♦ **Give the baby something to suck on**. Just take a guess why they call them "pacifiers." If you don't approve of pacifiers, you can either help the baby suck on his own fingers, or loan out one of yours (for more on pacifiers, see page 192).

♦ **Give the baby a bath**. Some babies find warm water soothing. Others freak out when they get wet. If you do decide to try bathing a crying infant, don't do it alone. Holding onto a calm soapy baby is no easy chore. Keeping a grip on a squirming, screaming, soapy baby takes a team of highly trained specialists.

♦ **Invest in a frontpack**. No matter how strong you think you are, carrying a baby around—even a newborn—is rough on the arms and back.

♦ **Take the baby for a walk or a drive**. A word of caution: this doesn't work for all babies. When she was an infant, my elder daughter used to fall asleep in the stroller or the car in a heartbeat. But the next one hated riding in the car, especially when she was tired, and cried even more whenever she saw her car seat. If you don't feel like going out, try putting the baby on top of a running washing machine or dryer—but *do not walk away*, even for a second. Alternatively, there are a number of inexpensive machines out that make thunder, rain, ocean, and jungle sounds that many babies find soothing. On the more expensive side is the SleepTight Infant Soother, a special device that, when attached to the baby's crib, simulates the feel (and sounds) of a car going fifty-five miles an hour. Call 1-800-NO-COLIC or go to www.colic.com for more information.

Coping with Crying

Starting at about two weeks of age, some 10–20 percent of babies develop colic—a word that strikes fear in the hearts of parents everywhere—crying spells that can last for hours at a time. Although many colicky babies limit their crying to certain times of the day, many others cry all day or all night or get progressively fussier as the day goes on. The duration and intensity of crying spells peaks at about six weeks, and usually disappears entirely within three months.

As hard as crying is on your baby, it's going to take a toll on you and your partner too. Here are some things that may help you cope:

♦ **Go to the drugstore**. Some parents have been able to relieve (partially or completely) their colicky infants with an over-the-counter gas remedy for adults. But before you give any medication to your child, talk to your doctor about whether she thinks taking this medication would help.

♦ **Tag-team crying duty**. There's no reason why both of you should have to suffer together through what Martin Greenberg calls "the tyranny of crying." Spelling each other in twenty-minute or half-hour shifts will do you both a world of good. Getting a little exercise during your "time off" will also calm your nerves before your next shift starts.

♦ **If you're bottle-feeding the baby, try changing his formula**. Some pediatricians suspect that colic may be linked to a milk intolerance and suggest switching to a non-cow's-milk formula.

♦ **Hold the baby facing you**. Put his head over your shoulder with your shoulder pressing on his stomach.

♦ **Hold the baby a little less**. I know this completely contradicts my suggestion a few paragraphs ago to hold the baby more, but some doctors believe that babies may cry because their nervous systems aren't mature enough to handle the stimulation that comes with being held and stroked and talked to. But don't do this unless your physician advises you to.

+ **Put a hot water bottle on your knees.** Place the baby facedown across it to warm his tummy, and stroke his back.

+ **Baby massage** (see pages 87–89).

+ **Try swaddling.** Being enveloped in a blanket may make the baby feel more comfortable.

+ **Let the baby "cry it out."** If you've tried everything you can think of and the crying has gone on for more than twenty minutes, put the baby in his crib and give yourself a break. If the baby doesn't stop screaming after five minutes, pick him up and try to soothe him again some other way for ten more minutes. Repeat as necessary. Note: The "crying it out" approach should be used only *after* you've tried everything else. Generally speaking, you should respond promptly and lovingly to your baby's cries. Several studies show that babies who are responded to in this way develop into more confident youngsters.

+ **Get some help.** Dealing with a crying child for even a few minutes can provoke incredible rage and frustration. And if the screams go on for hours, it can become truly difficult to maintain your sanity, let alone control your temper. If you find yourself concerned that you might lash out (other than verbally) at your child, call someone: your partner, pediatrician, parents, babysitter, friends, neighbors, clergy person, or even a parental-stress hotline. If your baby is a real crier, keep these numbers handy and see the section on anger (pages 267–270).

+ **Don't take it personally.** Your baby isn't deliberately trying to antagonize you. It's all too easy to let your frustration at this temporary situation wear away at your confidence in your abilities as a parent, and it could even permanently interfere with the way you treat your child.

Helping Older Kids Adjust to Their New Sibling

Handling your older children's reactions to their new baby brother or sister requires an extra touch of gentleness and sensitivity. Kids often start out wildly excited at their new status as big brother or big sister, but most will have some adjustment problems later on—as soon as they realize that the new kid is going to be sticking around for a while.

Some react with anger and jealousy. They may cry, have tantrums, and even try to hit the baby. They need to know immediately and in no uncertain terms that you understand how they feel and that it's okay to be mad and talk about how mad they are. It's even okay to draw hateful pictures or beat up a doll. But it's absolutely not okay to do anything to hurt the baby.

Others may react by regressing. My older daughter, for example, was completely potty-trained before her sister was born, but began wetting her bed again a few weeks after we brought the baby home. Some kids start talking baby talk again, suck their thumbs, need more bedtime stories and cuddling, or make demands for attention that you may not be able to satisfy.

Here are some ways you can help your older children cope with the big changes in their world:

♦ **Get them involved from the very start**. Our older daughter stayed at my parents' house while my wife was in labor with our younger daughter. But as soon as the new baby was born, we called and gave her the chance to break the news to everyone else that she was a big sister. We also had her come to the hospital right away (even though it was past her bedtime), where she got to hold her new sister "by herself."

If your older child comes to the hospital, keep the visit short. It won't take long for the initial excitement to wear off. And be sure to let him spend some time visiting with Mom, too. He may have been worried about her, and seeing her in a hospital bed, possibly with IV tubes hanging out of her arms, can be a scary sight.

♦ **Don't push too hard**. Letting the older sibling help diaper, bathe, feed, push the stroller, and clothe the new baby is a great idea if it helps bring him into the process by making him feel that the baby is "his." But don't force the older child to get too involved. It can make him feel as though you want him around only to wait on the more important new baby, which can make him resent the little interloper even more.

♦ **Prepare them for reality**. The first lesson is that infants aren't a whole lot of fun to have around for a little while. All they do is poop and cry and eat. They can't even play any games. It might be helpful to show your big kids their own baby pictures and talk to them about how they were when they were young and how you cared for them. Also, before going out as a family, warn your older child that everyone's going to be oohing and aahing over the baby, and he may feel a little left out.

♦ **Model good behavior**. Show your older kids the right ways to hold and behave with a new baby. Practicing with a doll is a great, risk-free way to get the hang of it—particularly the all-important head-supporting part. If you're bottle-feeding, show the older kids the right way to hold a bottle and how to recognize when the baby's had enough. Never, ever leave the baby unattended with an older sibling (unless you've got a teenager), and make sure the older child is always sitting down when holding the baby.

♦ **Be patient**. If your older child is angry or jealous, encourage him to talk about his feelings. If he's having trouble articulating them, you might offer a few suggestions ("Are you mad that that the baby is getting more attention than you are?") or have him draw pictures of how he feels. If your child is regressing, resist the urge to demand that he "grow up." Kids who adopt baby behavior are usually doing so because they figure that being helpless is a good way to get people to pay attention. So instead of snapping, point out some of the big-kid things they get to do that babies don't, such as using a fork and knife, riding a trike, putting on their own shoes, washing their own faces, going down a slide by themselves . . . .

♦ **Spend some extra time with them**. Your older child really needs to know that you still love him just as much as before. So make sure you get some private time together reading, going for walks, drawing, talking, seeing movies, or just hanging out. And make sure the big kid gets to spend some private time with Mom too.

♦ **Teach them about safety rules**. Your older children are probably going to want to hold and carry their new sibling. If you're going to allow it, they have to understand the proper way to hold a baby (supporting the head at all times), and they must go along with your rules about the whens and wheres. Children under about twelve shouldn't be allowed to carry a baby up or down stairs. And children under nine or ten should do all their baby holding sitting down.

Safety First

It may seem strange to talk about safety at a time when your baby is practically immobile and can't possibly get into any serious trouble. But even at this age babies can do the most surprising things. Here are a few precautions you should take now to start making your home a little safer:

♦ Avoid beanbags. Most beanbag chairs and baby rests have been taken off the market, but there are still plenty of them in garages all over the country. There is more than a coincidental link between beanbags and suffocation deaths.

♦ Never leave the baby's car seat—with the baby in it, of course—balanced on anything. A flailing arm or leg, even a sneeze, might move the car seat enough for it to tip over.

♦ Put together a good first aid kit. You can find a list of items on page 197.

♦ Take an infant CPR class. Instruction is usually available fairly inexpensively at your local Red Cross or YMCA.

♦ Take a quick look at the safety measures described in later chapters (pages 193–199, for example). Start putting together the materials you'll need and get into the habit of doing such things as pointing pot handles toward the rear of the stove.

MONTHS

First Smiles

What's Going On with the Baby

Physically

♦ By the end of this month, most of your baby's innate reflexes will have disappeared. Sad but true. Nevertheless, she still holds her arms and legs away from her body, and there's plenty of twitching to go around.

♦ Lying on her tummy, she can now easily hold her head up at a 45-degree angle. And when she's sitting (a position she probably prefers by now), she's a lot better at keeping her head straight.

♦ Your baby is now beginning to reach for objects. Grasping and unfolding her hands, which were once purely reflex actions, are slowly becoming voluntary. If she manages to grab something, she may be able to hold on to it for a few seconds before dropping it.

♦ The neurons in your baby's brain that govern vision are going through a major growth spurt. As a result, her vision is improving, and she's paying a lot more attention to what's going on in her world. And because you're such an interesting sight, she'll follow you with her eyes everywhere you go.

Intellectually

♦ As her brain develops, your baby will appreciate more complex patterns. Instead of the simple, relatively motionless outline of your face, she now prefers your eyes and mouth, which are constantly changing shape. Toward the end of this month she may begin to stare intently at very small items.

♦ If you touch her cheek now, she probably won't start sucking—an indication that she can now tell the difference between your finger and a milk-bearing nipple.

♦ She is also now able to accommodate herself to various situations. If you're holding her upright against your shoulder, she'll hold herself differently than if you're resting her on your knees.

♦ She gets excited when she sees familiar objects, but she has no sense of "object permanence" (which means that as far as the baby is concerned, anything she can't see simply doesn't exist). At the same time, though, she's developing a primitive understanding of cause and effect: when she cries, you take care of one of her needs.

Verbally

♦ Leaving behind the grunting and squeaking, your baby is expanding her vocabulary to include some delightful cooing (a combination of a squeal and a gurgle), as well as some impressive oohs, ohhs, and ahhs.

♦ Crying, however, is still one of her favorite ways of communicating.

Emotionally/Socially

♦ And now, the moment you've been waiting for: your baby is finally able to smile at you (sorry, but until now those things you thought were smiles were probably just gas), which she'll often do in response to something that pleases her.

♦ As she becomes more and more interested in learning about her world (a process that hopefully won't stop for the rest of her life), your baby will really enjoy regular changes of scenery.

♦ Her range of emotions is still fairly small, limited mostly to excitement and distress. But she's giving you a lot of hints about her future personality.

♦ She's awake about 10 hours a day; although she's stimulated more by touch than by social interaction, she'll stay awake longer if there are people around to amuse her.

What You're Going Through

Thinking about Sex

Most OB/GYNs advise their patients to refrain from intercourse for at least six weeks after giving birth. But before you mark that date on your calendar, remember that the six-week rule is only a guideline. Resuming intercourse ultimately depends on the condition of your partner's cervix and vagina, and, more important, on how you're both feeling. Many couples begin having sex again in as little as three or four weeks, but it's not at all uncommon for couples to take six months or longer to fully reestablish their prepregnancy sex life.

Many factors—both physical and psychological—influence when and how a couple decides to resume their sex life. Here are a few:

♦ When you had sex with your partner before, she was the woman you loved. Now she's also a mother—a thought that may remind you of your own mother and can be a big turn-off. At the same time, in your new capacity as parent, you may remind your partner a little too much of her own father. She may also find it tough to reconcile her roles as lover and mother, and may see herself as unsexual.

♦ Your partner may not have fully recovered from her episiotomy or C-section.

♦ Your partner may be embarrassed if milk leaks from her breasts when she's aroused. A lot of men find leaking breasts erotic. But if you don't—and she senses your feelings—she may worry that you don't find her desirable anymore.

♦ Some men have trouble coping with the idea that their partner's breasts and vagina can be functional as well as fun. And a lot of women find it difficult to think of their vaginas as sexual organs after seeing babies come out of them.

♦ You may resent your baby's unlimited access to your partner's breasts and feel that your partner is focusing more on the baby than on you.

♦ Your (or your partner's) motivation to have sex may have changed since your baby was born. If, for example, you or she were motivated to have sex because you really wanted to be a parent, sex after having a baby may feel a little anticlimactic, so to speak.

♦ Now that you have concrete proof (the baby) of your virility, you may feel more intimate with your partner than ever before.

Nonsexual and Almost Nonsexual Affection

Most adults have a limited repertoire of ways to please each other. But there are plenty of ways to be sensual short of intercourse. Hand-holding, back rubs, hair stroking while watching TV, or even gentle, nonsexual kissing are good for those times one of you isn't in the mood. If you're not in the mood but want to give—or receive—some nonsexual affection, tell your partner up front that there are no strings attached. Researchers have found that men and women who don't want sex are frequently afraid that the kiss or hug they need from, or want to give to, their partners will be misinterpreted as a sexual overture.

The First Time . . . Again

When you do finally get around to making love, you should expect the first few times to be a period of tentative rediscovery for both of you. Her body has changed, and she may respond differently than she used to. Some studies have shown that after giving birth, women experience a slightly decreased interest in vaginal stimulation and an increased interest in clitoral and breast stimulation. Also, women who experienced multiple orgasms before giving birth are less likely to do so, or will do so less frequently, now.

She may also be worried that having sex will hurt, and you may be afraid of the same thing or that those extra pounds she hasn't lost yet will interfere with her pleasure. Go slowly, take your cues from her, and give yourselves plenty of time to get used to each other again.

Sex researchers William Fisher and Janice Gray found that nursing mothers generally resume their sexual lives sooner than women who don't breast-feed. This is a little odd, considering that nursing mothers produce lower levels of ovarian hormones, which are responsible for producing vaginal lubrication. As a result, if your partner is nursing, her vagina may be much drier than before, making intercourse painful. Obviously, this doesn't mean she isn't aroused by you; it's simply a common postbirth condition. In situations like these, a little K-Y Jelly, Astroglide, or other over-the-counter lubricant will go a long way.

And while you're out buying lubricant, pick up a few boxes of condoms too. Despite what you may have heard about women *not* being able to get pregnant during the time that they're breast-feeding, the truth is that nursing is *not* an effective means of contraception. Your partner's periods will probably start up again between three and eight months after the birth. But since ovulation happens about two weeks before the period starts, she may not know that she's fertile again until it's too late. So unless the two of you really want two kids less than a year apart, get in the habit of using some kind of protection every time you have sex. Barrier methods (condoms or diaphragm) are probably best right now. But have your partner check with her OB to see whether any of the oral contraceptives are safe during breast-feeding.

When You and Your Partner Are Out of Sync

Just as you and your partner can't always agree on what movie you want to see or what you want to have for dinner, you can't expect that you'll both feel sexually aroused at the same time. She might want to make love at a time when you're simply too tired to move. Or you might want to have sex when she's feeling "touched out," having spent an entire day with a baby crawling all over her, sucking her breasts.

The months right after the birth of a baby are a particularly vulnerable time for your sex life. If you had great sex before or even during the pregnancy, don't take it for granted that everything will be as it was—you'll still have to work on it. And if your pre-baby sex life wasn't that great, don't count on it getting better anytime soon. Either way, here are a few suggestions that might help smooth over some of the rough spots you'll invariably encounter:

♦ **Figure out what, exactly, is motivating you to want to have sex**. That may sound ridiculous—you want to have sex because it feels good, right? Well, sort of. "Sex can be an expression of monogamy, intimacy, love, or even an affirmation of one's sexual identity ('I'm a man and this is what men do')," says Linda Perlin Alperstein, an associate professor at the University of California, San Francisco. "It can also be the only way some of us ever get held and touched lovingly in our culture." And for some people (this is pretty rare, though) sex is thought of exclusively as a way to reproduce.

♦ **Talk**. Most people—men and women—feel embarrassed to tell our partner exactly what we like and don't like. But doing so is absolutely essential— not only to getting your sex life back on track, but to the overall health of your relationship.

♦ **Negotiate**. If you really want to have sex, and she doesn't, ask her— without putting a lot of pressure on her—what, if anything, she'd be willing to do. Would she, for example, be willing to masturbate you? Would she hold you in her arms or let you touch her breasts while you stimulate yourself? It goes without saying (or at least it should) that you should be prepared to reciprocate. The object here is not to convince her to have sex with you; the two of you should be working toward creating an environment in which you both feel safe expressing your desires and in which each of you can turn the other down without fear of causing offense or hurting feelings.

♦ **Be completely honest**. If you and your partner agree that you'll hold each other like spoons and kiss, but that you won't touch each other's genitals, don't go over the line. Doing so will only make her tense and distrustful.

♦ **Change your attitude**. A lot of men have the idea that every erection has to result in an ejaculation. But is having an orgasm the only way to experi-

"You're not real experienced at this father business, are you?"

ence pleasure? Not a chance. Sometimes just getting aroused—and leaving it right there—can be fun.

♦ **Start dating again**. No, not someone else—your partner. Having a good sex life can certainly contribute to the happiness of your relationship, but even the wildest, most amazing sex doesn't guarantee anything. So make sure to set aside some time every day—even if it's only 15 minutes—to talk about life, work, movies you've seen, books you've read, politics, whatever. But *don't* talk about anything to do with your baby.

♦ **Ask for—and give your partner—some nonsexual affection** (see page 78).

Not Ready to Be a Father

One of the most consistent findings by researchers is that new fathers almost always feel unprepared for their new role. Personally, I would have been surprised if it were otherwise. When most of our fathers were raising us, a "good father" was synonymous with "good provider." He supported his family financially, mowed the lawn, washed the car, and maintained discipline in the home. No one seemed to care whether he ever spent much time with his children; in fact, he was discouraged from doing so, and told to leave the kids to his wife, the "good mother."

Yesterday's "good father" has now retroactively become an emotionally distant, uncaring villain. And today's "good father," besides still being a breadwinner, is expected to be a real presence—physically and emotionally—in his kids' lives. This, in a nutshell, is exactly what most new fathers want. Most of us have no intention of being wait-till-your-father-comes-home dads and want to be more involved with our children than our own fathers were. The problem is that we just haven't had the training. The solution? Quit complaining and jump right in. The "maternal instinct" that women are supposedly born with is actually acquired on the job. And that's exactly where you're going to develop your "paternal instinct."

Confusion

If there's one thing that set my first few months of fatherhood apart from the next few years, it was the confusing and often conflicting emotions I felt:

- ♦ On the one hand, I had a sense of incredible virility, power, and pride at having created a new life. On the other, I often felt helpless when I couldn't understand—let alone satisfy—the baby's needs.
- ♦ Most of the time I felt the most powerful kind of love for my tiny child. But sometimes I also felt ambivalent. And once in a while I felt a powerful anger—one that seemed to come out of nowhere—at the very same baby.
- ♦ Most of the time I felt particularly close to my wife—especially when we would admire our children together. But every so often I'd get suspicious that she loved them more than she did me.

Being confused leads a lot of guys to feel that there's something wrong with them. You'd be amazed at the number of questions I get via e-mail or in person, at workshops I do with fathers, that start with the same seven words: "Am I the only one who feels . . .?"

Before you go off and check yourself into a mental hospital, there are a few things you should know. First, being confused isn't abnormal at all. If you want proof, all you have to do is start asking a few of the other new dads you know whether they're feeling some of the same things you are. You'll probably find that (a) they have the same feelings you do, and (b) they also think they're abnormal. That begs the question: if almost everyone thinks he's abnormal, then isn't being abnormal the norm? If that doesn't reassure you at least a little, maybe this will: this state of confusion—and the accompanying suspicions about your sanity—usually disappear by the end of the third month.

Fears—Lots of Them

The combination of feeling unprepared and confused at the same time can be rather frightening, and the first few months of fatherhood are riddled with fears. Here are some of the most common:

♦ Fear of not being able to live up to your own expectations.
♦ Fear of not being able to protect your children from physical harm as they grow and develop.
♦ Fear of not being able to deal with the most basic parenting responsibilities: feeding, clothing, earning enough money, dealing with the baby's illnesses.
♦ Fear of not being able to shield your child from some of the more abstract horrors of modern life: poverty, war, disease, the destruction of the environment . . .
♦ Fear of simply not being "ready" to assume the role of father.
♦ Fear of picking up the baby because you think you might hurt her.
♦ Fear of your anger at the baby.
♦ Fear of not being able—or willing—to love the baby enough.
♦ Fear of not being in control (see pages 84–85).
♦ Fear of repeating the mistakes made by your own father (see pages 106–107).
♦ Fear that if you discuss your fears with your partner, she'll misinterpret them and think you don't love her or the baby.

Some fears—such as fear of poverty and war, or of not being ready—you just can't do anything about. But others you can. For example, fear of not being able

---

Don't Panic

Taken together, the feelings of unpreparedness, the fears, and the confusion so many new fathers experience can be overwhelming. Unfortunately, some men respond to this turmoil by running away—emotionally, physically, or both—from their kids and their partners. If you're feeling unable to deal with your anxieties and your feelings, do not run. Find yourself a more experienced father about your age and ask him to help you sort things out (see pages 186–188 for information on fathers' groups). If you can't find another father, talk to your partner. And if none of those alternatives work, find a good therapist, preferably one with experience dealing with men's concerns. Most important, remember that all this is absolutely normal, and that you're not the only one going through it. There is help out there; you just have to find it.

to handle the little things can be overcome by practice; fear of hurting the baby can also be overcome by spending more time carrying, stroking, picking up, and holding her—babies are not nearly as fragile as they look; and the fear of discussing things with your partner can be cured (to a certain extent) by taking a deep breath and telling her what you feel. She's going through many of the same things you are and will be relieved to find that she's not alone. Guaranteed.

Whatever your worries, you need to start by admitting to yourself that they exist and remembering that all new fathers are afraid sometimes. In his book *Fatherjournal*, David Steinberg eloquently describes coming to terms with himself and his fears. "I was going to be the perfect father: loving, caring, nurturing, soft. . . . I was going to do it right. . . . Tonight I see how scared I am. There is so much to do for this little creature who screams and wriggles and needs and doesn't know what he needs and relies on me to figure it out. . . . I need to accept my fear, my reluctance, my instinct to flee. I have to start from where I am instead of where the model new-age father would be."

Hey! Who's In Charge Around Here Anyway?

It's hard to admit, but like it or not, your baby's running your life. She cries, you pick her up. She's hungry, you feed her. She fills her diaper, you change it. She wants to play, you play. She needs a nap, you drive around the block twelve times until she falls asleep. She wakes up in the middle of the night, you're up too. The ancient rabbis of the Talmud described it pretty well. The first stage of life, they said, "commences in the first year of human existence, when the infant lies like a king on a soft couch, with numerous attendants about him, all ready to serve him, and eager to testify their love and attachment by kisses and embraces." It's all happening on your baby's schedule, not yours.

Being out of control is hard for anyone, but it's especially discombobulating for men, who are supposed to know everything and be in control all the time. Before my oldest daughter was born, I was incredibly anal about time; I always showed up wherever I was supposed to be exactly when I was supposed to, and I demanded the same from others. But, as you now know, going on a simple trip to the store with baby in tow takes as much planning as an expedition to Mount Everest. And getting anywhere on time is just about impossible.

You may be a great salesman or negotiator or a cult leader, but your ability to turn adults to your way of thinking won't work with a baby. Babies are, almost by definition, irrational and not at all interested in your timetables. In no time at all your baby will figure out what you're most rigid and impatient about, and she'll begin pushing your buttons. That leisurely walk in the park you planned might have to be cut short when the baby panics and won't stop crying after a friendly dog licks her face. Or you might end up having to stay a few extra hours at a friend's house so as not to wake the baby if she's sleeping or, if she's awake, not to upset her nap schedule by having her fall asleep in the car on the way home. And just when you think you've figured out her routines and the surefire tricks to comfort her or get her to sleep, she revamps everything.

So you've got a very Zen choice to make: you can either learn to accept change and bend, or you can break. It took a while, but I eventually learned that trying to be a father and Mr. Prompt at the same time just wasn't going to work. Most of the men I interviewed said basically the same thing: Since becoming fathers, they'd learned to be a lot more flexible and tolerant—not only of themselves and their limitations, but of other people's as well.

You and Your Baby

Awakening the Senses

Your baby was born equipped with the same five basic senses you were. And although they'll probably develop just fine without any outside intervention, gently encouraging them along by exposing your baby to a broad range of sensory stimulation can be a lot of fun for both of you. As we've already discussed, pay attention to your baby's cues and don't drag any of these activities out for more than a few minutes. If she's interested, she'll let you know by paying attention. If she's not, she'll let you know that too, by crying or fussing or turning away.

TASTE

By putting drops of various foods (in liquid) on babies' tongues, researchers have proven that babies have definite likes and dislikes. You're not going to try this, of course. At this age, your baby has no business eating anything but breast milk or formula. Save the experiments with real taste sensations for when you start introducing solid foods. (see pages 157–158). In the meantime, give the baby lots of different objects to put in her mouth. But be extremely careful that none of them has removable pieces or sharp edges, or is small enough to be a choking hazard. (Anything that can fit through the tube in a standard roll of toilet paper is too small.)

SMELL

Offer the baby a wide variety of things to smell:

♦ If you're cooking, let her smell the spices and other ingredients.
♦ If you're out for a walk, let her smell the flowers.

♦ Try some experiments to see whether she prefers sweet smells to sour ones.

♦ Be careful, though. Make sure she doesn't get any of these things in her mouth, and don't experiment with extremely strong smells. Also, stay away from ammonia, bleach, gasoline, paint thinner, pool or garden chemicals, and any other toxic materials you may have around the house.

VISION

Your baby's eyes are still getting used to being outside the womb, and she focuses best on objects that are 8–12 inches from her, so be sure to hold toys and other objects within that range.

♦ Play tracking games, moving objects slowly back and forth in front of her eyes. She may even begin to anticipate what you'll do next. You can also help boost her hand-eye coordination by holding an object within arm's reach and letting her try to grab it.

♦ Emphasize high-contrast (black and white or bright) colors. Regularly change the patterns and keep track of which ones she prefers. Over the course of the next few months she'll advance from simple shapes and patterns to more complex ones.

♦ Show her mirrors, pictures, and photographs.

♦ Regularly change the baby's position in her crib so that she has different things to look at. This is also a great time to hang a mobile.

♦ Take the baby out for a walk and let her see what's going on in the world.

TOUCH

♦ Expose the baby to as many textures as possible: the satin edges of her blanket; the plastic (or cloth) on her diaper; the family dog; a window; your computer keyboard; warm things and cool things; smooth ones and rough

No Baby Talk, Please

Whenever you talk to your baby, pay close attention to your voice. Your natural, conversational voice is best because it exposes the baby to English as it is actually spoken. For some reason I've never been able to understand, many people can't bring themselves to speak naturally to a baby. Instead, they smile the biggest fake smile they can and say things like "Cootchie-cootchie widduw baby-poo, can I pinchy-winchy your cheeky-weeky?" Is that really the way you want your baby to learn how to speak? Need I say more?

ones. Let the baby feel each object for as long as she's interested. It's a good idea to carefully wash the baby's hands after you do this, especially if you had her touch the family pet or anything else that could cause problems if she were to put her hands in her mouth or rub them in her eyes.

♦ Don't limit yourself to the baby's hands; you can gently rub objects on her cheeks, arms, or legs. (From a very young age, all of my kids loved me to rub the bottoms of their feet on my two-day beard growth.) Again, use common sense here. Be gentle and don't leave any objects with the baby.

HEARING

♦ Expose the baby to as wide a variety of sounds as possible: the radio; any musical instruments you have around the house; construction sites (if they're not too loud). Does your baby seem to prefer one kind of noise—or music— over another? If you do opt for music, don't feel limited to Mozart. Instead, let her listen to as many different styles as you can stand. Simple melodies and moderate tempi are best at this stage—very fast music may overstimulate her. And be sure to keep the volume down; babies' hearing is very sensitive and easily damaged by excessively loud noise.

♦ For fun, take a small bell, hold it behind the baby, and ring it gently. Does she try to turn around? Now move the bell to one side. Did she notice the change?

♦ Don't forget about your own voice. Make sounds, changing the pitch of your voice; sing; and even have leisurely chats (okay, monologues) with the baby.

♦ Play imitation games. Make a noise (a Bronx cheer is always a good place to start) and see whether the baby responds. It may take a few minutes or even a few days to get a reply. Once you do, try the same noise a few more times and then switch roles, having the baby initiate the "conversation" so you can imitate her.

Baby Massage

Many parents in other countries massage their babies every day, but in the United States the idea is just catching on. And in the eyes of some, it's about time. According to researcher Tiffany Field and other experts, massage may:

♦ Facilitate the parent-infant bonding process and the development of warm, positive relationships.

♦ Reduce stressful responses to painful procedures like vaccines (at least for the baby).

♦ Reduce pain associated with teething and constipation.

♦ Reduce colic.

♦ Help reduce sleep problems.

♦ Lower your stress levels while raising your self-esteem and self-confidence as a parent.

As fantastic as that all sounds, keep a lid on your expectations. While massage *may* provide some or all of the above advantages for some people, it may not be as successful for you. However, it's still a wonderful way of interacting with and getting to know your baby.

Sounds like it's at least worth a try, doesn't it? Let's start with a few general guidelines first:

♦ Schedule it. The best time is when both you and the baby are relaxed and calm and when you can have 10–20 minutes without interruption. Right after the baby's bath or right before putting her to bed are good, but you can do it anytime you want, as long as it's not right when you expect the baby to start fussing. Try to do at least a few minutes of massage every day (or split the duties with your partner).

♦ Find a warm room with a clean, flat surface you can put the baby on.

♦ Cover the surface with something soft and absorbent, since your baby will be naked.

♦ Sing or talk to your baby while you're doing the massage.

♦ Use firm but gentle pressure. Newborns don't like too light a touch—it seems like tickling and annoys them. At the same time, you're not doing deep-tissue, shiatsu, or Rolfing, so there's no need for any gouging, banging, or thumping.

♦ The first few times you massage your baby, do each technique once or twice. Go to two or three times after a few weeks, and even more if your baby really seems to love something you're doing.

♦ Pay attention to your baby's cues. If she seems unhappy, stop.

There are all sorts of techniques out there for doing baby massage. Here's my favorite:

1. Pour a few drops of vegetable oil into one palm, then rub your hands together to warm the oil.

2. With the baby on her back, start with her arms and legs, rolling each one between both of your hands the way you used to do when you made snakes out of clay when you were a kid.

3. Roll each of the toes between your thumb and forefinger in kind of a This–Little–Piggy fashion.

4. Put one palm on your baby's tummy, your little finger close to her rib cage.

Pressing firmly, move the hand downward. As soon as that hand reaches the pubic bone, repeat with the other hand. The complete motion is kind of like digging in the sand with your hands.

5. Alternatively (or in addition), place both palms on the baby's tummy, index fingers touching. Pressing firmly, move both hands out, as if parting the Red Sea.

6. Turn the baby over onto her tummy.

7. Starting with the back of the head, move your hands slowly, in one smooth stroke, all the way down to her heels.

8. Now do it again, except this time, use two or three fingers on each hand and make circles as you move from head to heels. Don't forget to massage the butt.

9. Using both of your thumbs, gently press on the bottom of each of the baby's feet, stroking from heel to toe.

Hey, What Happened to My Baby's Head?

Your baby's skull is made up of several bones that will remain somewhat flexible until she's two. For that reason, babies who lie on their backs for too long (particularly preemies) may develop a flat spot on the skull. In most cases, this kind of "positional molding" isn't anything to worry about. But if you don't deal with it relatively early, it can cause the ears and eyes to be out of alignment, or lead to even more severe facial deformities.

If your baby's head looks asymmetrical or you think she's got a flat spot, the best thing to do is to frequently switch her sleeping positions. Every time you put her down for a nap or for the night, put her in a different position in her crib (head toward one side, then the other). That way, even if your baby likes one particular view from the crib, she'll have to turn her head from side to side to see it.

As we've discussed, your baby should always sleep on her back. But you might want to put a small wedge pillow or a rolled-up receiving blanket behind her to keep her on a slight angle when she's sleeping. Check with your doctor first before you do this. When she's awake, have her spend plenty of time on her tummy (see page 90).

If you don't notice any improvement within a week, take the baby in to see her doctor. In very rare cases, a flattened head could be an indicator of a more serious condition that can be corrected only through surgery or by wearing a corrective headband or helmet.

The Importance of Squirming Around

Your two-month-old isn't really mobile yet. While on her back, she can raise her head to about 45 degrees, but rolling over is still a few months away. Nevertheless, your baby's muscles need a little exercise. Here are a few ways to help her get a workout:

♦ Stop swaddling (if you haven't already). Your baby needs to practice using her arms and hands, something she won't be able to do if she's all bundled up in a blanket.

♦ Encourage tummy time. Although your baby should always sleep on her back, make sure she spends plenty of time in other positions while she's awake. This will encourage her to use different muscles. Babies who don't get much tummy time don't learn to roll over as quickly as those who do (although does a month or two difference really matter? How many adults do you know who can't roll over from front to back or vice versa?) Spending time on her tummy gives your baby a little upper-body workout, strengthening her arms and neck muscles and encouraging her to use them more.

Introducing the Doctor

If you went to all your partner's prenatal doctor appointments, the schedule of visits to your baby's pediatrician will seem quite leisurely—only eight the entire first year (usually called well-baby checkups). Whether or not you got into the doctor-visit habit before the baby was born, make every effort to go to as many well-baby visits (and not-so-well-baby visits) as you can. Doing so is good for everyone; here's why:

♦ Your baby will know that she can turn to you for help and that you'll be there to comfort her when she needs it.

♦ Your doctor will be able to get some of your family history to apply to the baby. And since most of what pediatricians know about their young patients comes from what the parents tell them, your input doubles the amount of information the doctor can use to make a diagnosis.

♦ You'll be more in touch with your child and more involved in her life.

Most doctor visits will be pretty much the same: the nurse will try to convince the baby to lie flat enough to be measured, and to keep still on a scale long enough to get weighed. Then the doctor will poke the baby's stomach, measure her head, and ask you a series of questions about the baby's health. He or she may also ask you to immobilize the baby to facilitate a quick ear exam.

Between visits, keep a running list of questions and concerns you and your partner want to discuss, and don't be shy about going through every item. No one expects you to know everything. At this point, most new parents are worried about whether their baby is developing normally. Rest assured, even though well-baby visits may not seem all that thorough, your pediatrician is focusing on exactly that question.

Break out the needles

The big event at most doctor visits for the first several years are the immunizations, so if you're squeamish about needles, you'd better get over it. We'll

---

Immunizations

There has been a lot of controversy lately about immunizations (Are the vaccines themselves dangerous? Are the risks worth the rewards?), and a small but growing number of people are electing not to have their children inoculated. On pages 92–95 you'll find a chart listing the vaccines, the possible side effects, and what might happen to someone who's not inoculated. If you're thinking of skipping the vaccinations, keep these points in mind:

♦ Almost all public schools, and many private ones, require proof of vaccination before admitting a child.

♦ Not vaccinating your kids can be a viable option only if everyone else's kids are vaccinated, thus reducing the chance that your child will be exposed to health risks. This is known as "herd immunity": if enough people are immune, they'll protect the rest of the "herd." Imagine what would happen if everyone decided not to vaccinate.

♦ Today's vaccinations protect babies against almost a dozen diseases. Twenty-five years ago, they covered only four.

♦ Many vaccines work by introducing an *antigen* into the body. Antigens are incredibly tiny amounts of the actual disease they're supposed to protect against; they ready the body's immune system to attack similar (but much larger) invasions later on. Some people believe that too many antigens can overwhelm a baby's immature immune system. But thanks to a number of medical developments, babies are getting exposed to fewer antigens today than they were when you were immunized. In 1980, the pertussis vaccine alone had 3,000 antigens. Today, for example, it contains about five. And there are fewer than 130 antigens total contained in the 11 standard vaccines.

VACCINE	RISKS (👎) / REWARDS (👍)
Diphtheria, Pertussis, Tetanus (DTaP) or Diphtheria, Tetanus (DT): same as above, minus pertussis part for babies who have: ♦ history of seizures ♦ suspected or known neurological disease ♦ reactions to previous shot	👍 almost all protected after 3 doses plus booster 👎 you'll need to observe baby carefully for 72 hours after shot 👎 some fussiness, drowsiness, soreness, or a lump at injection site 👎 fever for 24 hours after the shot is common 👎 irritation of the brain occurs in 1 in 100,000 kids, and rarely (1 in 310,000), permanent brain damage results *Note:* Most of the risks are associated with the pertussis component. The only risk associated with the diphtheria and tetanus parts is local (injection site) swelling and slight fever
Hepatitis B—a noninfectious vaccine produced from cultures	👍 almost all children protected after 3 doses 👎 no adverse reactions, but occasional fussiness 👎 possible soreness at injection site, low-grade fever, or headache
Haemophilus (HiB)	👍 90–100 percent protection rate after the full series of shots 👎 soreness and/or lump at the injection site 👎 fever (rarely above 101 degrees) for 12–24 hours after shot
Measles	👍 over 95 percent protected after one dose 👎 10–20 percent have mild fever or rash 10 days after shot 👎 1 in 1,000,000 may develop a brain disorder

WHAT IT PREVENTS	RISKS IF BABY GETS THE DISEASE
Diphtheria, a severe respiratory illness; rare in the U.S.	♦ extremely contagious ♦ attacks the throat and nose, interferes with breathing, and causes paralysis ♦ damages heart, kidneys, nerves ♦ 10–35 percent death rate ♦ causes coughing so severe that the baby can't eat or breathe
Pertussis (whooping cough): prior to the invention of this vaccine, pertussis caused as many deaths as all other contagious diseases combined	♦ can cause brain damage, pneumonia, and seizures ♦ can cause death (1–2 percent) ♦ most severe in young babies
Tetanus (lockjaw), caused by dirt getting in cuts	♦ causes painful muscle contractions ♦ 20–60 percent of kids die
Hepatitis B	♦ important cause of viral hepatitis ♦ complications include cirrhosis, chronic active hepatitis, and liver cancer ♦ rare in children but an infected mom may pass it on to the kids via breast milk
Haemophilus Influenza type B, bacterial infection of children under 5	♦ causes 12,000 cases of meningitis and 8,000 cases of deep-seated infections (bones, joint, heart, lungs, blood, and throat) each year ♦ 5 percent mortality rate
Measles	♦ a most serious, common childhood disease ♦ high fever (103–105 degrees) and rash for up to 10 days ♦ may cause pneumonia or ear infection ♦ 1 in 100 kids becomes deaf or develops brain disorders

(continued on next page)

(continued from pages 92–93)

VACCINE	RISKS (👎) / REWARDS (👍)
Mumps	👍 99 percent protected after one dose 👎 rare fever, rashes, and swelling of glands after vaccination
Rubella	👍 over 95 percent protected after one dose 👍 getting it now protects future fetuses of girl babies 👍 children of pregnant women can be vaccinated without risk to mother 👎 1 percent of young children will have temporary leg, arm, or joint pain
MMR—measles, mumps, and rubella vaccines	👍 protection is as good as when vaccines are given separately 👍 side effects are the same as when given separately
Inactivated Polio Vaccine (IPV); an injection has replaced the riskier Oral Polio Vaccine (OPV), which you probably got (drops, usually in a sugar cube)	👍 very effective. No new cases of polio in the U.S. for over 25 years 👍 95 percent receiving all 3 doses are protected 👍 no common reactions 👎 1 in 4 million chance of paralysis
Chicken pox (varicella)	👍 extremely effective in preventing the disease 👎 soreness, fever, mild rash are common side effects 👎 seizures (1 per 1,000 vaccinations) and pneumonia are very rare
Pneumococcal Conjugate Vaccine (PCV)	👍 the best way to protect against pneumococcal bacteria, which is very resistant to antibiotics 👎 minor side effects include pain, swelling, fever

WHAT IT PREVENTS	RISKS IF YOU GET THE DISEASE
Mumps	◆ causes fever, tonsillitis, swollen cheeks, and swelling of salivary glands ◆ may cause irritation of heart, pancreas, or thyroid ◆ can cause permanent deafness and temporary brain disorder
Rubella (German measles)	◆ can cause birth defects in fetus of pregnant women ◆ symptoms are mild, often missed
Mumps, Measles, Rubella	
Polio	◆ causes paralysis of arms and legs ◆ interferes with breathing ◆ 1 in 10 kids with polio dies
Chicken pox	◆ Fever, tiredness, and 250–500 blistery spots ◆ Can cause skin infection, scarring, and pneumonia ◆ Rarely fatal (about six deaths per 100,000 infants)
Pneumonia and meningitis	◆ Causes meningitis, pneumonia, and blood infections, and is responsible for hundreds of deaths in the U.S. each year

discuss some specific medical questions in later chapters. But for now, here's a fairly typical schedule of well-baby checkups and the immunizations your baby will receive at each visit:

AGE AT TIME OF VISIT	VACCINATION(S) GIVEN
birth–2 weeks (before hospital discharge)	Hepatitis B, first dose (can be delayed for two months if the mother tests negative for the antigen)
2 months	IPV, PCV, DTaP, HiB, and first dose of Hepatitis B, if not already given earlier
4 months	IPV, PCV, DTaP, HiB, and Hepatitis B
6 months	IPV, PCV, DTaP, HiB, and Hepatitis B (flu shot optional)
12 months	MMR, Varicella, PCV, and TB test

But What Does "Normal" Mean?

At the very beginning of each chapter in this book, I discuss the developmental milestones that your baby will *probably* achieve by the end of that month. Keep in mind that these milestones are only guidelines and that not all babies the same age are in the same place at the same time. This is especially true if your baby was born prematurely.

To get a better handle on what's "normal" for a preemie, you'll need to use her adjusted age (that's her actual age minus the number of months she was born early). For example, a four-month-old baby who was born two months early would have an adjusted age of only two months and will be evaluated against two-month-old standards. Premature babies usually catch up to their agemates by the time they're two or three. But the more premature the baby, the longer it takes to pull even.

At this point, red flags that might concern your baby's doctor include:

♦ Not being able to hold her head up for at least a few seconds, holding her hands in fists most of the time, or general poor muscle tone.

♦ Asymmetrical movement. Does your baby seem to be using one leg or arm a lot more than the other? Most babies don't develop a true "handedness" until about age two. Some interesting research links asymmetrical movement with development of autism later in life.

♦ Absence of or extended persistence of various reflexes (see the chart on page 62–65).

A Few Important Health and Safety Issues

Getting your home completely childproofed is a process that never ends.

We'll talk extensively about it on pages 193–199, but there are a few things you should really take care of now.

- Turn your water heater down to 120 degrees. You may decide to take a shower or bath with your baby, and water hotter than that can cause permanent injury and scarring.
- Check out your baby's sleeping area. Whether she's in a bassinet, cradle, or crib, all of the following should apply:
  - The mattress should fit into the frame snugly enough that it's hard to get your hand into the gap.
  - If the crib is painted, make sure the paint is not toxic. Your baby's going to be chewing on it in a few months, and the last thing you want to worry about is poisonous paint chips.
  - The bars or slats on the crib should be no further apart than 2⅜ inches.
  - No pillows, blankets, or anything else that could possibly be a smothering hazard. It you're worried that your baby will get cold, put her in a warm sleep suit. If you're using crib bumpers or you've hung toys across the crib for the baby to swat at, make sure they are tied on very, very securely.

Is Your Baby Working the Graveyard Shift?

By the end of this month your baby's sleep and nap schedule should start to get a little more regular and predictable. Unfortunately, there's a pretty good chance that her schedule is going to be exactly the opposite of what you'd hoped it would be: she'll sleep more during the day and be up at night. In a way, this makes sense. While she was pregnant, your partner was probably awake during the day, and all of her movements rocked the baby to sleep. At night, though, when your partner slowed down, the baby woke. That's exactly why most pregnant women say that within a few minutes after lying down, the baby would start kicking up a storm.

Eventually, your baby will get her timetables straightened out and start living in your time zone. If you don't feel like waiting, there are a few things you can do that might help speed up the process:

- Wherever the baby sleeps, keep it as dark as you can all the time. All you need is a small nightlight so you don't stub your toes when you go in and out. If you need to, buy thick shades.
- Help the baby get lots of naps during the day. At this age she shouldn't be up for any more than an hour or two at a stretch. Although you might think that depriving her of daytime naps would exhaust her and make her sleep

Breast-feeding and Older Kids

Despite how wonderful breast-feeding is for the new baby, your older kids may see it as little more than an attempt to displace them from the center of the universe. And seeing Mom holding and cuddling and nursing often brings up all sorts of feelings—anger and jealousy being at the top of the list (see pages 73–74 for more on coping with this). Some new big brothers and sisters will want to be held the same way the baby is being held. Some will even want to nurse. If the older sibling is young enough, your partner may actually want to give in to the request. If so, it should only be on a very temporary basis. (Giving a teaspoonful or two of breast milk might be a better solution—most older kids won't like the watery consistency or the sweet taste.) Older children need to know that your partner's milk is for the baby and that big kids get to have—and do—lots of other things that newborns don't.

through the night, it doesn't work that way. Overtired babies actually wake up more than well-rested ones.

♦ Set a regular bedtime—7 P.M. is good—and start making it part of your routine. Again, keeping the baby up till midnight might seem like a good way to extend her sleep time, but it'll backfire.

♦ No playing around. When the baby wakes up at night, feed her, change her—without turning on the lights—and put her back to bed. No games, no stories. You want her to start making associations between dark and sleep.

You and Your Partner

No One Ever Told Me It Was Going To Be Like This. . .

During the first few days of parenthood, you and your partner may experience a kind of honeymoon period where you marvel at the little baby you made and feel closer to each other than ever before. Life seems as though it just couldn't get any better.

But as the days turn into weeks and months, the charm wears off and reality sets in. You're both getting used to a new schedule and new responsibilities. And instead of focusing on each other, as you used to do before you had kids, your world now revolves around the baby. You barely get any uninterrupted adult time together, and neither of you is getting your needs met. Throw in a little sleep deprivation and a few disagreements on parenting style, and you've got a perfect recipe for conflict.

As hard as all this is on you, it's probably even tougher on your partner, especially if you're back at work. Staying at home with a newborn is a thankless task, and your partner really needs to know that you appreciate what she's doing. Here's how you can get the point across:

♦ **Start off by coming right out and saying so.** Tell her she's a great mom, that you love her, that you're proud of her, and that you're amazed at how big the baby's getting on a diet of nothing more than the breast milk she's producing.

♦ **Buy her flowers**. Or send her faxes, bring little gifts for her and the baby, and call a few times a day to see how she's doing.

♦ **Take her out on dates**. That could mean anything from ordering in pizza to actually leaving the baby with a sitter for a few hours while the two of you go for a walk. In Oakland, where I live, there's a movie theater that sets aside two shows a week for new parents. The place is packed with moms, dads, and howling babies. But they crank up the volume and bring food right to your seat, and it's a great way to escape. I know there are similar theaters in other cities.

♦ **Encourage her to socialize**. As someone who's been a stay-at-home dad, I can tell you that spending all day alone with a baby can drive you nuts, no matter how much you love her. New moms' groups are everywhere, and they're a great way for women to hang out, talk about their problems, compare labor and delivery stories ("I was in labor for 14 hours and the pain was so awful I had to have an epidural." "Oh, yeah? Well I was in labor for 27 hours and I had the baby naturally." It gets worse from there). These groups also give new moms an opportunity to have a real conversation with someone who doesn't need a breast in her mouth to be happy.

♦ **Help her get some time to herself**. Take the baby, even if it's only for a half hour, and let your partner take a break. Don't be surprised if all she wants to do is shower and take a nap.

Library Books, Okay. But Can Fathers Be Renewed?

Well, according to sociologists, the answer is yes. A "renewed father" is a man who had children from a previous relationship, gets into a new one years later, and becomes a new dad all over again. (Actually, sociologists call these dads "recycled fathers," but that's such a horrible phrase that I changed it to "renewed" instead.) There are a lot of differences between renewed fathers and their nonrenewed brothers. First, the renewed dads tend to be more financially secure and less interested in career advancement. They also have more interest in— and more time to spend with—their young children. Overall, the older the father, the more relaxed, caring, flexible, and supportive he is, according to my colleague Ross Parke. Parke has found that men and women age differently. Women get more task- and goal-oriented as they get older, while men get more nurturing.

On the downside, renewed fathers don't usually spend as much time playing with their kids as younger dads who haven't turned themselves in for the deposit yet. But their intellectual level is still high enough to more than make up for the difference, says Parke.

In intact families, women whose husbands are involved fathers are generally happier and more fulfilled. But if you're a renewed dad, your new partner may have a very different experience. She may have been very supportive of your relationships with your older kids. In fact, seeing how you were with your kids might have been one of the things that attracted her to you in the first place. But now that she and you have a child, she may resent the time that you spend with your other kids, fearing that you won't be as attentive to your new family.

Being a renewed dad can bring up other potentially sticky problems as well. A lot of new dads I've interviewed complain that new moms act as though they know a lot more about parenting than dads do. They jump in to soothe the crying baby, change the diapers, and give very specific instructions for everything else, from bottle feeding and getting the baby to sleep to dressing and bathing. The fact that mom and dad came into parenthood with equal amounts of experience doesn't seem to matter. What these dads resent most of all is not being allowed to learn the way their partners did, by making mistakes.

But if you're a renewed dad, there's an excellent chance that you really do know a lot more about parenting than your partner does. After all, you've been through it all before, and you probably still remember what babies need and how to give it to them. You're more relaxed around the baby and not nearly as worried as your partner about every little thing.

Here's where the problem comes in. Being a brand-new mom is sometimes tough because our society gives women the message that if they aren't fantastic, loving, caring, nurturing mothers right from the start, they've failed. So imagine how she feels when Mr. Experienced Dad comes along, reversing the traditional roles, and already knows better than she does how to soothe and feed and carry and dress the baby.

From my own experience, I can tell you that what you need to do if you're in this situation is back off. Bite your tongue and let your partner make her own mistakes. It's how you learned what you know, and it's what you'd want her to do for you if the situation was reversed.

MONTHS

Let the Games Begin

What's Going On with the Baby

Physically

♦ As more and more of his reflexes disappear, your baby's body is changing. He can now keep his hands open (instead of in tiny fists), and when you put him down on his tummy, he extends his legs instead of automatically rolling up into a little ball like a pill bug. But he can't yet tell one side of his body from the other, and he moves both legs or both arms together. By the end of this month, though, he'll realize that the two sides can be controlled independently.

♦ He can roll from his back to his side, and when he's on his tummy, he can lift his head and lean on his elbows. Sometimes he may arch his back and raise his head and legs off the floor and rock like a little seesaw.

♦ When you pull him from a reclining position, he'll try to stand up, pressing his feet against whatever he was lying on. If you hold him upright, he may be able to "stand."

♦ His head is bobbing around a lot less, although it still needs support, and if you can get him into a sitting position, he can probably sit fairly well for a few seconds before keeling over.

♦ Your baby reaches for things with both hands and is getting much better at grasping things (although he still misses a lot). This is a development that some experts believe is a new reflex, designed to develop your baby's hand-eye coordination. "Everything that the child grasps is brought to the eyes and everything he sees evokes an effort to grasp," says child psychologist Peter Wolff.

Intellectually

♦ Moving objects are a source of nearly endless fascination. Your baby will follow with his eyes and head an object moving slowly from one side of his head to the other. If you drop something, he'll stare at your empty hand, wondering where the object went—but not knowing anything at all about gravity, he won't follow the object as it falls.

♦ One day your baby will catch sight of his own hand on its way into his mouth. Until this very moment, he had no idea that the thing he's been sucking on for the past few months actually belongs to him. Best of all, he now realizes that objects (or at least his hand) can exist for at least two reasons at the same time: to look at and to suck on.

♦ As a result of this startling, and incredibly important, revelation, your baby will spend as much as 15 minutes at a stretch intently staring at his squiggling fingers and then shoving them into his mouth. He'll repeat the process over and over and over.

♦ The baby is now able to tell the difference between various objects; he prefers circular shapes to stripes and complex patterns to simple ones.

♦ He is also able to make associations between certain objects and qualities linked to them. For example, he may associate your partner with food and you with play, and will react differently to each of you.

Verbally

♦ Although most of your baby's vocalizing is crying, he's making some delightful, soothing, ooohs, aaaahs, and other single-syllable sounds.

♦ He's now beginning to use his vocalizing for a purpose—if you listen carefully, you should be able to tell the difference between his " Feed me now!," "Put me down, I want to take a nap," and "Change my diaper" cries.

♦ He's now also attentively listening to all the sounds around him and distinguishes speech from any other sound.

Emotionally/Socially

♦ At this point your baby's schedule of eating, sleeping, diaper filling, and being alert is getting fairly regular.

♦ When it comes to people, he has strong likes and dislikes, crying or calming down depending on who holds him. He'll also smile or laugh at familiar people, and stare at strangers.

♦ He's very perceptive about your moods and will react to them. If you're tired and anxious, he'll be harder to calm and soothe, but if you're calm and happy, it'll be easier.

♦ He'll stare, absorbed in his surroundings, for several minutes at a time. He wants to interact with people and may stop what he's doing (which is usually sucking something) and listen if you talk to him.

What You're Going Through

Worry, Worry, Worry

A lot of new dads find themselves obsessed with worry about the health of their infant. In most cases, these worries are completely irrational. However, every year about 150,000 babies in the United States alone are born with serious birth defects, and about 8,000 don't live past the first year. But the thing that worries dads most is SIDS (sudden infant death syndrome), which is the sudden, unexpected death of an otherwise healthy baby. Striking one out of every thousand babies (about 7,000 per year), SIDS is the most common cause of death of children between one week and one year old. Although government and private agencies spend millions of dollars each year in the fight against SIDS, scientists have been unable to figure out what, exactly, causes it. And there's no medical test to determine which babies are at the greatest risk. Here is what scientists do know:

♦ SIDS is most likely to strike infants two to four months old.
♦ Ninety percent of deaths happen by six months, but SIDS still strikes children up to one year old.
♦ It is more likely to occur to boys than girls, to preterm babies, to multiple-birth babies, and to babies from low-income homes or homes in which a parent or caretaker smokes. African-American and Native American babies are over twice as likely to die of SIDS as white babies. Bottle-fed babies are also somewhat more likely to die from SIDS, but not because of the bottle-feeding itself. Bottle-fed babies are more likely to have been born prematurely or have mothers who smoke, which are more accurate risk factors.
♦ SIDS is more common in cold weather, when respiratory infections and overheating are more common. Both have been linked to SIDS.
♦ SIDS is *not* caused by colds, other minor illnesses, or by any immunizations.
♦ There's even a theory that SIDS may be caused by babies' dreams. Australian researcher George Christos has suggested that babies may stop breathing when they dream they're back in the womb, getting all the oxygen they need from their blood, and don't have to breathe on their own.

Although two-thirds of all SIDS babies have no risk factors, there are still a few things you and your partner can do to minimize the risk:

♦ Make sure your baby sleeps on his back. When my oldest daughter was born in 1990, the then-current wisdom was that babies should sleep on their tummies because of the risk of choking if the baby spit up. But in 1992, the American Academy of Pediatrics debunked the spit-up theory and started recommending that parents put babies to sleep on their backs. The number of cases of SIDS immediately dropped by 50 percent. If your baby has been sleeping on his stomach, it's not too late to change (sure, he's been doing it all his life, but still, it's only been three months).

♦ Don't smoke, and don't let anyone else smoke near the baby.

♦ Don't overdress the baby (see the section on dressing, pages 120–121).

♦ Have your baby sleep on a firm mattress: no pillows, fluffy blankets, cushiony sofas, waterbeds, thick rugs, or beanbags. Make sure the mattress fits snugly into the crib so that the baby can't slip between the mattress and the crib frame. And take out of the crib all the plush animals, extra blankets, and other things that might accidentally cover the baby.

♦ Breast-feed.

♦ Don't panic. Although SIDS is a horrible, devastating experience for any parent, remember that 999 out of 1,000 babies *don't* die of it.

Coping with the Death of a Child

Losing a child is every parent's worst nightmare, something no one who hasn't experienced it can possibly imagine. It can bring up grief, anger, denial, and even feelings of guilt at not having been there enough or inadequacy at not having been able to prevent the death.

Researcher Kim Wendee Schildhaus studied how couples adapt to and cope with the loss of a child and keep their marriage alive. She found that, as in most areas of parenting, men and women coped with the loss of a child differently. Women had two basic needs: one was to focus on the surviving children, if any; the other was support systems. Men did what men usually do: they tried to ignore their feelings and dove headlong into their jobs. It's as if they tried to make up for having failed (only in their eyes) as a protector by succeeding as a breadwinner. Unfortunately, that isn't an effective way of coping with grief—either in the short or the long term. "Grief will change you," adds Amy Hillyard Jensen, author of *Healing Grief*. "But you have some control over whether the changes are for better or worse."

Besides being devastating to the parents, losing a child to SIDS or some unexpected medical condition can also destroy the marriage itself. But it

Grief: Not for Women Only

For better or worse, men and women are socially and culturally conditioned to behave in certain ways in certain situations. Men are brought up to be tough, strong, competent, knowledgeable, and in control of our emotions. Weakness—especially tears—is discouraged. Anger and frustration are okay, but sadness and pain are not. This kind of socialization is very effective in a lot of ways. But when we face some kind of emotional upheaval, such as the loss of a child, too many of us have no idea how to react. Instead of acknowledging our grief and dealing with it, we ignore it. Instead of getting help, we pull away from the people closest to us. The results can be physically, emotionally, and psychologically dangerous—to ourselves and to those who love us.

Men have some very specific needs when it comes to grieving. Here are some wonderful ideas suggested by the SIDS Alliance in Baltimore:

♦ Talk to your family—especially your wife. "Grief is the stone that bears one down, but two bear it lightly," said William Hauff, a nineteenth-century author. Let people know you're doing as much as you can and let them know how they can help you.

♦ Have quality "alone" time. You need time to sort through all the questions running through your brain. Think about keeping a journal.

♦ Decrease your social activities. Many men seek out new hobbies or other activities, but these only detract from the grieving you really need to do.

♦ Cry. It's just about the hardest thing to do for most of us, but don't try to keep down that lump in your throat or swallow your tears. Crying releases some tension and can actually make you feel better.

♦ Get angry. Anger is a natural part of the grieving process, and holding it back or ignoring it won't make it disappear. There's nothing wrong with being angry; it's what you do with the feeling that counts, so find a way to express your anger that won't hurt others. Exercise is perhaps the best outlet for it.

♦ Find a support system. For many men, asking for help is even tougher than crying. But research has shown that what men find most helpful is a caring listener, someone patient, someone, perhaps, who is going through (or has recently gone through) the same experience. Local hospitals are an excellent source of referrals to support groups. So is the SIDS Alliance, which has counselors available twenty-four hours a day. You can reach them at (800) 221-SIDS (7437). The SIDS Alliance also has resources on its Web site, www.firstcandle.org, as does GriefNet.org.

doesn't have to. Kim Schildhaus identified a number of factors shared by couples who adapted to their loss and stayed together.

+ They accept different ways of grieving and allow each other space in the relationship without making judgments. Men and women must accept each other's individual style.
+ They believe in and utilize family support networks, asking for help when needed, accepting it when offered.
+ They have other children to focus on.
+ They concentrate on work, job, career.
+ They agree that the death of the child was the most tragic loss imaginable, and that the thought of losing the spouse too is unbearable.
+ They develop new friendship networks that include other parents who've lost children.
+ They get therapy.
+ They keep the memory of the deceased child alive.
+ They communicate with each other.

Examining Your Relationship with Your Father

As you continue to grow and develop as a father, you may find yourself spending a lot of time thinking about your own father. Was he the kind of dad you'd like to use as a role model, or was he exactly the kind of father you don't want to be? Was he supportive and nurturing, or was he absent or abusive? One way or another, it is the relationship you had with your father when you were young that sets the tone for your relationship with your own children.

Depending on your perspective, this is either good news or bad news. If you are satisfied with your relationship with your dad, and you'd like to be the kind of father he was, you don't have much to worry about. "A cohesive boyhood home atmosphere in which the father and mother worked together," writes researcher John Snarey, "predicts that the boy who grew up in it will provide more care for his own children's social-emotional development in adolescence."

But if your relationship with your father wasn't everything it should have been, you may be afraid that you are somehow destined to repeat your father's mistakes. And you may have started to act accordingly. If your father was abusive, for example, you may worry that you'll do the same, and you may emotionally and/or physically pull back from your baby as a way of protecting him.

If you find yourself doing—or not doing—things with your baby out of fear, you can relax. At least a little. Dr. Snarey found that new fathers seem to take the good from their fathers and throw away the bad. In fact, many new fathers

Well, Dad, I'll tell you: Every time I face a dilemma about parenting, I ask myself, "What would Dad do?"... And then I do the opposite.

SIPRESS

are able to turn to their advantage the example of a less-than-perfect relationship with their fathers. Here are some common scenarios:

♦ Men whose fathers were distant or non-nurturing often provide high levels of care for their children's social-emotional and intellectual-academic development in adolescence.

♦ Men whose fathers provided inconsistent or inadequate supervision tend to provide high levels of care for their children's physical-athletic development in childhood.

♦ Men whose fathers used or threatened to use physical punishment that instilled fear in them as boys generally provide high levels of care for their own children's physical-athletic development in childhood.

Taking On More Responsibility

Whenever I ask men to tell me how their lives have changed since they became fathers, some variation on the phrase "I'm more responsible" almost always comes up in the first sentence or two. Of course, that phrase doesn't mean the same thing to everyone. Here are a few of the most common definitions I've heard:

♦ **Being more involved at home**. That could mean doing more housework, sharing the child care with your partner, planning and cooking more meals, doing more laundry, and so on.

♦ **Getting real**. One new father, a man who had been out of work for four years, said that becoming more responsible meant looking more realistically at his employment situation. "I just have to lower my sights," he said. "I can't hold out for the exact position I want."

♦ **Looking at things from other people's perspectives**. A lot of guys admit that they were somewhat selfish and self-centered before having kids, according to Rob Palkovitz, a researcher who did an exhaustive study of how fatherhood changes new dads. This isn't necessarily a negative thing; it's simply an acknowledgment that having people depend on you and putting their needs before your own isn't something that comes naturally to most people before they become parents. What's especially interesting is that, according to Palkovitz, getting married didn't trigger this same realization.

Issues for Adoptive Fathers

Adopted children and their adoptive fathers develop in very much the same ways as biologically related fathers and kids. Many experience feelings of inadequacy at not having been able to produce their own children, although by the time the child enters preschool, most have gotten over their feelings about infertility and shelved their fantasies of having a biological child. Instead, they're "coming to see themselves as they really are, the eminently entitled and very 'real' psychological parents of their adoptee," writes adoption expert Gordon Finley.

This might seem pretty simple, but it's usually not. For many parents, adoption is a second choice, a decision reached only after years of unsuccessfully trying to conceive on their own and after years of disappointments and intrusive, expensive medical procedures, says researcher Rachel Levy-Shiff. Infertility can make you question your self-image, undermine your sense of masculinity (how can I be a man if I can't even get my partner pregnant?), force you to confront your shattered dreams, and take a terrible toll on your relationships—with your wife and, perhaps more important, with your adopted child. If you're having trouble accepting that you won't be having biologically related children, I urge you to talk to some other people about what you're feeling. Your partner certainly has a right to know—and she might be feeling a lot of similar things. In addition, the agency you're working with will probably have a list of support resources for adoptive fathers. Give them a try.

♦ **Honing your skills as a role model**. Almost everything you do will influence your child. He'll be imitating your mannerisms in a few months, and the moment he learns to talk, he'll start repeating back all those swear words you thought he wouldn't understand. That's bad enough, but how are you going to feel when he pretends to smoke a cigarette or drink a beer or copy any of your bad habits? "A DWI would put a hardship on the family," said one new father who quit having a few drinks before driving home from the golf course. And of course *you've* never fudged on your taxes, but some guys, who did before they had kids, don't anymore. Rob Palkovitz found that a lot of dads gave up destructive or risky behavior, criminal activity, and even drug abuse. I got better at obeying the speed limits (or trying to) and stopped accelerating at yellow traffic lights. For you, it might mean anything from giving up bungee jumping or alligator wrestling to reducing the aggressiveness of your investments.

♦ **Living the healthy life**. Many also change their attitude about their health. Most men don't go to the doctor (for themselves, anyway) unless a women in their life forces them. But having kids often motivates us more than we or anyone else can. All of a sudden being around for our kids seems a lot more important. We may start exercising more regularly, eating better, and even cutting down on the amount of junk food that makes its way home from the grocery store.

♦ **Thinking about religion or spirituality**. About 80 percent of the men in Rob Palkovitz's study and a similar majority of the dads I interviewed said that they'd made some kind of shift in their basic values or life priorities. Also, since teaching right from wrong is such a stereotypical dad thing, it's not surprising that a lot of new dads spend some time thinking about how they're going to handle those tough questions when they start cropping up. In some cases this means increasing church or synagogue attendance and/or planning to send their kids to religious school. About half of Palkovitz's sample didn't make any changes at all. Religion was already central in their lives, or they'd had such bad experiences as kids or young adults that they were turned off for good. Younger fathers in particular were less likely to take any big steps either way. Their religious and spiritual views tend not to be as fully developed, and they're not as sure as more mature dads what they're embracing or rebelling against.

You and Your Partner

Heigh Ho, Heigh Ho, It's Back to Work She Goes

With more and more women in the workforce, there's a lot of pressure on new moms to go back to work. That explains why a third of them are on the job again only six weeks after giving birth, and two-thirds are working after 12 weeks.

While some of these women are glad to be back at work, a large percentage are anything but glad. In fact, a lot of them are just plain miserable, worried that they've failed as mothers, and wishing they'd win the lottery so they could quit their jobs. This can be a very tough time for your partner, and she's going to need your help and support to get through it. Here's what you can do:

♦ **Be flexible.** When it comes to coming up with an acceptable work-family balance, your partner may not be operating completely rationally. Let me give you an example of what I mean. Before my youngest was born, my wife and I discussed having her stay home full-time for five months, work part-time for four months, and then transition to full-time. All that changed when the baby was born. All of a sudden she didn't want to go back to work at all. But in the interests of being able to make our mortgage payment (California real estate is outrageously expensive), she decided to do a full year part-time before going to full-time. Everything changed again after her first week back at the office. Now she decided that she wanted to stay part-time until the baby entered preschool.

Obviously, you and your partner have to keep talking about this stuff. And you have to find a reasonable (and fiscally responsible) way of making sure that everyone's needs are met, or that they're at least taken into consideration. That means listening to each other carefully and respectfully and acknowledging the pressures that each of you face.

♦ **Get your child-care situation in order.** Fear that the baby won't be adequately cared for is what many new mothers find most unsettling about going back to work.

♦ **Take the pressure off her.** In most families, regardless of how enlightened and egalitarian they want to be, working mothers still do most of the work at home. Because so much of women's identity is tied up in motherhood, your partner may try to do more than she can really handle—just to show herself and anyone else she thinks might be paying attention. Don't let her. Instead, anticipate what has to be done and take care of it in advance. Simple things like making sure the table is set and dinner is ready when she comes home are great and will do wonders for her mood. If you get home later than she does, make a habit of doing something nice for her on a regular basis. Massages, a few hours alone with you, and even renting a video and snuggling up on the couch will really help. And make sure that you remind her frequently what a great mom she is even though she has to be away.

♦ **Let her spend more time with the baby**. If you and your partner are both working, you're both going to miss your baby, and you're both going to want to spend time with him from the moment you walk in the door. Be a nice guy and let your partner have first dibs. This is especially important if she's still nursing; her breasts may be ready to explode by the time she gets home, and she may need to have the baby Hoover her out.

Breast-feeding and the Working Mother

As we've talked about earlier, in a perfect world your partner would breast-feed exclusively for six months and then do a mix of breast milk and other food for the following six months. Unfortunately, most of us live in an imperfect world. Brian Roe and his colleagues at Ohio State found that over half of mothers who returned to full-time work within 12 weeks of giving birth stopped nursing. Of the women who hadn't gone back to work at 12 weeks, only 35 percent had stopped breast-feeding.

Fortunately, breast-feeding and work don't have to be mutually exclusive. You or your child-care provider could bring the baby to your partner's office so she can feed him there. But that's a fairly rare situation. The more likely scenario involves your partner expressing milk from her breasts, which the baby will be able to drink while your partner is at work.

There are two basic ways to express breast milk: manually or with a pump. The manual option is kind of like milking a cow and is one of the many reasons I'm glad I'm a man. Pumps tend to be either battery-operated or electric and can handle one or both breasts. As you might guess, electric pumps can be expensive ($200–$250 to purchase a typical double pump), but they're a lot faster and a lot more convenient, and most women find that the expense is well worth it, especially if they're planning to pump for more than a few weeks.

Using an electric pump can be uncomfortable and will take a lot of getting used to. (If you're wondering why, go ahead and give it a try. I was curious myself, and one morning when I was alone in the house, I lifted up my shirt, turned on the pump, and positioned the suction devices on my chest. The shock of having both nipples nearly sucked off my chest was matched only by my embarrassment when I looked up and saw my wife standing there. For weeks afterward she'd break in to giggles every time she looked at me.)

I'd suggest that you rent a pump for a month or so before you buy. You should be able to get one through your local La Leche League chapter or the hospital where your partner gave birth. One important note on pumps: if a friend or relative offers to let you have or borrow her breast pump, respectfully decline. Unlike with rental pumps, there's no way to properly clean the machine's internal mechanism, and there's a slight risk of infection.

A few more pumping/work-related things to keep in mind:

♦ **Introduce your baby to a bottle now if you haven't done so already**. If you wait too long, you may miss your window of opportunity. Some babies may get used to the feel of a silicone nipple, but others, like my middle daughter, may absolutely refuse. Filling the first few bottles with breast milk will up your chances that the baby will take the bottle. Also, start the bottle when your baby is just a little hungry instead of ravenous. A very hungry baby won't be in the mood to participate in your little experiment and will demand the real thing.

♦ **Get some practice**. If at all possible, you should do the bottle-feeding. Your baby associates your partner's smell with feeding, and if she tries to give him a bottle, he may refuse, preferring what she's got in her blouse to what she's got in her hand.

♦ **Help her arrange things at work**. If she's planning to pump at work, at the very least she'll need a private place to plug in and a refrigerator or some other way to keep the expressed milk cold. In 2002 the state of California enacted the California Lactation Accommodation Law, which requires employers to provide nursing employees a reasonable amount of break time and the use of a private room. A number of other states have similar laws on the books.

♦ **Learn how to store and retrieve expressed milk**. Here are the basic requirements:
    ♦ Breast milk can be stored at room temperature for 8-10 hours.
    ♦ It can be refrigerated for no longer than a week.
    ♦ If your partner is freezing the milk, do so within 48 hours of pumping. Also, make sure she gets bags that are specially designed to store milk. The ones at Walgreen's or Target are usually about half the price of the ones that the pump manufacturers sell.
    ♦ Milk can stay in the freezer section of your fridge for up to three months. If you have a stand-alone freezer, you may be able to go as long as 6–12 months.
    ♦ To thaw, put the bag of milk in a container of warm water. It's best not to use an oven to do your defrosting, but if you do, don't boil the milk. Also, never warm milk in the microwave—besides possibly

interfering with the health benefits of the milk, microwaves often heat unevenly, meaning that while some of the milk feels fine to your touch, other parts could be hot enough to hurt your baby.

♦ After thawing, milk can stay in the refrigerator for up to 24 hours but should not be refrozen.

♦ Before giving milk to the baby, swirl it around to mix the cream back in with the rest of the milk.

A Work-Family Solution You Might Not Have Thought Of

On pages 172–182 we'll discuss a number of the child-care options you and your partner will have to sift through sometime soon. But what if you'd both really prefer to have your child raised in the arms of a loving relative? Most families that make the decision to have a parent stay home automatically assume that it has to be Mom. Sometimes, though, that just doesn't work. Your partner might have a more stable career than you, make more money, or simply have no interest in staying home. Well, all is not lost. If you and your partner truly want to have your children raised by a parent, it may be up to you.

Now before you throw this book down and run screaming out of the room, take a minute to consider the idea. Actually, take longer than that—take at least as much time considering this option as you would any other. You may find that it's not as crazy as it sounds. Let's start with some of the benefits:

♦ You won't have to agonize over picking the right babysitter or nanny or day-care center.

♦ You'll get a wonderful opportunity to get to know your child.

♦ You'll be giving your child what you and your partner agree is the best possible upbringing.

♦ You'll be able to help your partner's career and give her some peace of mind at the same time.

Deciding to be a stay-at-home dad is a decision that will affect everyone in your family. If you're even remotely considering it, start by asking yourself the following very important questions:

♦ **Can we afford it?** Going from two incomes to one will probably require some major changes in your lifestyle. But it can be done. If you're really committed to the idea, there are all sorts of ways to cut your expenses, including buying food in bulk, eating out less often, raising your insurance deductibles, taking vacations closer to home, making presents instead of buying them, getting rid of the housekeeper, and moving to a smaller house or a place where the cost of living is lower.

♦ **Can I take the career hit?** This is a big one, since earning power and masculinity are inextricably linked in so many people's minds. ("If I'm not a good provider, I'm not a good man/father," the thinking goes.) If you can get over this one, you may still be able to keep a finger or a foot in the work world by teaching, consulting, writing, or starting a home-based business. But be realistic. If you decide to reenter the workforce later, that employment gap on your résumé could cause you some problems with potential employers, many of whom may be a lot more traditional than you.

♦ **Can I handle it?** Staying home with a child is a lot more work than you think. It can also be a bit lonely. According to researcher Robert Frank, about two-thirds of stay-at-home dads feel isolated, but only one-third of stay-at-home-moms do. There's not a lot of social support for men who decide to stay home, and you won't see many other guys around who are doing it. You'll also probably find that women—moms, nannies, babysitters—tend not to welcome men into their groups at parks or playgrounds or malls and the other places people take their kids during the day. And you'll have to get used to the funny looks and stupid comments you'll hear from people who see you with your kids in the middle of the day. Several stay-at-home dads I've interviewed have told me that it's actually easier to tell people that they're unemployed than to deal with the raised eyebrows and "Where's the mother?" questions.

   In reality, you won't be quite as alone as it might seem. At least 2 million stay-at-home dads are doing it every day, and the number is rising all the time. There are also a lot of great resources out there. On the Web, www.slowlane.com is fantastic, with lots of articles by and for stay-at-home dads, as well as links to dads' groups all over the country. Who knows? You may find one right around the corner.

♦ **Can our relationship handle it?** Bucking gender stereotypes is often easier for women than it is for men. But having the freedom to choose between pants or dresses is hardly the same as going back to work while you take care of the baby. Unless the two of you can speak openly and honestly with each other about what you're feeling, your relationship could be severely hurt.

You and Your Baby

Let the Games Begin

Playing with your baby is one of the most important things you can do for him. Researchers have found that early parent-child play can speed up the attachment process. In addition, kids who play a lot—especially with their dads—as babies are more attentive and interactive as they grow up, and end up with higher self-esteem than kids who don't get as much physical activity. But before you mount that basketball hoop, remember that at this stage of life babies have literally just discovered themselves, and watching and experimenting with their own little bodies is quite enough to keep them occupied for a big chunk of their waking time.

At this age, you are your baby's first toy, and the first "game" you play with him starts with nothing more than his giving you a smile. If you respond nicely, he'll smile at you again. After repeating this a few times (it may even take a few days), your baby will learn that what he does can lead to a response from you. That seemingly simple realization is the basis for any kind of meaningful interaction your baby will have with other people.

Nuts and Bolts

Now that your baby has developed some control over his hands, this is the perfect time to introduce some rattles, or keys, or other similar toys. Early this month he'll probably tentatively reach for interesting-looking objects with both hands at the same time. Within a few weeks he'll start using them independently. Whether he's using one hand or two, just make sure that whatever you give him is soft enough that he can smack himself in the head without doing any damage—he's going to be doing that a lot. If he's not quite ready to actually grab anything, you can still have fun by simply holding a toy nearby and encouraging him to reach for it. Just don't take it personally if your gesture is completely ignored.

Make sure you set aside at least a few minutes a day to play with your baby. Don't worry about getting bored or needing any fancy equipment—you can have plenty of fun just walking around keeping up a running commentary on everything you see. Sing some songs or do some baby weight lifting: Lie on your back, holding the baby chest-to-chest. Then lift him straight up, saying "Up" and lower while saying "Down." Be sure to watch out for the drool.

A fun experiment: Tie one end of a ribbon loosely to the baby's ankle and the other to a mobile. Make the ribbon taut enough so that if the baby moves his leg, he'll also move the mobile. After a few minutes, most (but definitely not all) babies at this age will begin to see a cause-and-effect relationship developing and will begin to move the tied leg more than the other. Move the ribbon to the other leg, then to the arms, and see how well the baby adapts. A note of caution: *never* leave the room—even for a minute—with the baby tied to the mobile.

Music

While it's way too early to start private cello lessons, it's not at all too early to start making music a part of your baby's life. Babies come prewired for music. Studies have shown that babies who listened to music while still in the womb (which they can do anytime after about 24 weeks) often stop crying and focus when they hear a familiar song. If you pay attention, you'll notice that he already has a rudimentary sense of rhythm. Lay him on the floor and turn on the stereo (not too loud, please). Notice how he moves his arms and legs rhythmically—not in time to the music, but definitely in response to it. Here are a few things to keep in mind as you're thinking about introducing your baby to music:

♦ Kids are surrounded by language from their first days (in fact, there's plenty of research showing that kids respond to linguistic rhythms and patterns they heard even before they were born). And since kids learn music in much the same way as they do language—by listening and absorbing— play as much music as you can. But don't go crazy. Your baby—just like you—needs some regular downtime.

♦ Play a wide variety of music. Major or minor keys, fast or slow tempos, and the types of instruments are not important at this stage. For some reason, babies seem to prefer simple melodies to more complex ones, so save the fusion jazz for later. Stay away from anything that's very loud or might startle the baby. And pay attention to your baby's reactions. Do his movements change as you change the style of music?

♦ Select music you like too (after all, you'll be listening as well).

♦ Some babies this age may try to imitate tones they hear. This is, however, extremely rare.

♦ It doesn't have to be expensive. Kindermusik (www.kindermusik.com) and Music Together (www.musictogether.com) offer music-related programs all over the country for kids of all ages. Check the Web sites to see whether there's a franchise near you. They, along with the Mozart Effect people (www.mozarteffect.com), also sell some excellent CDs of music that babies really like. That said, you can accomplish the same thing at home with the CDs in your own collection. Just follow the guidelines above.

♦ Have fun. Although music has been shown to stimulate brain development in infants, don't try to raise the next Beethoven. Just enjoy yourself and make sure your baby's doing the same.

Reading: From Birth through Eight Months

Feeling a little silly about the prospect of sitting down and reading to your baby? Consider this: "When children have been read to, they enter school with larger vocabularies, longer attention spans, greater understanding of books and print, and consequently have the fewest difficulties in learning to read," writes Jim Trelease, author of *The Read Aloud Handbook*.

Still not convinced? How about this: 60 percent of prison inmates are illiterate, 85 percent of juvenile offenders have reading problems, and 44 percent of adult Americans do not read a single book in the course of a year. Clearly, reading is an important habit to develop, and it's never too early to start.

What to Read When

For the first few months of your baby's life, your reading probably won't seem to be having much effect on him. Sometimes he'll stare at the book, sometimes not. Once in a while a flailing arm might hit the book, but it's completely accidental. It doesn't really matter what you read at this stage, just as long as you do it. It's a great opportunity for you and the baby to snuggle together and for him to get to know the rhythm and feel of our language.

At about three months, your baby may start holding your finger while you read to him. While it doesn't seem like much, this tiny gesture is a clear indication that he's starting to become aware of the book as a separate object and that he likes what you're doing. Look for books with simple, uncluttered drawings as well as poetry and nursery rhymes.

At four months, your baby will sit still and listen attentively while you're reading. He may even reach out to scratch the pages of the book. Don't get too excited, though—he's a while away from being able to identify anything on the page. Nursery rhymes, finger plays (this little piggy went to market and so on), and books with pictures of other babies are big hits at this stage.

At about five months most babies are just starting to respond to your pointing. There are two ways to take advantage of this new development: first, watch your baby's eyes, then point to and talk about what he is already focusing on. Second, point to something and encourage the baby to look where you're pointing. It's now time for the seven Rs: rhythm, rhyme, repetition, repetition, repetition, repetition, and repetition.

At six months babies will respond to what you're reading by bouncing up and down or chuckling before you get to a familiar part of the story. If you've been reading regularly to your baby for a few months, you may notice that he has developed clear preferences for books and will let you know which one he wants you to read. A word of warning: at this age babies have an irresistible need to put everything into their mouths, and books are no exception. But first they'll want to scratch, tear, pat, rub, hit, and get into a serious tug-of-war with you over the book. To avoid these problems before they start, give your baby something else to put in his mouth while you're reading to him, and try to distract him with noise books (the cow says "moo," the airplane goes "whooosh"). Just in case your baby manages to outfox you, keep those family heirlooms far away, and stock your shelves with board and cloth books.

At about seven months your baby's grabbing and tearing are now slightly more purposeful, and you may notice an occasional attempt to turn pages. It will be another month or two, though, until he's actually able to do so. Plot is pretty well wasted on babies this age. But he'll like books with brightly colored pictures of familiar objects, as well as those that encourage you to make different sounds or funny voices.

READY, SET . . .

Here are a few things to keep in mind when you're getting ready to read:
  ♦ Select a regular place for reading.
  ♦ Set aside a regular time, when you will be able to devote your full attention to the baby and the book. Just before or just after a nap is usually good.
  ♦ Try to read for at least fifteen minutes each day. Be prepared: you may have to do this in several installments. Kids' attention spans average only about three minutes at this age, but vary widely (my oldest and youngest daughters would sit in my lap for an hour at a time, but the middle one couldn't sit still for more than three seconds).
  ♦ Use lots of vocal and facial expression.
  ♦ You don't have to finish the story. Reading to your child is for him, not for you. So if he arches his back, squirms, lurches forward, or does anything to let you know he's not happy, stop immediately—you're wasting your time. If you don't, the baby will begin to associate reading with discomfort.
  ♦ Make it interactive. Take plenty of short breaks from the text to point out interesting things going on in the illustrations and to ask questions ("Where's the piggy hiding?" "What does the big bad wolf say?").
  ♦ Don't read things that are developmentally inappropriate. It's not so much the actual content as the tone of your voice. So unless you plan to act out all the parts in *War and Peace*, stick with kids' books.

A list of appropriate titles follows. This is by no means definitive. With about five thousand new children's titles published each year, the pool of good books never stops growing. I strongly urge you to get to know your local librarians, who are always up to date, or to subscribe to *Children's Literature* (www.childrenslit.com), a wonderful newsletter that reviews current children's books.

. . . G O !

GENERAL INTEREST FOR THE FIRST SIX TO EIGHT MONTHS

All Fall Down, Helen Oxenbury (board book)

Baby Animal Friends, Phoebe Dunn (board book)

The Baby (and others), John Burningham

Baby Farm Animals, Garth Williams

Baby's Book of Babies, Kathy Henderson

Baby's First Words, Lars Wik

Baby's First Year, Phyllis Hoffman

Baby's Home, Tana Hoban

Chugga-Chugga-Choo-Choo, Kevin Lewis (board book)

First Things First, Charlotte Voake

Funny Faces, Nicola Tuxworth (board book)

Goodnight Gorilla, Peggy Rathman

Hand Rhymes, Marc Brown

Happy Baby, Angie and Sage

How Big Is a Pig? Clare Beaton

I See (and others), Rachel Isadora

Pat the Bunny, Dorothy Kunhardt

Pat the Cat, Edith Kunhardt

Peek-a-Moo, Marie Torres Cimarusti (board book)

Peek-a-Who, Nina Laden (board book)

Spot's Toys, Eric Hill

This Is Me, Lenore Blegvad (board book)

Ten Little Babies, Debbie MacKinnon (board book)

Welcome, Little Baby (and others), Aliki

What Do Babies Do? Debby Slier (board book)

What Is It? Tana Hoban (board book)

MOTHER GOOSE, LULLABIES, POETRY AND SONGS, FINGER PLAYS

These are great for kids of all ages. Start now and find some favorites.

The Baby's Bedtime Book, Kay Chorao

Eyes, Nose, Fingers, and Toes, Judy Hindley

A First Caldecott Collection: "The House That Jack Built" and "A Frog He Would A-Wooing Go"

A Second Caldecott Collection: "Sing a Song of Sixpence" and "Three Jovial Huntsmen"

A Third Caldecott Collection: "Queen of Hearts" and "The Farmer's Boy"

The House that Jack Built, Janet Stevens

The Mother Goose Treasury, Raymond Briggs
Old Mother Hubbard, Alice and Martin Provensen
The Random House Book of Mother Goose, Arnold Lobel
Read-Aloud Rhymes for the Very Young, selected by Jack Prelutsky
Ring a Ring O-Roses, Flint Public Library
The Complete Story of the Three Blind Mice, John Ivimey
Three Little Kittens, Lorinda Cauley
Trot Trot to Boston: Play Rhymes for Baby
Singing Bee! A Collection of Favorite Children's Songs
Tail Feathers from Mother Goose: The Opie Rhyme Book, Iona and Peter Opie
Tomie De Paola's Mother Goose, Tomie De Paola
A Week of Lullabies, Helen Plotz
Wendy Watson's Mother Goose, Wendy Watson

Hittin' the Road

One of the great myths about babies is that you have to bundle them up like Nanook of the North every time you take them out of the house. Here's the truth: overdressed babies are at risk of getting heat stroke, which can result in abnormally high fevers and even convulsions. This risk is especially high if you're taking the baby out in a sling, backpack, or frontpack, where he'll be even hotter.

Of course, underdressing can be a problem, too. The answer is to dress your baby just as you would dress yourself (except that you're probably not going to wear any of those cute little booties). When the weather's cold, it helps to dress the baby in various layers rather than one or two very heavy items. That way you can remove a layer or two if the baby gets overheated.

Most important, because you're the grown-up, you're going to have to pay close attention. If you underdress your baby, he'll probably let you know about it; babies usually complain loudly when they're too cold. Babies who are too hot, though, tend not to complain, preferring instead to lie there listlessly.

SUMMER

For the first six months, your baby should be kept far away from direct sunlight. Because babies' skin is at its thinnest and lightest during this period, even a little sun can do a lot of damage. This applies to babies of all races and skin tones.

When you go out, dress your baby in lightweight and light-colored long-sleeved shirts and long pants. From the time they were a few months old, none of my kids would let me put any kind of hat anywhere near them. But if you

Sunscreen

Until she's six months old, don't use any sunscreen on your baby at all
(that's why it's so important to keep infants out of the sun). They are
usually filled with chemicals and frequently cause allergic reactions.

After six months, the risk of an allergic reaction from sunscreen is
much lower, but stick with one that's unscented, alcohol- and PABA-free,
and hypoallergenic, or made specially for infants. Hawaiian Tropic,
Johnson & Johnson, and Water Babies all make acceptable formulas.

Lube your baby up with sunscreen about half an hour before going
outside, and add some more every three hours or so. Pay special
attention to feet, hands, legs, and arms—even if they're completely
covered. Socks can roll down, and sleeves and pant legs can hike up all
by themselves, exposing baby's skin to the elements.

can get your baby to wear a cute hat with a wide brim, so much the better. And
if you're brave enough to try putting sunglasses on her, get the kind that shield
her eyes from UVA and UVB rays. For extra protection, consider getting a para-
sol or sunshade for your stroller and try to stay indoors during the hottest parts
of the day (about 11:00 A.M. to 3:00 P.M.).

When you're putting together your supplies for an outdoor summertime
excursion, throw in a sweater, a pair of socks, and some warm pants for the
baby. Sounds a little strange, but if you step into any kind of air-conditioned
building (such as a supermarket or your office building) after having been outside for a while, you're going to feel awfully cold—and so will the baby.

Oh, and by the way, if you were thinking that your baby can't get a sunburn
on a cloudy or overcast day, think again. Studies have shown that 60 percent of
the sun's UV rays make their way down here, regardless of clouds, fog, or anything else.

Skin Problems

SUN

Despite all your precautions and good intentions, your baby may still end up
with a minor sun-related condition:

♦ **Sunburn.** If it's minor, cover the affected area with a cool compress. If there
  are blisters, if the baby is running a fever, or if he's listless or nonresponsive,
  call your doctor immediately.

♦ **Prickly heat (heat rash).** A direct result of overdressing, prickly heat looks like tiny red blisters on a flushed area. It occurs anywhere sweat can build up: where the neck meets the shoulders, under the arms, inside elbows and knees, inside diapers. If your baby has heat rash, try to keep him as cool as possible. Lotions and creams probably won't help much, but putting a cool, damp washcloth or some cornstarch on the affected area may make your baby more comfortable.

INSECTS

The sun isn't the only potentially dangerous element that comes out in the summer. Here are some tips for preventing your baby from being consumed by bugs:

♦ Don't use any kind of scented powders, lotions, or even diaper wipes. Bugs love them.

♦ Avoid insect repellent if at all possible. A long-sleeved shirt and long pants can provide just about the same level of protection and are a lot easier on infant skin.

♦ Stay away from clothes with floral patterns: most bugs aren't smart enough to tell the difference between a real flower and your equally delicious flower-covered child. Light colors are far less attractive to bugs than dark colors.

♦ When outside, consider getting some insect netting to drape over the stroller. Inside, position a fan so it blows across the baby's crib. Mosquitoes and other insects prefer stagnant air to a breeze.

DIAPER RASH

You can prevent sunburn or insect bites, but no matter what you do or how hard you try, one of these days your baby is going to get diaper rash. In the pre-disposable-diaper era, when a baby urinated, the moisture stayed right there against his skin. Partly because of the acid in urine and partly because it's uncomfortable to sit in something wet, the baby would soon start complaining. And if he made what my oldest daughter used to call "a big dirty" (a bowel movement), he'd be even more uncomfortable and would "speak up" even sooner. This raised the chances that he'd get changed fairly quickly.

With disposables, however, a lot of the moisture is whisked away from the baby (just like they say in the commercials) and converted into some kind of nonliquid gel. Still, the digestive acids in the baby's waste, especially in his stool, continue to irritate his skin until—voilà!—diaper rash. But because the baby isn't uncomfortable enough to complain, his diapers somehow don't manage to get changed quite as often.

A Little Diaper-Changing Fireworks

In 1999, English housewife Jill Furlough got a fright late one night when she saw green sparks shooting out of her sleeping baby's disposable diaper. She called the diaper manufacturers, who assured her that the sparks were the result of triboluminescence, an extremely rare—and perfectly harmless—buildup of energy probably caused by the friction of the baby's bottom rubbing against the inside of the diaper. (It's actually exactly the same chemical reaction that produces the sparks you see when you bite down on a Wintergreen LifeSaver in a dark room. Unlike static electricity, it doesn't generate any heat.) The boy apparently slept through the entire episode, and there's no record of any injury to anyone.

Just about the only thing you can do to keep diaper rash to a minimum is to check your baby's diapers every few hours and change them even if they're only slightly wet. Also:

♦ If you're using cloth diapers, don't use rubber or plastic pants. Your baby's bottom needs as much air as it can get.

♦ When diaper rash develops, let your baby frolic for a few minutes sans diaper (on a towel, perhaps, just in case). The extra air circulation will help.

♦ Apply some diaper cream with each change, but be especially gentle: irritated skin doesn't like to be rubbed. A piece of advice: after you've applied diaper rash cream to the baby's bottom, wipe any residual cream on your fingers onto the inside of the diaper before fastening it.

Notes:

Born to Be . . .

What's Going On with the Baby

Physically

♦ She can now track moving objects, coordinating the activities of her eyes and head as well as an adult can.

♦ She's making better use of her hands, using them to finger each other, to grasp small objects (most of which immediately end up in her mouth), and generally to bring the world to her, since she still can't go to it. But she hasn't yet figured out what to do with her opposable thumb. So, for the next few months at least, she won't be using it much, making her grasping a little clumsy. She can retain objects in her hands voluntarily although letting go is still a problem.

♦ By the end of this month, though, she'll have figured out that the two sides of her body are separate—a discovery she's glad to demonstrate by passing things back and forth between her hands. But she hasn't completely discovered how to separate them. When picking something up with one hand, she'll make the same grasping motion with the other.

♦ While on her tummy, she can lift her head 90 degrees and prop herself up on her forearms. And if you've had her spend a lot of time on her tummy, she may even be able to roll from front to back, although she won't be able to do it regularly for another month or so. She can, however, roll onto her side and may occasionally surprise herself by ending up on her back.

♦ She still tries to stand when you pull her up (don't let her do this for more than a second or two; her hips aren't strong enough to support the weight). And when she's sitting, her back is straight and her head hardly wobbles.

Intellectually

♦ Your baby now knows her hands and feet are extensions of herself. She'll spend a great deal of time every day staring at her hands and using them to explore her face, her mouth, and whatever other parts of her body she can reach.

♦ She's beginning the long process of understanding cause-and-effect relationships. If she accidentally kicks a toy and it squeaks, she may try to kick it again, hoping to get the same reaction. Similarly, she knows what a breast (or bottle) is for and may get excited when she sees one.

♦ She's begun to draw small distinctions between similar objects and can clearly tell the difference between a real face and a picture of one. She is also starting to differentiate herself from some other objects in her world. She may, for example, find a special toy particularly soothing.

♦ She's learning that objects (and people) have labels and may occasionally respond to her own name.

Verbally

♦ She's trying as hard as she can to speak, using her tongue and changing the shape of her mouth. And, if she's got something on her mind, she may take the initiative and start a "conversation" with you. If she really wants to chat, she'll be very upset if you aren't focusing all your attention on her.

♦ If you wait a few seconds after saying something to her, she may "answer" you, making ample use of her expanding vocabulary of squeals, chuckles, chortles, giggles, and clicks.

♦ When she hears a sound—especially a voice—she actively searches for it with her eyes.

Emotionally/Socially

♦ Overall, your baby is a pretty happy kid. She smiles regularly and spontaneously, enjoys a rousing game of peek-a-boo, and anticipates pleasurable encounters by vigorously kicking her arms and legs. She may also use the full-body wiggle as a signal for "do it again" or "pick me up."

♦ She's so anxious to socialize that she can actually suppress other interests in order to play. If you talk to her while she's eating, for example, she'll gladly stop for a few minutes to talk.

♦ She now tries to extend her playtime by laughing or holding her gaze on a desired object, and she may protest loudly if you stop doing what she wants you to.

♦ Despite this hedonistic streak, she's still got clear preferences among playmates (including toys). Some will be able to soothe her, others won't.

♦ This is an extremely busy developmental time for your baby, and you may notice some interruption in her sleep patterns as she wakes up in the middle of the night to practice her new tricks.

What You're Going Through

Reevaluating Your Relationship with Your Job

Remember the shift in focus and priorities we talked about last month—from self to family? Well, once that shift has begun, the very next thing most new fathers do is take a long, hard look at their jobs. In a small number of cases, fathers make a renewed commitment to their jobs—longer hours, increased productivity, more responsibility—motivated by a need to provide for their growing families. It's far more common, however, for new dads to try to balance work and family by finding ways to reduce or restructure their work hours.

Seventy percent of working dads—regardless of their occupation or socio-economic status—say they experience work/family conflict, according to the Families and Work Institute. But it's an uphill battle; 57.6 percent of Americans polled by the National Center for Fathering felt that employers don't recognize the strain fathers face when trying to balance work and family demands. Interestingly, more established dads (age 45–54, earning more than $40,000 per year, college-educated) were almost 30 percent more likely to feel that way than less established dads (age 18–24, making less than $40,000 per year, high-school education).

Still, a number of national polls have found that men all over the country are willing to put their money where their dissatisfaction is, turning down promotions or transfers that would reduce the time they spend with their families. In one recent Harris poll, 80 percent of men aged 20 to 39 said that having a work schedule that allows them to spend time with their family is more important than doing challenging work or earning a high salary. And 70 percent of men in their 20s and 30s said they'd be willing to give up some of their pay in exchange for more time with their families.

Unfortunately, not everyone is quite so bold. Some men interviewed for the Families and Work Institute study said that they "had told friends at work they were going to a bar when in fact they were going home to care for their children."

Coming to Terms with Breast-feeding

Before their babies are born, nearly all expectant fathers feel that breast-feeding is the best way to feed a baby and that their partners should do so as long as possible. After the baby comes, new fathers still feel that breast is best, but many are also feeling a little ambivalent.

Most new fathers feel that breast-feeding "perpetuates the exclusive relationship the mother and infant experienced during pregnancy," writes Dr. Pamela Jordan, one of the few researchers ever to explore the effects of breast-feeding on men.

Given all this, says Dr. Jordan, a new father is likely to experience:

♦ A diminished opportunity to develop a relationship with his child.

♦ A sense of inadequacy.

♦ A feeling that the baby has come between him and his partner.

♦ A feeling that nothing he does to satisfy his child can ever compete with his partner's breasts.

♦ A sense of relief when his partner weans the baby, giving him the opportunity to "catch up."

♦ A belief in what Jordan calls the "hormonal advantage theory"—the idea that women are born with certain knowledge and skills that give them an advantage in parenting, including guaranteed success with breast-feeding.

Whether or not you're experiencing these or any other less-than-completely-positive feelings, there's a good chance that your partner is having a few ambivalent feelings of her own about breast-feeding. Here are some of the things she may be feeling:

♦ Exhaustion. It may look easy and relaxing to you, but nursing a baby is tough work.
♦ Despite the images of smiling, happy nursing mothers, your partner may not be enjoying the experience. And if she isn't, she may be feeling guilty or inadequate. (Just goes to show you that fathers aren't the only ones boxed in by socialization.)
♦ She may resent the way nursing interferes with some of the other things she'd like to do.
♦ She may want to run as far away from the baby as possible. If so, she's also likely to feel guilty or selfish (socialization again . . . mothers are always supposed to be happy to be with their children).
♦ She may not be interested in answering your questions about the process. (I

SIPRESS

had a million for my wife: How does it feel? How much comes out in each feeding? Does the milk come out from one hole or more than one?)

If your partner is breast-feeding, there's no question that you're at a bit of a disadvantage when it comes to feeding the baby. There are, however, a few ways you can help your partner and yourself make the experience as pleasant an experience as possible for everyone:

♦ You can bottle-feed your baby with breast milk if your partner is willing to express some. But don't insist on this. Many women find expressing milk— manually or with a pump—uncomfortable or even painful (see pages 111–112 for more on this).

♦ Don't take it personally if your baby doesn't seem interested in taking a bottle from you. Some babies need a few days to get used to the idea of sucking on a silicone nipple instead of a real one. Other babies, like my second daughter, simply refuse to take a bottle at all. But don't give up without a fight. Silicone nipples—like real ones—come in all sorts of shapes and sizes. So you may have to do a little experimenting before you and your baby discover the kind she likes best (which may or may not have anything in common with the kind you like best).

♦ Make sure you get some private time with your baby for activities that provide regular skin-to-skin contact, such as bathing, cuddling, playing, putting to bed, and even changing diapers. This can help your partner by giving her some needed time off, and you by making you feel more needed and important.

♦ Compare notes with other men whose partners breast-fed their babies.

Worried That Your Life Will Never Be the Same Again (It Won't)

Before my first child was born, just about everybody my wife and I knew with kids pulled us aside and tried to warn us that our lives would change forever once we became parents. They told us about how hard it is to shift from worrying only about ourselves to being responsible for the safety and well-being of a completely helpless little person. They told us that we'd lose a lot of sleep and even more privacy. And they told us that we'd better go to a lot of movies and read a stack of books, because we might not have another chance for a while. Everything everyone said was absolutely correct, but none of it really prepared us for our transition to parenthood.

What I often find most interesting about the changes I underwent when I became a father is the way my memories of my prefatherhood past have been subtly altered. It's not that I can't or don't remember life before children, it's just that that so much of my identity is tied up in being a father that my child-less life, in retrospect, seems somehow incomplete. Most of the new dads I've interviewed expressed the same kinds of feelings.

I have clear, fond memories of taking long walks on the beach by myself, sleeping in all day, and going out at midnight for a beer with friends—things I haven't done much since becoming a father. It's as though those things happened to someone else, however. I don't really miss my other life, but in a way I wish I could have shared it with my children (not the beers, perhaps, but the walks on the beach and the sleeping in).

Rethinking What It Means to Be a Man

There are two major reasons why so many of us would prefer to drive ten miles down the wrong road rather than stop and ask for directions. First, from the time we were little boys, we've been socialized to associate knowledge with mas-culinity—in other words, real men know everything, so admitting to being lost is a sign of weakness (and, of course, a lack of masculinity). Second, we've also been socialized to be strong, independent, and goal-oriented, which makes ask-ing for help a sign of weakness (and, again, a lack of masculinity). Nothing in the world can bring these two factors into play faster than the birth of a baby. Because of the near-total absence of active, involved, nurturing male role mod-els, most new fathers can't seriously claim that they know what to do with a new baby (although never having cooked before didn't prevent my father from mak-ing all sorts of wild claims about his culinary skills; boy, was he wrong).

Getting help seems like the obvious solution to the ignorance problem, but most men don't want to seem helpless or expose their lack of knowledge by asking anyone—especially their partner. Now toss in a few more ingredients:

♦ The confusion and fears we've been feeling lately.
♦ The prevailing attitude that a man who is actively involved with his children—especially if he's the primary caretaker—is not as masculine as his less-involved brothers.
♦ Cultural messages that tell us that we have to explore our "feminine" side or be more maternal in order to be better fathers.

It's easy to see how the whole experience of becoming a father can lead so many new fathers to wonder secretly (no one would ever openly admit to having these thoughts) whether or not they've retained their masculinity. All too often the result of this kind of thinking is that fathers leave all the child-rearing to their partners and thereby leave their kids essentially without a father.

So you have a choice. Either accept the hardest yet most rewarding challenge you'll probably ever face by becoming an actively involved father and taking on a significant share of the responsibility for raising your children, or take the easy way out and leave it all to someone else. What would a "real" man do?

You and Your Baby

Your Baby's Temperament

Nearly fifty years ago a husband-and-wife team of psychiatrists, Stella Chess and Alexander Thomas, came up with a theory that children are born with a set of nine fundamental behavioral and emotional traits that they called "temperamental qualities." These qualities, which experts now believe remain fairly consistent throughout life, combine differently for each child and determine, to a great extent, a child's personality and whether he will be "easy" or "challenging." In addition, Chess and Thomas found that a child's temperament has a major influence on his parents' behavior and attitudes.

Over the past few decades, Chess and Thomas's original research in temperament has been expanded, refined, and improved upon by all sorts of people. But one thing that hasn't changed at all is how understanding about temperament can truly change your life by helping you to accept your child (as well as yourself) for who she is. Here, then, are the nine temperament traits, adapted from Chess and Thomas, the Temperament Program at the Center for Parenting Excellence, and the work of Jim Cameron, head of the Preventive

The Nine Temperament Traits of Babies

APPROACHING BABIES
- separate easily from parents
- are excited to meet and interact with new people
- love to try new foods
- seem perfectly at home in new situations

WITHDRAWING BABIES
- are usually shy, cling to their parents in new situations or around strangers
- have difficulty separating from parents
- need time to warm up to new experiences
- may be extremely picky eaters and spit out unfamiliar food

FAST-ADAPTING BABIES
- fall asleep easily and without fussing, no matter where they are
- don't mind changes in routines
- can be fed easily by different people
- don't mind being handled by different people or passed around
- smile back quickly when talked to
- seem perfectly delighted to be wherever they are

SLOW-ADAPTING BABIES
- may refuse to fall asleep in a strange place (or even a moderately familiar one like Grandma and Grandpa's)—only their own cribs will do
- take a long time to get back to sleep after being awakened
- don't like being picked up and held by strangers
- take a long time to warm up to new situations, and once upset, may take a long time to calm down

LOW-INTENSITY BABIES
- display their emotions, but are often hard to read
- have subdued moods
- seem fairly nonchalant

HIGH-INTENSITY BABIES
- react strongly (positively or negatively) to strangers, loud noises, bright lights
- do everything—shrieking with delight or crying—so loudly it hurts your ears
- let you know, in no uncertain terms, when they're hungry, thirsty, or uncomfortable

POSITIVE-MOOD BABIES
- laugh and smile at just about everything
- are happy even when having their diapers changed
- enjoy being able to do new things
- seem genuinely happy to see you

NEGATIVE-MOOD BABIES
- cry when being changed
- are fussy or cranky most of the time
- whimper or cry a lot, sometimes seemingly for no reason
- complain during hair-brushing

LOW-ACTIVITY BABIES
- seem content to lie still while nursing or getting changed
- will sit calmly in the car seat
- prefer less physical play (swings instead of wrestling)

HIGH-ACTIVITY BABIES
- move around a lot while sleeping, frequently kicking their blankets off
- squirm and wiggle while awake, and are hard to dress, change, bathe, or feed
- often reach physical developmental milestones earlier than lower-activity kids

PREDICTABLE BABIES

+ get hungry, tired, and move their bowels at about the same times every day
+ love regular eating and bedtime schedules
+ don't like to have their routines messed with

UNPREDICTABLE BABIES

+ have absolutely no respect for your schedule
+ have frequent sleep problems, get up several times during the night, and may or may not take naps during the day
+ may not be hungry at mealtimes and may want to eat at different times every day
+ have irregular bowel movements

HIGH-SENSORY-THRESHOLD (OBLIVIOUS) BABIES

+ love loud events (basketball games, circuses, bands . . .)
+ aren't bothered by wet or dirty diapers
+ are emotionally stable
+ can't always differentiate between two voices
+ aren't bothered by clothing labels, bright lights, scratchy fabrics, or even pain

LOW-SENSORY-THRESHOLD (VERY AWARE) BABIES

+ are easily overstimulated
+ are awakened easily by a gentle touch or lights being turned on
+ may get extremely upset at loud noises
+ notice tiny variations in the taste of food
+ are extremely uncomfortable in wet or dirty diapers
+ are very sensitive to fabrics, labels, and the fit of their clothes

LOW-DISTRACTIBILITY BABIES

+ are quite hard to soothe once they're upset
+ seem completely oblivious to interruptions (noise, familiar voices) when involved in something important (like nursing)

HIGH-DISTRACTIBILITY BABIES

+ have short attention spans
+ are easily distracted while nursing
+ are easily soothed when upset and quickly stop crying when picked up
+ can turn from tears to laughter on a dime

HIGH-PERSISTENCE BABIES

+ are able to amuse themselves for a few minutes at a time
+ like to practice new motor skills (like rolling from front to back) over and over and over
+ pay close attention (for more than a minute) to rattles and mobiles
+ pay close attention to other children when playing
+ cry when you stop playing with them

LOW-PERSISTENCE BABIES

+ need constant attention — can't amuse themselves for very long in crib or playpen
+ have short attention spans and are frustrated easily, even by simple tasks
+ quickly lose interest in playing, even with favorite toys
+ won't spend much time working on new skills (rolling over, sitting up)

Ounce, a nonprofit mental health organization for children. The chart on pages 132–133 has a lot of examples that will give you a good idea of what each of the nine traits looks like. When you're done reading it, take the quiz below.

1. **Approach/Withdrawal**: Your baby's usual initial reaction to unfamiliar situations, such as meeting a new person, tasting a new food, or being in a new situation.
2. **Adaptability**: Similar to Approach/Withdrawal, but deals with your child's longer-term reactions to changes in routines or expectations, places, and ideas.
3. **Intensity**: The amount of energy your baby commonly uses to express her emotions—both positive and negative.
4. **Mood**: Her general mood—happy or fussy—over the course of a typical day.
5. **Activity level**: The amount of energy she puts into everything she does.
6. **Regularity**: The day-to-day predictability of your baby's hunger, sleeping, and filling diapers.
7. **Sensitivity**: Your baby's sensitivity to pain, noise, temperature change, lights, odors, flavors, textures, and emotions. Note: it's quite possible for her to be highly sensitive to one sensation (bright lights, for example) but not at all sensitive to another (noise).
8. **Distractibility**: How easy it is to change the focus of your baby's attention.
9. **Persistence**: Similar to Distractibility, but goes beyond the initial reaction and concerns the length of time your baby will spend trying to overcome obstacles or distractions.

Now that you know what to look for, spend a few minutes rating your baby on the following scale. And have your partner do it, too.

TRAIT	RATING						
Approach/Withdrawal	Approaching	1	2	3	4	5	Withdrawing
Adaptability	Fast	1	2	3	4	5	Slow
Intensity	Low	1	2	3	4	5	High
Mood	Positive	1	2	3	4	5	Negative
Activity Level	Low	1	2	3	4	5	High
Regularity	Predictable	1	2	3	4	5	Unpredictable
Sensitivity	Oblivious	1	2	3	4	5	Very Aware

Distractibility	Low	1 2 3 4 5	High
Persistence	High	1 2 3 4 5	Low

If you have a lot of 1s and 2s, you're one lucky guy. You've got an "easy" child (about 40 percent of parents do), and having an easy child is, well, easy. Your baby's always smiling and happy, she sleeps through the night, eats at the same time every day, and loves playing and meeting new people. When she does get upset or fussy, you can usually calm her down almost immediately. You're madly in love with your baby and you're feeling confident about your parenting skills.

However, depending on the situation, 1s and 2s might actually be "undesirable" traits. For example, as noted in the chart on pages 132–133, a low distractibility baby (who would score 1 or 2) won't be upset by noises but will be hard to soothe and a highly distractible baby (who would score 4 or 5) may not be able to sit still but will be easy to soothe.

If you ended up with a lot of 4s and 5s, you most likely have a "challenging" child (only about 10 percent of parents do), and things are not nearly as rosy. She doesn't sleep through the night, has trouble eating, freaks out at the slightest noise or change in her surroundings, cries for hours at a time (and nothing you try seems to make it any better), and is generally fussy. Meanwhile, you're exhausted and depressed, angry at the baby for her "malicious" behavior, embarrassed at the way people stare at your unhappy child, guilty about your unparental feelings, and jealous of your friends and their easy babies. In short, you're not finding your parenting experience very satisfying, you're discouraged and frustrated, and you think you must be a complete failure as a father. You may even feel trapped and fantasize about running away.

As bad as it sounds, there are some things you can do to help you overcome a lot of your frustration and negative feelings:

♦ Recognize that challenging children are challenging because of their innate makeup. Their temperament exists at birth. It's not their fault, it's not your fault, and it's not your partner's fault. It's just the way things are.

♦ Stop blaming yourself, your partner, or your baby. There's probably nothing wrong with any of you. Your baby is who she is, and there's very little you can do about it. The problem is that the way you're interacting with your child simply isn't working.

♦ Get to know your child's—and your own—temperament and look for similarities and differences, or what some people call *goodness of fit*. If you're both Highly Distractible, you may never get through that book you're reading —and neither of you will care. But if you're Highly Approaching

ENFANT TERRIBLE.

MUELLER

and the baby is Highly Withdrawing, you may have some real problems taking her to meet your boss for the first time.

At the very least, these steps will enable you to modify your approaches to your child's behavior and to anticipate and avoid conflicts before they occur. The result will be a far happier, more loving, and more satisfying relationship with your child. Guaranteed.

Putting Your Knowledge of Temperament to Good Use

Following are some of the most common temperament traits you're likely to encounter during your baby's first year, along with some suggestions for how to handle them.

INITIAL WITHDRAWAL/SLOW ADAPTABILITY

Just because your baby is shy, spits out new foods (which you probably won't be giving her for another few months), and refuses to play with new toys doesn't mean she'll never change. The key is to introduce things slowly and to be patient. For example, introduce new foods a few times at different meals, and give the baby a chance to "meet" a new toy from a distance before letting her touch it.

Your Withdrawing/Slow-Adapting baby will probably begin experiencing stranger anxiety (see pages 209–210) earlier—and it will last longer—than babies who are more Approaching and Fast-Adapting. Tell new visitors, and even those the baby knows a little bit, to take it easy when approaching her, not try to pick her up right away, and not take it personally if she screams or cries.

Your baby will eventually get used to new things—it'll just take her a little while. One thing you can do is frequently expose her to new situations and experiences so she can get used to the idea. But be careful. Your Withdrawing/Slow-Adapting baby has a tendency to get overstimulated, so recognize those symptoms and be prepared to get her back to something more familiar if necessary.

Also, think about your baby's temperament before making any major changes in your appearance. Shaving your beard, getting a haircut, or even replacing your glasses with contact lenses can trigger a strong negative reaction. When my oldest daughter was six months old, her babysitter—whom she absolutely adored—got a haircut, and it took her more than a week to recover.

HIGH INTENSITY

Some babies just make a lot of noise, and short of leaving the room or getting earplugs (both of which are perfectly reasonable approaches), there's not much you can do about it. Just make sure you can tell the difference between a shrill, eardrum-destroying *happy* shriek and a shrill, eardrum-destroying *unhappy* one. And watch out if you're tickling your baby with your nose—her mouth is very, very close to your ears.

NEGATIVE MOOD

Not much can make you happier than going out with a smiling, happy baby. But a baby who isn't a smiler, and who whimpers and cries all the time, can be a real challenge to your self-confidence. It's hard to take pleasure in a baby with a Negative Mood, or even to feel proud of her. And it's certainly tempting to think that if the baby doesn't smile at you all the time, she doesn't love you.

If you're feeling this way, resist the urge to get angry with your baby for her whining, or to "get even" with her by withholding your love. (I know it sounds silly, but it happens.) The truth is that the lack of a smile probably doesn't mean anything at all. And the whining will subside as your baby's verbal skills improve, enabling her to get your attention in more productive ways.

HIGH ACTIVITY

Because your High-Activity baby will spend her sleeping moments doing laps in her crib, it's important to install some big, soft bumpers (pads designed to protect babies' heads from banging into the bars). Just make sure they're securely attached to the sides of the crib so they don't become a smothering hazard. If your baby is really, really active you might want to put some rubber stops underneath the crib's wheels because energetic kicking and bouncing can actually move the crib. (Believe me, it's quite a shock to walk into your baby's room first thing in the morning and find that she—and her bed—aren't where you left them.) For that reason, it's especially important that you remove anything from inside the crib (or nearby) that could possibly fall on top of the baby's head.

Never, never leave your baby unattended—even for a second—on a changing table or bed; she could very well roll off (this applies to all babies, but especially to Highly Active ones). Once, when my oldest daughter was seven months old, I was tickling her in her bassinet when the phone (located about three feet away) rang. I stepped over, said "Hello," and heard a loud thump behind me: my daughter, who had never given any indication that she knew how to pull herself up, had done exactly that, and toppled over the side of the bassinet. No harm was done, but we put that bassinet into storage and didn't take it out again until the next baby came.

Your High-Activity baby may sometimes be too busy to be held or cuddled and may squirm and cry until you put her down. It's easy to take this as a rejection, but don't. Just try to do your holding and snuggling at times when she's likely to be more receptive, such as first thing in the morning or just before bed.

UNPREDICTABILITY

Since your Unpredictable baby seems to be eating, sleeping, and filling her diaper at random, it's up to you to try to establish a regular schedule. Although she may not want to eat, try to feed her something at times that are more convenient for you. If you schedule meals at the same times every day, you may be able to help her create a modified routine.

Routines are important for bedtime too. When you go into her room at night, don't turn on the lights, don't pick her up, don't play, and get out as soon as you can. Once you stumble on a getting-back-to-sleep routine, stick with it (although be prepared: what works with an Unpredictable baby one day may stop working a day, a week, or a month later).

If your baby's sleep irregularities are truly serious, you and your partner should divide up the night, each taking a shift while the other sleeps. If that doesn't help, talk with your pediatrician about a mild sedative—for the baby, not you.

LOW SENSORY THRESHOLD

For the first few months of a Low-Sensory-Threshold baby's life, you'll never know what's going to set her off. Sounds, smells, and sensations you might hardly notice can cause her to explode into tears: so can turning on the car radio, the crowd applauding at a basketball game (yes, you can take babies to basketball games), even too many toys in her crib.

One way to make your baby's life a little less jarring is to modify the amount and type of stimulation in her environment. Avoid neon colors when decorating her room, get opaque drapes to keep daytime light out during naptime, and don't play actively with her right before bedtime. When dressing your baby, stay away from tight clothes, brand-new clothes (they're often too stiff), wool, synthetic fabrics, or anything with a rough texture. Cotton blends usually offer the best combination of washability and softness. And be sure to clip off scratchy labels and tags.

HIGH DISTRACTIBILITY AND LOW PERSISTENCE

This combination of characteristics isn't usually a challenge until babies get active. Your Highly Distractible/Low Persistence baby gets bored easily and may want constant attention from you. She may also take forever to eat, stopping every thirty seconds to follow a fly as it zips through the room or to check out a shadow on the wall. If she's being breast-fed, this will probably bother your partner more than you.

This discussion of temperament should be enough for you to identify and begin to deal with your child's behavior patterns. But if you're seriously concerned about your child's temperament, check out the Resources section of this book.

You and Your Partner

Sex

On average, couples resume having sex about 7 weeks after the birth of the baby. But it may be a lot longer than that before your prebaby (and prepregnancy) sex life returns. If your partner is breast-feeding, she's also producing hormones that may mildly suppress her desire. That helps explain why a majority of women don't recover their sex drives for as long as six months after giving birth. For most couples, though, the biggest obstacles are fatigue and time.

Getting your physical relationship back to normal is going to take patience, communication, and some careful planning. Here are a few things that may give your sex life the jump start it needs:

- **Go for quality over quantity.** Just because you can't have sex three times a week doesn't mean you have to give up altogether. You may only be able to fit in a few rolls in the hay a month, but make them count.

- **Keep it regular.** When it comes to sex, it's use it or lose it. Your sex organs are muscles, and they need some regular working out to operate at peak capacity. In addition, long breaks can cause your hormone levels to change, which can reduce your desire.

- **Start early and build from there.** When she gets out of bed, tell your partner how good she looks; if you see her naked, compliment her body; flirt with her and let her catch you peeking down her shirt over breakfast; rub up against her as you walk past each other in the hallway; and make a few sexy phone calls to her during the day. By the time you get home, you'll be all over each other.

- **Think like teens.** Watch some porn videos together, grope each other in the back seat of the car, or have sex on the sink in the bathroom of a friend who's invited you over for dinner.

- **Be good to yourselves.** Both of you should you eat right, exercise at least three times a week, get plenty of sleep, and have at least five minutes alone a few times a week to just get your thoughts together.

"And so the big bad wolf ate Little Red Riding Hood, Hansel and Gretel, Cinderella, and the three little pigs, and that was the end of fairy tales forever. Now good night!"

♦ **Reach out and touch each other.** When you were younger and more awake, the need to touch your partner was sparked by desire. Now that you're a dad, things have changed and the order is reversed. Touching, holding, stroking, and kissing each other—even if you aren't really into it when you start—can actually *produce* the desire, which in turn will make the kissing and fondling more intense, which could lead to other things...

Finally, as mentioned earlier, don't forget the contraception. Condoms are best until your partner's doctor tells her that anything else is okay.

Thyroid Problems

For up to six months after birth, 5 to 10 percent of women experience *postpartum thyroiditis*, an inflammation of the thyroid, a gland that produces hormones that are involved in almost every organ and system in our body. In particular, thyroid hormones are involved in regulating your temperature, metabolism, weight, muscle strength, digestion, heart and lung function, mood, and overall mental state.

Postpartum thyroiditis causes no pain but produces a number of symptoms, including anxiety, emotional instability, muscle fatigue, lack of energy, and depression. The problem is that every one of those symptoms is also a perfectly normal part of your partner's postpartum recovery. However, by this point, she should have been over most of them, so if you recognize any, it's worth discussing them with your partner's doctor. Most of the time, the condition will take care of itself within a few months, but sometimes it requires some medical treatment. Diagnosing it definitively may require some tests that use radioactive isotopes, which are a big no-no if your partner is nursing because traces can be passed to the baby through the breast milk.

Family Matters

Sleeping Tight

We all love our children, but let's face it, sometimes we want them to go to sleep—and stay that way for a while. There are all sorts of factors (many of which are beyond your control) that influence whether your child will be a "good" sleeper or a "bad" one. Fortunately, though, there are a few rules of thumb that can help tilt the odds in your favor:

♦ Don't become the baby's sleep transition object. Baby's last waking memory should be of her crib or something familiar in it (blankie, toy, a picture on the wall). That way, if she wakes up in the middle of the night, she'll see the familiar object and be able to associate it with sleep. If you were the last thing she saw before dropping off, she'll want you again, even if you happen to be sleeping.

♦ It's perfectly natural for babies to fuss or be restless for fifteen or twenty minutes after being put down. (Please remember that fussing is one thing, screaming is another. If the baby begins to really wail, pick her up and soothe her, but try to get her back in her crib while she's still awake. It's absolutely impossible to spoil a baby by picking her up or soothing her in the first three or four months of life.)

♦ Keep nighttime activity to a minimum. Whether your baby is sleeping with you or not, she needs to learn that nighttime is for sleeping, not for playing.

♦ Don't turn on the lights. If the baby wakes up for a middle-of-the-night breast or bottle, do it in the dark.

♦ Don't change diapers unless you absolutely have to (such as when you're trying to treat a particularly nasty case of diaper rash or if the baby is wearing cloth diapers; if she's wearing disposables, she'll be perfectly fine until the morning).

♦ Establish a routine. You'll need to make up your own, depending on what works best for you. Here's a fairly simple routine that is good for babies this age as well as for toddlers: change diapers, get sleepsuit on, read a story or two, go around the room and say "goodnight" to all the toys and animals, give a kiss goodnight, and into bed.

♦ When your baby is about six months old, start leaving the door to her room open. Kids that age get scared if they feel they're trapped in a small space, especially if they aren't sure you're just outside the door.

♦ In case of nightmares or other middle-of-the-night scares, respond promptly and be as reassuring as possible. Unless your child is hysterical with fear, try to keep things brief and resist the urge to take the baby out of the crib. You can do a lot of soothing by rubbing her back or head—all from your side of the bars.

♦ Make sure the baby doesn't get overtired during the day. This means making sure she has plenty of naps—preferably one within 60–90 minutes after eating—and goes to bed early.

♦ During the day, gently wake up—and entertain—your baby if she tries to nap more than two or three hours at a stretch. The idea is to make her longest sleep of the day occur at night.

But What About Those Middle-of-the-Night Wake-Ups?

The most common reason babies wake up in the middle of the night is that they want to eat. If your partner is breast-feeding, do everything you can to stay in bed and let her handle things. I realize that this sounds positively insensitive, but the truth is that there's really nothing you can do to help out short of bringing the baby to her. If your partner wants some adult company (and who wouldn't?), try not to give in. Instead, offer to give her a few extra hours of sleep while you handle the early-morning child-care shift (which usually lasts a lot longer than a 2 A.M. feeding).

Of course, if you're bottle-feeding your baby (either with formula or expressed breast milk), you should do your fair share of the feedings. And since there's no sense in both you and your partner getting up at the same time, you should be able to negotiate breakfast in bed (or at least a couple of hours of sleep) on those days when you do the 2 A.M. feeding.

Sometimes, no matter what you do, your baby is going to wake up at two or three in the morning for no other reason than to stay awake for a few hours and check things out. When this happens, keep your middle-of-the-night encounters as boring as possible. Until they're old enough to have sex, kids need to know that nighttime is for sleeping.

Sleeping Arrangements

As hard as it may be to imagine, there exists a rather basic parenting issue that regularly generates even more controversy than circumcision or the disposable-versus-cloth-diapers debate: whether or not to have your child sleep in the same bed as you and your partner.

Fortunately (or unfortunately, depending on where you stand on the issue), there's absolutely no consensus on which view is the "right" one. And just to

Naps and Sleep Schedules

At four months your baby has probably only recently settled into a regular sleep routine. Every baby has her own sleeping schedule, but a typical one for a baby this age might include a ten-hour stretch at night plus, if you're lucky, two two-hour naps—one midmorning, the other midafternoon. Or it might be only a 5-hour stretch at night plus four or five 30-minute naps. Keep an eye on these naps, however; if they get too late, they may start upsetting the night-sleeping routine. You can't expect a baby to take a nap from 4 to 6 P.M. and then go to bed for the night at 7.

make sure that there's no real way to decide this issue once and for all, there's very little serious scientific data supporting either position.

Our older daughter slept in a bassinet in our room for a month or so until we moved her into her own room. The middle one slept in bed with us for six months before being asked to leave. Personally, I kind of liked being able to snuggle up with a warm, smooth baby, but after being kicked in the head, stomach, back, face, and chest every night for six months, I was glad to go back to an adults-only sleeping arrangement. The youngest baby also started off in our bed but moved to her own room after only 6 weeks or so.

Here are some of the most common issues that come up in discussions of the family bed:

+ **Independence.** Proponents of *cosleeping* or *the family bed* point to the fact that in most countries (comprising about 80 percent of the world's population), parents and children sleep in the same bed. They claim that kids are being forced to be independent too early and that human evolution simply can't keep pace with the new demands our culture is placing on its children. They maintain that before a child can become independent, she must feel that the world is a safe place and that her needs will be met. Kids who sleep in a family bed, in this view, turn out to be more independent, more confident, and more self-assured than those who don't. Critics, however, say that what works in other countries doesn't always work here. In America early independence is critical, and babies should therefore quickly learn to be away from their parents, especially if both work and the children have to be in day care.

+ **Sleep—the baby's.** Despite what you might think, cosleeping children tend to sleep more lightly than children who sleep alone (blankets rustling and parents turning over in bed wake them up). But light sleeping isn't necessarily a bad thing. In fact, there seems to be a correlation between lighter sleep and a lower incidence of SIDS.

+ **Sleep—yours.** It's perfectly normal for even the soundest-sleeping kids to wake up every three or four hours for a quick look around the room. The vast majority (about 70 percent) soothe themselves back to sleep after a minute or two. But about 30 percent will spot something they just have to play with (you or your partner, for example), and they're up for hours.

+ **Safety.** Many parents are afraid that they'll accidentally roll over on their sleeping child if the whole family is sharing the same bed. While this is a perfectly legitimate concern, most adults—even while asleep—have a highly developed sense of where they are. It's probably been quite a while since you fell out of bed in the middle of the night.

♦ **Sexual spontaneity**. No kidding. But there are plenty of other places to make love besides your bed.

♦ **Breast-feeding**. There's no question that it's a lot easier for a nursing mother to reach across her bed for the baby than to get up and stagger down the hall. Some research indicates that this may encourage mothers to breast-feed longer. Problems arise, however, when fathers feel (and they often do) displaced by the nursing baby and decide that the only place to get a good night's sleep is on the couch.

A Few Things to Consider If You're Thinking about Sharing Your Bed with Your Child

♦ Keep politics out of your decision-making. Sleep with your child because you and your partner want to, not because you feel you have to.

♦ Don't be embarrassed. You're not being soft, negligent, or overindulgent—it's a choice made by millions of fine parents.

♦ Make sure your bed is large enough to accommodate everyone. (But no waterbeds—baby could roll between you and the mattress.) Put the bed against the wall and have the baby sleep on the wall side, or get a guard rail if she's going to sleep on the outside edge. And remember, overly soft mattresses, comforters, and pillows may pose a risk of suffocation.

♦ Make sure everyone's toenails are trimmed.

♦ Rethink your decision right now if you're obese, you drink, or take any medication that might make you hard to wake up, or if you're generally such a sound sleeper that you're worried you might roll on top of your baby without noticing.

♦ Think before you start. Once your baby has been sleeping in your bed for six to eight months, it's going to be awfully hard to get her out if you change your mind.

A Few Things to Consider If You're Thinking about Not Sharing Your Bed with Your Child

♦ Don't feel guilty. You're not a bad or selfish parent for not doing it.

♦ There is absolutely no evidence that sleeping with your child will speed up the bonding/attachment process.

♦ It's okay to make an occasional exception, such as when a child is ill or has had a frightening experience.

♦ If you're making your decision because of safety issues, you may be able to compromise by setting up the baby's crib in your bedroom or by getting a "sidecar"—basically a three-sided crib that attaches to the side of your bed.

Work and Family

What's Going On with the Baby

Physically

♦ This month's big discovery is, yes, toes. And just as your baby spent hours fondling and sucking his own fingers, he'll repeat the process with his lower extremities.

♦ He's getting a lot stronger and is now able to roll from his stomach to his back at will. He can also get himself from his tummy to his hands and knees. Once there, he may rock back and forth as if anxious for some kind of race to begin.

♦ When you pull him to a standing position, he'll try to help you out by leaning his head forward and bending at the waist. Once standing (which he can do quite well as long as you hold on), he may stamp his feet up and down.

♦ He's almost able to sit without support and can now pick up objects while sitting.

♦ His hands continue to get more coordinated. His aim is still a little iffy when he reaches for things, but he now plays with a toy in either hand and can turn his wrist (it's harder than it sounds) to get a better look at what he's picked up. He may even be able to hold on to his own bottle.

♦ There are now longer and more regular intervals between feedings and bowel movements.

Intellectually

♦ For the past four months, your baby was content to sit back and stare at objects or to have you put them in his hand. But no longer. In an attempt to actively engage in his world, he's energetically starting to reach for things. Watch carefully as he looks back and forth between an object and his hand—inching the hand slowly toward the object. That may not sound like much to you, but he's learning that objects exist that are separate from him.

♦ Handling and turning an object teaches your baby that even though something looks different from different angles, its shape remains the same.

♦ With these newfound skills, your baby will now get excited by seeing only a small part of a familiar object and will try to move small obstacles out of his way. He's also learning to anticipate the direction that objects move, and he may lean over to find a toy he's dropped instead of staring at his hand. But if the object is out of his sight for more than just a few seconds, it ceases to exist and he forgets about it.

♦ Amazingly, he can also make estimates about speed and distance. In one fascinating study, babies who heard a sound that appeared to come closer to them leaned back to get out of the way of what they thought was a threat.

Verbally

♦ It's finally happened: your baby is babbling. Besides the vowel sounds (*eee*, *aaa*, *ayy*) he's been making, he's added a few consonants (*bbb*, *ddd*, *mmm*) to the mix.

♦ He's found his voice's volume switch and will practice modulating his shrieks, coos, and yelps.

♦ Although he's still trying to imitate more of the voice sounds you make to him, the noises he produces sound nothing like actual language.

♦ He's so delighted with his newfound language skills that he'll babble for 20 to 30 minutes at a stretch. Don't worry if you're not there to enjoy it—he's perfectly content to talk to his toys or, in a pinch, to himself.

♦ He may understand, and respond to, his name.

Emotionally/Socially

♦ He's capable of expressing a growing number of emotions: fear, anger, disgust, and satisfaction. He'll cry if you put him down and calm if you pick him up.

♦ He has—and readily expresses—strong preferences for toys and people, pushing away what he doesn't want. He also deliberately imitates faces and gestures.

♦ If he feels you're not paying enough attention to him, he'll try to interrupt whatever you're doing with a yelp or a cry. If he does start crying, you can usually stop his tears just by talking to him.

♦ He knows the difference between familiar people and strangers, and associates friends with pleasure.

♦ Unfortunately, he doesn't remember that his friends started off (to him, at least) as strangers. Consequently, he's a little slow to warm to new people. That can be tough on you if you're trying to show people what a fantastic baby you have, but it's a positive developmental sign. We'll talk more about stranger anxiety in the next chapter.

♦ He may spend some time trying to soothe himself—either by talking to himself or by clutching a favorite toy.

What You're Going Through

Worried about Doing Things Wrong

Just a few months ago your baby didn't make very many demands, so satisfying them wasn't all that tough. But now his needs are far more complex, and at times you may feel that it's nearly impossible to react promptly and appropriately.

With so much to respond to, it's perfectly normal to worry that you're not reading your baby's signals correctly and that you're doing everything wrong. These feelings, of course, are made worse by a baby who won't stop crying (a

Mom probably wouldn't buy us one, but you have to learn to make your own choices, Dad.

SIPRESS

reflection of inadequate fathering skills?) or by a dissatisfied or seemingly hostile look on the baby's face (possibly a reproach for some terrible mistake that you made).

Perhaps the best way to overcome your worries is to spend more time with the baby. The more practice you get, the better you'll be at understanding the baby's "language" and the more confident you'll be in responding.

Also, learn to go with your gut feelings. There's almost always more than one solution to a given problem, and you'll undoubtedly settle on a good one. Even if you make a few mistakes, they aren't likely to have any long-term effects. After all, just because your partner burps the baby over her shoulder doesn't mean you can't do it with the baby sitting on your knees.

It's also important that you stand your ground. Many women have been raised to believe that if they aren't the primary caregiver, they've failed as mothers. In some cases, that leads the mother to act as a gatekeeper, not sharing in the parenting and actually limiting the dad's involvement to an amount she feels isn't a threat. If you're feeling left out, talk to your partner right away. Chances are she's not doing it deliberately. And give her time to learn that you're serious about wanting to be an equal participant, and that you're ready and able to do the job.

Of course, if you're really sure you're making serious mistakes, ask for some help. But spending too much time analyzing things and worrying that you've done something wrong can get you into trouble. According to psychiatrist Stanley Greenspan, excessive worrying can destroy your self-confidence and lead to doing nothing at all or to adopting a hands-off attitude toward the baby. (That way, the twisted logic goes, at least you won't make any more mistakes.) This, of course, can have a decidedly negative effect on your baby's development—and on your development as a father.

Finally, before you toss in the towel, consider this: If you think you're having trouble reading your baby's signals, how can you be so sure that his crying and odd looks mean all the horrible, negative things you think they do?

Striking a Balance between Work and Family
Most new fathers feel torn between two options that seem mutually exclusive: protecting and providing, and being an involved, nurturing dad. Of course, the percentage of your time you spend on each option will change as your children get older and as other circumstances change. Finding the perfect balance is something you'll be working on for the rest of your life.

As mentioned in the previous chapter (page 126), most men place a high value on their family life and claim that they're willing to make sacrifices to spend more time with their children. But by six months after their children's birth, about 95 percent of new fathers are back working full-time. (At about the same time, only 36 percent of new moms are working full-time, and another 17 percent are working part-time.)

At first glance it seems that there's a major contradiction between what men say and what they do. But researcher Glen Palm found that the work/family trade-off isn't nearly so cut-and-dried. Many new fathers, Palm says, are "taking time off from friendships, recreation, and sleep to devote to their children, while they continue the time commitment to a full-time job." Clearly there's something keeping fathers from spending less time at the office. One explanation, of course, is financial. Since the average working woman makes less than the average working man, if one parent is going to take time off from work, many families conclude that they can better survive the loss of the woman's salary. Another important explanation is that in our society men and women have very different choices about the relative value of career in their lives.

Basically, we simply expect men to show their love for their families by providing for them financially. "To many people, 'working mother' means conflict," says the Fatherhood Project's Jim Levine. "But 'working father' is a redundancy." Perhaps the most interesting explanation (and my favorite) for why we keep fathers tied to their jobs and away from their families is offered by anthropologist Margaret Mead: "No developing society that needs men to leave home and do their thing for society ever allows young men in to handle or touch their newborns . . . for they know somewhere that if they did the new fathers would become so 'hooked' they would never go out and do their thing properly." I know exactly what she means.

Just because most fathers are trapped at the office doesn't mean that they aren't affected by what's going on at home. As it turns out, men are just as likely as women to suffer from *work-family spillover*—family pressures intruding on work, and work pressures intruding on family life. And working moms and dads are equally likely to say that trying to manage the spillover causes them a lot of stress.

Making Some Changes

Although you may never be able to resolve your work/family conflicts completely, there are a few ways you can maximize your time with your family, minimize your stress, and avoid trashing your career.

When the first edition of this book came out in 1997, alternative work-scheduling options were fairly rare. But today, employers are a little more open-minded—perhaps in response to the estimated *90 percent* of parents who say they want access to more flexible options. According to the Society for Human Resource Management, two-thirds of employers offer flexible schedules, a third offer compressed workweeks, 41 percent allow at least some telecommuting, and a quarter offer job sharing. Those numbers (with the exception of job sharing) are about 50 percent higher than they were in 1998.

Let's take a look at these options in a little more detail.

FULL-TIME OPTIONS

If you can't (or don't want to) reduce your hours, you may still be able to build a little flexibility into your schedule. Options include:

- **Flex time**. You'll still work the same number of hours, but you might, for example, start at 5 A.M. and go home at 1 P.M. instead of the usual 9 to 5. The schedule you come up with will depend on what works for you, your employer, and your coworkers.
- **Compressed work week**. The basic idea is that you put in extra hours on certain days in exchange for a day off. Typical arrangements include 4 ten-hour days per week, or working an extra hour every day for nine days and taking a day off every two weeks.
- **Alternate work week**. You still put in your 40 hours, but you might work Wednesday through Sunday and take Mondays and Tuesdays off.

"It's your husband. The baby won't burp for him."

PART-TIME OPTIONS

If you can afford to, you might want to consider one of the following alternatives:

♦ **Job sharing**. You and another person divide up the responsibilities of the job. You would probably use the same office and desk. A typical job-share schedule might have you working two days one week and three days the next, while your workplace partner does the opposite. Or one of you might work the mornings and the other afternoons. Either way, be very careful to negotiate a continuation of your health benefits. Many employers drop them for less-than-full-time employees.

♦ **Switch to part-time**. This is more or less the same as job sharing, except you won't have to share a desk with someone else. Again, make sure you're clear on how many hours you need to work so you don't lose your benefits.

♦ **Become a consultant to your current employer**. This can be a great way for you to get a lot of flexibility over your workday. There are also lots of tax advantages, particularly if you set up a home office (see more on this in the next section). At the very least, you'll be able to deduct auto mileage and a hefty percentage of your phone and utility bills. But be sure to check with an accountant first; the IRS uses certain "tests" to determine whether someone is an employee or a consultant. If, for example, you go into the office every day, have a secretary, and get company benefits, you're an employee. Also, remember that if you become a consultant, you'll lose your benefit package. So be sure to build the cost of that package (or the amount you'll have to pay to replace it) into the daily or hourly rate you negotiate with your soon-to-be-former employer.

WORKING AT HOME (TELECOMMUTING)

All the options above involve making changes to your schedule. But this one involves changing your location.

Far too many managers believe in the importance of daily "face time" (actually being seen at the office). The truth is that face time is highly overrated and often unnecessary. In all the years I've been writing, I've worked for dozens of magazines and newspapers and a number of publishers, most of which are several thousand miles from my home. And in most cases I've never even met my editors. I'm certainly the first to admit that being a writer isn't a typical job. But millions of Americans (engineers, computer programmers, and just about anybody else who sits at a desk) do work that doesn't require their physical presence in any particular place at any particular time. If you're not a construction worker or a retail salesman, you might be a prime candidate for telecommuting.

Now don't get too excited: it's not as if you and your boss will never see each

If You're an Employer (or a Supervisor)

Most companies still look at flexible or alternative workplace schedules as a "women's issue," which means that they rarely, if ever, consider that a lot of fathers might need the same benefits. The ultimate responsibility for changing this Neanderthal attitude and helping men get more involved with their families rests at the top—with you.

+ **Change your own schedule**. Many of your male employees will be reluctant to approach you with proposed schedule changes because they're afraid of jeopardizing their career. So if you know someone has just become a father, raise the issue with him first. Chances are he'll be grateful.
+ **Make some changes**. If you have enough employees, organize classes and support groups for new parents. Even if you don't have many employees, you can still offer free (or subsidized) on-site or near-site child care. You can also encourage your employees to take advantage of part-time, job-sharing, or flexible scheduling options. Overall, your company's policies should recognize that all parents (as opposed to just mothers) are responsible for their children's care and development.
+ **Don't worry about the cost**. Companies with family-friendly policies find that the costs of implementing such programs are more than compensated for by increased morale and productivity, reduced absenteeism, and lower turnover. They're also a great recruiting tool.

other again. Most telecommuters are out of the office only a day or two a week. Like the other flexible work options discussed in this chapter, telecommuting is designed to give you more time with your family. But if you think you'll be able to save money on child care or have your baby sit on your lap while you crunch numbers, you're sorely mistaken.

Besides the convenience aspect, one of the major advantages of telecommuting is that you don't have to shave and you can work in your underwear. There are, however, a few disadvantages. Primary among them is lack of human contact: you may hate that train ride into the city or the annoying guy in your carpool, but after a few months alone in your house, you might actually miss them. You might also miss going out to lunch with your coworkers or even just bumping into them in the halls. And if you have a tendency to be obsessive about your work (as I do), you'll have to train yourself to take frequent breaks. I can't tell you how many times I've realized—at ten o'clock at night—that I haven't eaten all day and that the only time I went outside was to take the newspaper in from the porch.

Making the Proposal

The decision to try one of these workplace alternatives (or any other one you can come up with) can be huge. So before you march into your boss's office, do the following:

♦ Figure out with your partner which arrangement works best for you and your family.

♦ Be as specific as possible about the days and times you're proposing to work as well as how long you anticipate needing the revised schedule.

♦ Get a group of people with similar concerns to approach your boss at the same time. That way no one will be able to accuse you of asking for preferential treatment. Start by asking other dads with young kids as well as working mothers.

♦ Look at things from your employer's point of view. Unless you work for a nonprofit, your company is in business to earn money. And to do that, your boss has to be sure that what needs to be done will actually get done. So give your employer all the details about how you'll be able to accomplish the various tasks you have, how often you'll be in touch, and how your boss and coworkers can reach you in case of emergency. The more secure your employer and coworkers feel, the more supportive they're likely to be.

♦ Experiment. If your employer is skeptical, suggest trying it out for a few months. Then get together to evaluate how well your proposed arrangement met everyone's needs.

♦ Sell the benefits. Employers that offer flexible, family-friendly benefits enjoy better employee morale, reduced absenteeism and turnover, increased job satisfaction and creativity, lower real estate costs and other overhead, and an increased ability to recruit and retain high-quality people.

Putting It All Together

No matter how you try to keep your work life separate from your family life, there's going to be plenty of spillover between the two. This isn't necessarily a bad thing. In his four-decade-long study of fathers, John Snarey found that, "contrary to the stereotype of rigid work-family trade-off, a positive, reciprocal interaction may exist between childrearing and bread-winning."

Other researchers have come to similar conclusions. "Before they became fathers, men did not appear to be conscious that home and work life often require different personal qualities," writes Phil Cowan. After becoming fathers, however, many men "described new abilities to juggle conflicting demands, make decisions, and communicate quickly and clearly both at home and at work. . . . Some described themselves as more aware of their personal relationships on the job, and more able to use some of their managerial skills in the solution of family problems."

You and Your Family

Caught between Two Families

Integrating your old and new families can be enormously complicated—for your kids, your new partner, and you. Most older children feel somewhat abandoned and jealous when a younger sibling comes along. But if they aren't living with you full-time, these feelings may get kicked to an even higher level when you start a new family. They may feel that your loyalty and your love (and sometimes your money) will be spent on your new baby, the one who's with you all the time, and they may resent having to share those things with anyone. They may also see how much more involved you are with their new half-sibling and resent that you weren't that way with them. (This may or may not reflect reality, but your kids' feelings are just as real either way.)

Children of divorce almost always harbor a secret (or not-so-secret) hope that their parents will get back together. But your having a new family with a woman who's not their mother may make them confront their dashed hopes. At the same time, your new family may disrupt your older children's loyalties. On the one hand, they'll continue (as they should) to feel deeply loyal to their mother. On the other hand, they'll feel a naturally growing allegiance to the baby and to their stepmother. But as those newer relationships deepen, the children may feel guilty that they're abandoning their mother—as if in allowing themselves to be part of a new family, they have to stop loving her. This can sometimes make them lash out at you, the baby, and/or your partner. In their minds, if it weren't for all the changes that have been forced on them, life would be great—or at least not any worse than it was before.

This is almost exactly what happened with me. My two older kids are with me half the time, and we have a very close relationship. That's a wonderful thing for the three of us, but it sometimes makes my new wife feel excluded, as though she has me only 50 percent of the time. And she naturally worries about whether I'm going to have time (and love) enough for her and the child we have together.

As tough as your renewed fatherhood status is for your children and your partner, it's no less difficult for you. The nice, linear progression of your development as a father has been derailed. Usually, you get married, have kids, the kids grow up and get married, and they have kids of their own and make you a grandfather. But if you're a renewed dad, you're literally in two places at the same time. You're still on your original track with your older children, but you're also starting the process all over again with your new family.

Sometimes it's easy—and fun—to be on both tracks. Having been through it before will probably make the early stages of fatherhood less stressful and more relaxing. Other times, however, you'll feel as though your two tracks are on a collision course with each other. As I discussed earlier, your new partner may interpret your laid-back attitude as a lack of interest or excitement. But the more time you spend with your new family, the more abandoned and resentful your older kids may feel, jealous of the things they never got. You might feel guilty too, about not having been a better dad the first time around. But the more time you spend with your older children, the more your new family will feel excluded.

All in all, you're in a tough spot, and you'll have to figure out a way to juggle the often conflicting needs of your two families in a way that works for everyone—including you. But whatever you do, don't give in to pressure or temptation to sever ties with your older children. They need you, and you need them, even if you don't get to see each other as often as you'd like.

Your challenge is to create a new family unit, one that integrates your older children, your new child, and your partner. Notice that I'm *not* saying to make the older kids part of your new family or to make the new family part of the old one. Either of those approaches will make one group or the other feel second best. Instead, both groups have to understand that they're part of something bigger and that your loyalties are not divided but are spread out evenly.

You and Your Baby

Green-Eyed Babies?

Older siblings aren't the only children who get jealous. There's actually some indication that babies as young as five months may too. Sound crazy? Well, consider this: British researcher Riccardo Draghi-Lorenz asked 24 mothers of five-month-old babies to show affection to another baby and to talk with another adult while their baby watched. The results weren't pretty: over half of the babies got upset and cried when Mom cooed or tickled or cuddled with another infant. But when the mothers were schmoozing with adults, only 10 percent of the babies cried.

This bit of information probably isn't going to do much to change your behavior. But if you're in a situation where you're likely to be interacting with your baby's tiny peers, just be aware of how he might react.

Time for Solids

When I was a baby, the current wisdom about introducing solid foods was to do it as early as possible, often as soon as five or six weeks. One of the explanations was that babies who ate solid foods supposedly slept longer than those on bottles (almost no one was being breast-fed then). Today, people are more interested in the baby's health than in whether he sleeps through the night (which eating solid food doesn't affect anyway), and most pediatricians now recommend that you delay introducing solids until your baby is 6 months old if he's being breast-fed; possibly as soon as 4 months if he's bottle-fed. The recommended delay may be even longer if you or your partner has a history of food allergies (for more on that, see page 159).

Even if you're tempted to start solids earlier than four to six months, resist. Here's why waiting a little longer is a good idea:

- It may protect against illness. Introducing solid foods before 16 weeks has been linked to a greater risk of developing respiratory illness (such as asthma) in childhood, and to weight problems throughout life.
- If you, your partner, or an older child has Type I diabetes (sometimes called *juvenile diabetes*), timing is especially important. Two very recent studies found that at-risk babies who first ate cereals or other foods containing gluten before four months or after seven months had a far higher risk of developing diabetes than babies who started on solids within the traditional four-to-six-month window.
- Because younger babies' digestive systems are immature, they can't digest proteins, starches, or fats until they're at least six months old. Before then, solid foods—along with their nutrients—pass undigested through their systems.
- If the baby isn't ready, he may choke on the food.
- Feeding solids may fill up the baby and make him drink less formula or breast milk, which could deprive him of the calories and nutrients he needs.
- It can reduce the likelihood of the baby developing allergies later on.
- Breast- and bottle-feeding is a great opportunity for parents to cuddle with their babies, although it's nearly impossible for you to cuddle the baby while your partner is breast-feeding.

♦ With breasts, there's nothing to clean up; with bottles, only the bottle. But with solids, you have to wash spoons, dishes, high-chair trays, bibs, and perhaps even the floor and nearby walls.

If your baby was born prematurely, check with your pediatrician before introducing solids. You'll still probably start when his *adjusted age* (see page 96) is six months. (If he's five months old now and was born six weeks early, his adjusted age, for food introduction purposes, is only three and a half months.

Here's how you can tell if your baby is really ready for solids:

♦ His weight has doubled since birth (indicating that he's getting plenty of nutrition).
♦ He's very underweight for his age (indicating that he's not getting enough nutrition).
♦ He's drinking more than a quart (32 ounces) of formula or breast milk per day.
♦ He chews on nipples (either your partner's or the bottle's) while sucking.
♦ He stares intently at you, smacks his lips, or drools when you're eating.
♦ He can sit by himself or with support and has good head control.

Remember, introducing solids does not mean that breast- or bottle-feeding will end (see pages 275–281 for information on weaning). In fact, most of your baby's nutrients will still come from milk or formula for a few more months.

Getting Started

Getting your baby to eat solid foods isn't going to happen overnight. For starters, most of what he's had in his mouth thus far has come out again looking pretty much like it did when it went in. Now a full spoon is going in and an empty one is coming out. Second, he'll probably take a few days to get used to the strange new taste and texture. Then he's got to figure out how to move it from the front of his mouth to his throat (liquids kind of know where to go by themselves), where he can swallow it. Here's the way to do it:

♦ Offer new foods at a time when the baby isn't too tired, too fussy, or too hungry.
♦ Set aside a lot of time. It could take you 10 or 15 minutes to work your way through a single teaspoon of food.
♦ Make sure your baby is properly strapped into a high chair; you don't want to do this on your lap. Also, put a bib on the baby unless you enjoy doing laundry.
♦ Your baby's first food should be an iron-fortified, single-grain cereal (no, not

Allergies and Intolerances:
What They Are and How to Prevent Them

Despite the claims of about 25 percent of American parents, fewer than 5 percent of children under three are truly allergic to any foods. True allergies are abnormal responses by the immune system to ingested proteins. The most common symptoms are nasal congestion, asthma, skin rashes (eczema and hives), chronic runny nose or cough, vomiting, and severe mood swings. In contrast, symptoms such as headaches, excess gas, diarrhea, or constipation are generally caused by intolerances, which are usually the result of an enzyme deficiency.

While you may be tempted to say, "What's the difference? A reaction is a reaction," the distinction between an allergy and an intolerance is critical and subtle. Allergies often begin in infancy and get progressively worse with each encounter with the offending food. Intolerances don't. Fortunately, most kids—except those allergic to peanuts and fish—outgrow their allergies altogether by age five. (Only about 2 percent of children over five have true food allergies.)

The consensus among pediatricians is that the way to deal with allergies and intolerances is to prevent them before they happen. Complete prevention, of course, is impossible. But here are a few things you can do to better the odds:

♦ Breast-feed your baby and withhold solid foods for at least four to six months.

♦ If your partner has a history of true allergies, she should reduce or completely eliminate high-risk foods (see page 161) while breast-feeding.

♦ Introduce only one new food at a time. That way, if your baby has a reaction, you'll know right away what caused it.

♦ After introducing a new food, wait three to five days before introducing another.

♦ If your baby has any of the negative reactions mentioned above, eliminate the food right away and call your pediatrician. He will probably tell you to take the baby off the food and reintroduce it in six months. By then, your baby may have built up the necessary defenses.

Cheerios)—oatmeal or barley. For the first few days, add breast milk or formula—but not cow's milk—to make the cereal especially liquidy. Thicken it up as your baby gets used to it by adding a little less milk. You don't have to follow the exact instructions on the package—a teaspoon is plenty for the first few days—what 's important is the ratio between the cereal and milk or formula (usually 1:3).

♦ Watch out for constipation. Most parents start their babies on rice cereal, and most of those babies immediately get constipated. If this happens, stop the rice and start the baby on fruit until the problem resolves itself. (The best fruits for this purpose start with the letter "p"—pears, prunes, peaches, plums, (a)pricots—for *poop*.) Once the baby's intestines are flowing again, reduce the fruit and add back some cereal (stay away from rice this time). Adjust the mix as needed to keep the baby regular.

♦ Use a plastic-coated spoon to serve. He'll probably spend some time chewing on it, and regular metal utensils are hard on gums. And be sure to have a *washable* toy that the baby can play with while you're feeding him. In a few years you're not going to want him to play around while he's eating. But for now, if his hands are busy with a toy, they won't be trying to grab the spoon out of your hand.

♦ Do *not* try to feed your baby solid foods through a bottle with an enlarged hole in the nipple. (Don't laugh—people do it all the time.) The object is to get the baby to eat with a spoon.

♦ Never force the baby to eat. If he turns his head away, refuses to open his mouth, or spits out whatever you've given him, it's time for a break.

♦ Three days after you actually manage to get some cereal down the baby's throat, start adding vegetables—one at a time, three to five days apart. Make sure the baby gets a good mix of yellow (carrots, squash) and green (peas, spinach, zucchini) veggies. Many people prefer to make bananas baby's first non-cereal food. The problem with bananas is that they are fairly sweet, and babies may become so fond of them that they won't be interested in any other foods you may introduce thereafter. Plus, like rice, the other traditional first food, bananas are constipating.

♦ After a week or so on vegetables, introduce non-citrus fruits (again, one at a time, three to five days apart). Until he's a year old, your baby can't digest raw apples, but unsweetened applesauce is okay. Hold off on the oranges for a few more months (the citric acid can cause painful diaper rash).

♦ If you absolutely must give your baby juice (see page 47 for a few reasons *not* to), be sure to dilute it at least fifty-fifty with water.

♦ Don't add sugar or salt to any foods. Your baby doesn't need either one.

♦ Try not to feed the baby right out of the jar unless he's going to eat the whole thing. The bacteria in his mouth can contaminate what's left.

♦ When your baby is about seven months old, introduce yogurt. It's an important source of protein and can easily be mixed with other foods. Although most babies like yogurt, none of mine did, and we had to trick them into eating it by putting a blueberry (always a favorite food) at the back of the spoon.

♦ Breads and cereals (yes, Cheerios are okay now) are next, followed by shredded meats if you want.

♦ At about nine months, introduce some mushy finger foods.

♦ At about one year, your baby can eat almost any kind of food, but in small pieces. Some foods, such as grapes, raw carrots, nuts, and hot dogs, can still present choking hazards.

♦ One big warning: Do not give your baby honey or corn sweeteners for at least the first year. They often contain tiny parasites that an adult's digestive system exterminates with no problem. But the baby's still-immature system won't be able to handle the chore.

I Wanna Do It Myself

When your baby is ready to feed himself, he'll let you know, usually by grabbing the spoon from your hand (babies are quicker than you'd think) or mushing around anything that's dropped onto the high-chair tray. When this happens, prepare yourself; in the course of the next few weeks, your baby will discover the joys of sticking various kinds of food in his nose and eyes, under his chin, behind his ears, and in his hair. And it won't be much longer until he learns to throw.

One way to minimize the mess is to put a large piece of plastic under the high chair; a large trash bag cut open along the side is good. But don't relax

MOST ALLERGENIC FOODS	LEAST ALLERGENIC FOODS
♦ Egg whites	♦ Rice
♦ Wheat and yeast	♦ Oats
♦ Milk and other dairy products	♦ Barley
♦ Fish	♦ Carrots
♦ Tree nuts (pecans, walnuts)	♦ Squash
♦ Shellfish	♦ Apricots
♦ Peanuts and soy beans	♦ Peaches
♦ Citrus fruits	♦ Pears
♦ Berries	♦ Apples
♦ Tomatoes	♦ Lamb
♦ Chocolate	♦ Veal

Two Small Warnings

First, when you begin giving your baby solids, he's going to make an incredible array of faces: horror, disgust, fear, betrayal. Try not to take them personally—he's just reacting to the new and unknown and not criticizing your cooking.

Second, don't make a ton of food the first few times. You'll probably end up feeding the baby the same spoonful over and over again (you put some in his mouth, he spits it out; you scrape it off his cheek and put it in his mouth again . . .). This can be frustrating, but try to remember what comedian Dave Barry once said: "Babies do not take solid food through their mouths. . . . Babies absorb solid food through their chins. You can save yourself a lot of frustrating effort if you smear the food directly on your baby's chin, rather than putting it in the baby's mouth and forcing the baby to expel it on to its chin, as so many uninformed parents do." The solution: be patient and keep your video camera ready at all times.

yet; your baby will soon learn to use his spoon as a catapult to launch food beyond this protective boundary. There's really nothing you can do about this, so avoid wearing your best clothes while the baby is eating. You might also want to consider feeding the baby while he's wearing only a diaper. He's going to need a shower after almost every meal anyway so you might as well save yourself the trouble of having to wash his clothes too.

Making Vs. Buying

Jarred food is convenient but can be expensive—especially if you're going with one of the organic brands. A cheaper but less convenient alternative is to make your own. It's easy, really. After all, the major ingredient of most baby food is cooked vegetables. You can even do it in bulk. All you have to do is boil some vegetables, blend or mash them up, and pour them into an ice-cube tray. Whenever you need to, just pop out a cube, thaw, and serve.

Even though making your own sounds like a much healthier way to feed your baby, jarred food may be better, largely because it doesn't taste as good. Here's what I mean: as recently as 5 years ago, a lot of jarred baby food was filled with preservatives, chemicals, dyes, and other nasty stuff. But today man-ufacturers have cleaned up their act, and jars are filled with an additive-free, mashed version of whatever's on the label (besides the picture of the baby). It's also usually very bland, at least to the adult palate.

When you make your own baby food, though, it's so tempting to toss in a little olive oil, a few seasonings, and all sorts of other things to make it taste better. That's great—if *you're* planning to eat the food. But what your *baby* needs right now (and that's what it's all about, right?) is bland. Seasonings, especially salt, aren't good for him. So save the curries and butter and sugar until he's a little older. Of course, if you plan to eat your baby's leftovers, season them up as much as you want—just as long as you do it after he's finished.

A word of caution: Microwaves heat food unevenly, leaving hot spots right next to cold ones. So if you're using a microwave, make sure you stir well and test anything you're planning to give the baby.

Notes:

Gaining Confidence

What's Going On with the Baby

Physically

♦ By the end of this month she'll probably be able to sit by herself in "tripod position" (feet splayed, hands on the floor in between for balance). She may even be able to right herself if she tips over and pull herself to a sitting position if you grasp her hands.

♦ She can turn herself from back to front or front to back at will, and may even be able to propel herself short distances (usually backward at first) by creeping or wiggling. Be prepared, though: she'll be demonstrating a lot of these new moves when you're trying to change or dress her.

♦ She can probably get herself to her hands and knees and will spend hours rocking back and forth, picking up an arm here, a leg there—all in preparation for crawling.

♦ She can clap her hands and bang two objects together. And whatever isn't being banged is sure to be in her mouth.

♦ She can now look at one thing and reach for another and can probably pass objects back and forth between her hands.

Intellectually

♦ With so many new things to do and learn, your baby is now awake about 12 hours a day and spends most of that time finding out about her environment by touching, holding, tasting, and shaking things.

- Your baby recognizes her name and, if she's not too busy, may turn her head toward you if you call her.
- The idea that she is separate from other people and other objects is slowly sinking in. But she still thinks she has absolute control over all she sees or touches. As if to rub it in, she'll endlessly drop toys, dishes, and food from her high chair and revel in the way she can make you pick them up.
- Another way your baby demonstrates her complete power over the world and everything in it (especially you) is to cry for attention whether she needs any or not. Both these activities show that your baby is able to formulate plans and can anticipate the consequences of her actions.
- She's developing a solid sense of the way things should be. For example, she loves to look at drawings of faces, but if you turn the drawing upside down or mix up the features, she'll get very confused. She'll also get confused if she sees a picture of you but hears someone else's voice.

Verbally

- She's now more regularly adding consonants to vowels and creating single-syllable "words" such as *ba, ma, la, ka, pa.*
- She's getting pretty good at imitating sounds and also tries—with some success—to imitate your inflections.
- She's getting so familiar with language that she can easily tell the difference between conversational speech and any of the other noises you make. She might, for example, laugh when you start making animal noises. And she definitely prefers listening to her native language over a foreign one.
- She's also learning to like other sounds; music in particular will cause her to stop what she's doing and listen.

Emotionally/Socially

- Until this month, your baby really didn't care who fed her, changed her, played with her, or hugged her, just as long as it got done. But now, for about 50–80 percent of babies, who satisfies their needs is almost as important. You, your partner, and perhaps a few other very familiar people may now be the only ones your baby will allow near her without crying. This is the beginning of stranger anxiety.
- She's still very social and will smile at everyone (as long as you're nearby). She even smiles and laughs when looking at that "other" baby in the mirror.
- She'll wave her arms to let you know to pick her up, cling to you when you do, and cry if you take away a toy or stop playing with her.

♦ Despite all this, she's still incredibly curious in new situations, and will spend as much as ninety minutes taking in her surroundings.

♦ Her range of emotions is getting broader. She can, for example, express real anger if you do something she doesn't like, such as try to put her in a car seat or stroller or down for a nap.

What You're Going Through

Growing Up

There's nothing quite like having a kid to make you realize that you're a grown-up. It also makes you realize that besides being a son, you're also a father. That may sound like a painfully obvious thing to say, but you'd be surprised at how many men have a hard time with the concept. After all, we've spent our whole lives looking at our fathers as fathers and at ourselves as sons.

Here's how a friend of mine described becoming aware that he had made the transition: "One day I slipped my arm into the sleeve of my jacket and my father's hand came out the other side." You'll know it's happened to you when you use a phrase that your father used but that you haven't heard for twenty years. Or when you suddenly find yourself doing or saying one of the dozens of things your dad did that you swore you'd *never* do when you became a parent. Don't be embarrassed; it happens to all of us.

Feeling Like a Father

Most men (and women) see the father's role as that of a teacher of values and skills. Besides being a little limiting, there's really nothing wrong with that attitude—except that it puts dads with infants in a tough spot. Teaching requires communicating and interacting, which is hard to do when the student is a baby who's completely helpless and essentially nonresponsive. The result is that since they can't teach, a lot of new dads don't feel particularly fatherly.

But by the time your baby is six months old, she's no longer unable to communicate. She turns her head when you call her, she gets excited when you walk into the room. And when you wrestle with her, build a tower together, or tickle her, she'll give you a smile that could melt steel—a smile that's only for you. Your baby's reactions and "praise" may not seem like much, but whether you realize it or not, they're making you feel confident that she needs you and that you're playing an important and influential role in her young life. You're finally starting to feel like a father now; and the more you and your baby interact, the more you'll feel that way.

Jealousy

"The single emotion that can be the most destructive and disruptive to your experience of fatherhood is jealousy," writes Dr. Martin Greenberg in *The Birth of a Father*.

There's certainly plenty to be jealous about, but the real question is: Whom (or what) are you jealous of? Your partner, for her close relationship with the baby and the extra time she gets to spend with her? The baby, for taking up more than her "fair share" of your partner's attention and for getting to spend more time with her breasts than you do? The babysitter, for being the recipient of the baby's daytime smiles and love—tokens of affection you'd rather were directed at you? Or maybe it's the baby's carefree life and freedom from responsibility. The answer, of course, is: All of the above.

Like most emotions, a little jealousy goes a long way. Too much can make you feel competitive toward or resentful of your partner, the babysitter, even the baby. Do you feel you need more attention or emotional support from your partner? Do you need more private time with the baby? Whatever or whomever you're jealous of, it's critical to express your feelings clearly and honestly and to encourage your partner to do the same. If for some reason you feel you can't discuss your feelings on this issue with your partner, take them up with a male friend or relative. You'll be surprised at how common jealousy is. Jealousy's "potential for destruction," writes Greenberg, "lies not in having the feelings but in burying them."

Gaining Confidence

I don't remember every day of my children's childhoods, but there's one day in particular—when my older daughter was about six months old—that I recall quite clearly.

It really wasn't all that different from any other day. I gave her a bottle and dressed her. When she threw up all over her clothes, I dressed her again. Five minutes later she had an explosive bowel movement that oozed all the way up to her neck, so I cleaned her up and dressed her for the third time. Over the course of the day I probably changed five more diapers and two more outfits, gave her three bottles, calmed her from crying four times, took her in and out of the car eight times as I drove all over town doing errands, put her down for two successful naps, during which I managed to do a few loads of laundry and wash the dishes. I even managed to get some writing done.

All in all, it wouldn't have been a very memorable day if it weren't for what happened at the end of it. As I sat in bed reading, I remember thinking to myself, "Damn, I'm really getting a pretty good handle on this dad stuff." The truth is that I was. And by now, you probably are too. Things that would have had you panicking a few months ago now seem completely ordinary. You've learned to understand your baby's cues, you can predict the unpredictable, and those feelings of not being able to do things right are nearly gone. You probably feel more connected and attached to your baby than ever before. The feeling is one of confidence and stability, and signals that you've entered what some sociologists and psychologists refer to as the "honeymoon period" with your baby.

The calmness and smoothness of this period can (but doesn't always) spill over into your marriage as well. It's a time when a lot of men say that their relationships with their partners have gotten "easier," and that they feel a sense of truly being a family. I'll talk more about your relationship with your partner on pages 281–282.

You and Your Baby

Playing Around
As your baby develops her reaching, grabbing, and shoving-things-into-her-mouth skills, she'll gradually lose interest in face-to-face play and become more focused on the objects around her (or at least the ones she can reach) and on exploring her environment.

The first, and perhaps most important, lesson your baby will learn about objects is that she can, to a certain extent, control them (unless they happen to be cats; then she's out of luck). Of course, this startling epiphany comes about as a complete accident: you put a rattle in her hand, and after swinging her arms around for a while, she'll notice that the rattle makes some noise. But over the course of several months, your baby will learn that when she stops flailing, the rattle stops rattling and that she can—just because she wants to—get it to rattle again, and again, and again.

Your baby will learn quite a bit about objects all by herself. But if you're interested, there are a number of games you can play with her that, besides being fun, will encourage object awareness and perception.

REACHING GAMES

To encourage your baby to reach and to expand her horizons, try holding attractive toys just out of her reach: above her head, in front of her, to the sides. See how close you have to get the toy before she makes her move. Remember, the object here is not to tease or torture the baby, it's to have fun. You can add another layer of complexity by putting the out-of-reach object on a blanket or towel. Then slowly pull the blanket and show her how it gets closer.

TOUCHING GAMES

Try this: Let your baby play with a small toy without letting her see it (you might want to do this in the dark or with her hands in a paper bag). Then put that toy together with several other toys she's never played with. Many babies this age will pick up the familiar toy. Although this may sound fairly easy, it isn't. You're asking your baby to use two senses—touch and vision—at the same time, and to recognize by sight something she's touched but not seen. If your baby isn't ready for this one, don't worry. Just try it again in a few weeks. It's a concept that can take a while to develop.

IF . . . THEN. . . GAMES

There are thousands of things you can do to reinforce cause-and-effect thinking. Rattles, banging games, rolling a ball back and forth, and splashing in the pool are excellent. So is blowing up your cheeks and having the baby "pop" them with her hands. Baby gyms—especially the kind that make a lot of noise when smacked—are also good, but be sure to pack them up the moment your baby starts trying to use the gym to pull herself up; they're meant to be used while sitting or lying down and aren't sturdy enough to support much weight.

OBJECT PERMANENCE

When your baby is about six or seven months old, the all-important idea that objects can exist even when they're out of sight finally starts sinking in.

♦ Object permanence develops in stages. If you're interested in seeing how, try this: Show your baby a toy. Then, while she's watching, "hide" it under a pillow. If you ask her where the toy is, she'll probably push the pillow out of the way and "find" it. But if you quickly move the toy to another hiding place when she's not looking, she'll continue to look for it in the first hiding place.

♦ Peek-a-boo and other games that involve hiding and finding things are great for developing object permanence. Peek-a-boo in particular teaches your baby an excellent lesson: when you go away, you always come back. This doesn't sound like much, but making this connection now lets her know she can count on you to be there when she needs you and will help her better cope with separation anxiety (see page 216).

TRACKING GAMES

Hold an object in front of the baby. When you're sure she's seen it, let it drop out of your hand. At five or six months, most babies won't follow the object down. But starting at about seven months, they'll begin to anticipate where things are going to land. When your baby has more or less mastered this skill, add an additional complication: drop a few objects and let her track them down. Then hold a helium balloon in front of her and let it go. She'll look down and be rather stunned that the balloon never lands. Let her hold the string of the balloon and experiment.

Another great tracking game involves your baby's newly developed abilities to track moving objects even when they're out of sight part of the time. Put your

GOOD TOYS	BAD TOYS
♦ Blocks	♦ Anything made of foam—it's too easy to chew off pieces
♦ Dolls with easy-to-grasp limbs	
♦ Real things: phones, computer keyboards, shoes, and so on	♦ Anything small enough to swallow, having detachable parts, or small enough to fit through a toilet paper tube
♦ Toys that make different sounds and have different textures	
♦ Musical toys	♦ Anything that could possibly pinch the baby
♦ Balls	♦ Anything that runs on electricity
♦ Sturdy books	♦ Stuffed animals and other furry things that might shed (stuffed animals that don't shed are fine)
	♦ Toys with strings, ribbons, elastic—all potential choking hazards
	♦ Walkers (possibly—see page 194)

Give the Kid a Break

Don't feel that you have to entertain your baby all the time. Sure it's fun, but letting her have some time to play by herself is almost as important to her development as playing with her yourself. And don't worry; letting her play alone—as long as you're close enough to hear what she's doing and to respond quickly if she needs you—doesn't mean you're being neglectful. Quite the opposite, in fact. By giving her the opportunity to make up her own games or to practice on her own the things she does with you, you're helping her learn that she's capable of satisfying at least some of her needs by herself. You're also helping her build her sense of self-confidence by allowing her to decide for herself what she'll play with and for how long.

baby in a high chair and sit down at a table facing her. Slowly move a toy horizontally in front of her a few times. Then put a cereal box between you and the baby and move the ball along the same trajectory but have it go behind the box for a second or two. Most 6-month-olds will look ahead to the other side of the box, anticipating where the ball will emerge. If your baby's still having fun, try it again, but this time, instead of keeping the ball on the same path, make a 90 degree turn and bring the ball out from the top of the box.

You can do the same kind of thing during games of peek-a-boo. Step behind a door so the baby can't see you. Then open the door a little and poke your head out. Do that in the same place a few times and then higher or lower than where she was expecting to see you. Most babies find this endlessly amusing.

Again, if your baby doesn't respond to some, or any, of the activities suggested here, don't worry. Babies develop at very different rates, and what's "normal" for your baby may be advanced—or delayed—for your neighbor's. And keep in mind that you don't need to spend a lot of money on fancy toys. When my oldest daughter was about this age, one of her favorite toys was a plastic dish-scrubbing pad. And I remember taking her to FAO Schwartz in New York—zillions of fantastic toys everywhere—and thinking that she was going to want to play with everything. But all she wanted to do was play with the price tags. (She's a teenager now, and I look back at that experience as a warning—she still spends an awful lot of time looking at price tags....)

You and Your Partner

Overcoming Tension

As I mentioned earlier, this is a time when a lot of new parents start feeling a little less strain in their relationship and a lot more like a family. Of course, this isn't true for every couple; some are still feeling a lot of tension, which can sometimes translate into lack of satisfaction with the relationship (we'll talk more about this on pages 281–282). If you're feeling this way, wake up.

As it turns out, men's satisfaction with their relationships is a major factor in determining how involved they are with their children. The more satisfying the relationship, the more involved and happy you'll be in your fathering role. But the more unhappy and volatile your relationship, the less involved you'll be, and the lower the quality of that involvement.

Oh, and in case you thought you could keep the quality of your marriage a secret from your baby, forget it. Eleven-month-olds, for example, are less likely to look to their fathers for help in novel situations (such as seeing an unfamiliar person) when their fathers are in distressed marriages.

Family Matters

Finding Quality Child Care

Most parents instinctively feel (and there's plenty of research to back them up) that to have one or both of them care for their baby in their own home would, in a perfect world, be the best child-care option. But most couples can't afford the traditional dad-goes-to-work-while-mom-stays-at-home option or the less traditional mom-goes-to-work-while-dad-stays-at-home scenario. So chances are that, sooner or later, you'll need to consider some form of day care for your child. Here are some of the options and their advantages and disadvantages.

IN-HOME CARE

In-home care is probably the most convenient option for parents. You don't have to worry about day-care schedules, and your baby can stay in the environment to which she's become accustomed. In addition, your baby will receive plenty of one-on-one attention, and because she remains at home, she will be less exposed to germs and illness.

Leaving your child alone with a stranger can be daunting and traumatic, especially the first time. On the one hand, you might be worried about whether you really know (and can trust) the caregiver. You might also be worried—as I was—that no one will be able to love or care for your child as well as you and your partner. On the other hand, you might experience what psychologist Lawrence Kutner calls the "natural rivalry" between parents and caregivers. "As parents, we want our children to feel close (but not too close) to the other adults in their lives," he writes. "We worry that, if those attachments are too strong, they will replace us in our child's eyes." Fortunately, no one will ever be able to replace you—or your love. But there are many wonderful caregivers out there who can give your baby the next best thing.

If you do go this route, I'd strongly suggest that you have the caregiver keep a log of the basic goings-on in your baby's life: naps (when and how long), feedings (including how much), diaper (when, how many, contents), and overall behavior. This may sound incredibly anal, but it's actually quite helpful. It's especially important, for example, to know if the baby's gone a few days without filling a diaper, isn't napping, or is gradually losing interest in food.

Ideally, your sitter should tell you these things, but she may forget to, or you may forget to ask. Plus, having a log is a good way to remind the sitter when the baby needs to eat (if you're on a strict schedule) or when to give her medicine. Having a written record of these things can help you track them over time. In the unlikely event that something *is* wrong, being able to tell your pediatrician what's been going on will help him diagnose the problem.

You can keep your own log on a pad of paper—just make columns for each of the things you want to keep track of and write the time in hour increments down the side. Day-at-a-time calendars work well too. A more expensive but extremely well organized (and very attractive) alternative is the Baby Tracker, which combines calendar, logbook, and gentle reminders in one place. They're available at www.timetoo.com.

To Put Your Mind at Ease. Sort of.

Finding the perfect day-care situation for your baby is a big job, and you and your partner need to take it seriously. Of course, it isn't made any easier by the stories you hear all the time about babysitters or day-care providers who were caught beating or abusing the children they were supposed to have been caring for. It's enough to scare the hell out of anyone.

Even though those kinds of incidents are fairly rare, you're still going to want to eliminate as much of the risk as possible. Here are a few ways you can do this:

♦ Hire people you know and trust. If you have good friends or relatives who rave about the day-care center or nanny or babysitter they sent their children to, take that into consideration. But you should still meet with the person (or check out the center) to make sure that the fit is right for your baby and your family.

♦ Only consider licensed facilities. Anyone working at a state-licensed facility should have gone through a background investigation. You'll need to check with your state's licensing agency to verify that the facility is licensed and to get an idea of how thorough the screening process is. See the Resources section for more.

♦ If you're hiring an individual, go through an agency. Many—but not

HOW TO FIND IN-HOME CAREGIVERS

The best ways to find in-home caregivers are:

♦ Word of mouth

♦ Agencies

♦ Bulletin boards (either the cork kind or the Internet kind; caregivers can respond to your ad, or you respond to theirs)

The first thing to do is to conduct thorough interviews over the phone—this will enable you to screen out the obviously unacceptable candidates (for example, the ones who are only looking for a month-long job, or those who don't drive if you need a driver). Then invite the ones who make the first cut over to meet with you, your partner, and the baby in person. Make sure the baby and the prospective caregiver spend a few minutes together, and pay close attention to how they interact. Someone who approaches your baby cautiously and speaks to her reassuringly before picking her up is someone who understands all—agencies will screen applicants. At a minimum they should get a driving record and criminal background check.

♦ Do some investigating on your own. Some states have a centralized place to do background checks—district attorney, child abuse registry, sex offender registry—and if you can't do it, you can hire companies that will do it for you; you'll need the applicant's full name, social security number, and driver's license number.

♦ Get a nannycam. There are literally dozens of options. Cameras can be mounted in obvious places so the caregiver can see them or hidden inside clock radios, stuffed animals, or something else. Some are black and white, others are color; some make a tape that you have to review later, others can broadcast the images to your office computer or PDA.

The most important thing you can do is to trust your gut. If a day-care center or an individual gives you a funny feeling—even if it, or she, came with the most glowing recommendation—move on to the next option. The same goes with background checks and electronic surveillance. If someone won't cooperate, that should be a red flag. And if you're suspicious enough of a sitter to consider installing cameras in your home, maybe you should find someone else.

and cares about your baby's feelings. And someone who strokes your baby's hair and strikes up a "conversation" is a far better choice than a person who sits rigidly with your baby on her knee.

Another good "test" for potential caregivers is to have them change your baby's diapers. Does the applicant smile or sing or try some other way to make getting changed interesting and fun for the baby, or does she seem disgusted by the whole thing? And be sure that she washes her hands when she's done.

When you've put together your list of finalists, get references—and check at least two (it's awkward, but absolutely essential). Ask each of the references why the babysitter left her previous jobs, and what the best and worst things about her were. Also, make sure to ask the prospective caregiver the questions listed on page 176.

When you make your final choice, have the person start a few days before you or your partner return to work so you can all get to know each other, and of course, so you can spy.

To Grandmother's (or Grandfather's) House We Go

If your parents, in-laws, or other relatives live in the neighborhood, they may provide you with a convenient, loving, and low-cost child-care alternative. According to a 2003 survey by the U.S. Census Bureau, about 21 percent of children under five years old are being cared for by their grandparents while their parents are working—half of them in their grandparents' homes. Other relatives account for an additional 8 percent of all child-care arrangements for preschoolers.

If you're counting on your baby's grandparents for child care, be as appreciative and respectful of their time as you possibly can. While most grandparents are usually delighted to spend time with their grandchildren, they're also entitled to enjoy their retirement and spend their time the way they'd like to. However, they may be reluctant to say anything to you out of fear of offending you. So come right out and ask them directly whether you're asking too much. And here's something else to think about: a recent study published in the *American Journal of Public Health* found that women who care for grandchildren nine hours a week or more had a 55 percent increased risk of heart attacks.

WHAT TO ASK THEM

Here are a few good questions to ask prospective in-home caregivers. You may want to add a few more from the sections on other child-care options.

♦ What previous child-care experience have you had (including caring for younger relatives)?

♦ What age children have you cared for?

♦ Tell us a little about your own childhood.

♦ What would you do if . . . ? (Give several examples of things a child might do that would require different degrees of discipline.)

♦ When would you hit or spank a child? (If the answer is anything other than "Never," find yourself another candidate.)

♦ How would you handle . . . ? (Name a couple of emergency situations, such as a gushing head wound or a broken arm.)

♦ Do you know baby CPR? (If not, you might want to consider paying for the caregiver to take a class. The Red Cross usually offers them.)

♦ What are your favorite things to do with kids?

♦ Do you have a driver's license? Insurance?

♦ What days/hours are you available/not available? How flexible can you be if an emergency arises while we're at work?

♦ Are you a native speaker of any foreign language?

♦ Can you cook? (My wife left recipes for our nanny to make during the baby's naps.)

OTHER IMPORTANT ISSUES TO DISCUSS

♦ Compensation (find out the going rate by checking with other people who have caregivers) and vacation.

♦ Willingness and/or ability to take care of more than one baby. Doing a "nanny share" with someone in your neighborhood can reduce the cost for both families and provide a playmate for the babies at the same time.

♦ Telephone privileges.

♦ Complete responsibilities of the job: feeding, bathing, diapering, changing clothes, reading to the baby, and so on, as well as what other chores (light housekeeping, cooking) will be expected while the baby is sleeping.

♦ English-language skills—particularly important in case of emergency (you want someone who can accurately describe to a doctor or 911 operator what's going on).

♦ Immigration/green card status (more on this and other legal complications below).

♦ You might want to draw up a contract listing all of the caregiver's responsibilities—just so there won't be any misunderstandings.

♦ U.S. weights and measures. Sound silly, but if your caregiver is going to cook for you, make sure she knows the difference between a teaspoon and a tablespoon, and between a cup and a pint. We had some very odd-tasting dishes before we figured out that our Azerbaijani nanny didn't have any idea.

LIVE-IN HELP

Hiring a live-in caregiver is like adding a new member to the family. The process for selecting one is similar to that for finding a non-live-in caregiver, so you can use most of the questions listed above for conducting interviews. After you've made your choice, try out your new relationship on a non-live-in basis for a few weeks, just to make sure everything's going to work out to everyone's satisfaction.

FAMILY DAY CARE

If you can't (or don't want to, or can't afford to) have someone care for your child in your home, the next best alternative is to have your child cared for in

Au Pairs

Au pairs are usually young women who come to the United States on year-long cultural exchange programs administered by the U.S. Department of State. Legally, au pairs are nonresident aliens and are exempt from social security, Medicare, and unemployment taxes (see page 180 for more on taxes and payroll).

What an au pair provides is up to forty-five hours per week of live-in child care. If she's responsible for a child under two, she must have at least 200 hours of documented infant-care experience. But she's not allowed to care for a child under three months old unless you, your parents, or some other responsible adult is in the home. In exchange, you pay a weekly stipend (currently about $150 and tied to the minimum wage) as well as airfare, insurance, the first $500 toward her education, program support, and full room and board. On average, having an au pair will set you back about $13,000 for the full year.

You can hire an au pair through one of only a handful of State Department-approved program sponsors who screen au pairs and host families and match them up. The most current list is on the State Department website (see Resources, page 299, for the URL). You could hire one through a non-approved organization, but the au pair would be subject to immediate deportation and you to a $10,000 fine.

Having an au pair can be a wonderful opportunity for you and your baby to learn about another culture. One drawback, however, is that they can stay only a year; then it's *au revoir* to one, *bonjour* to another. In addition, it's important to remember that from the young woman's perspective, being an au pair is a cultural thing. In theory she's supposed to do a lot of child care, perhaps some light baby-related housekeeping, and take six semester hours of academic credit. But in reality she may be far more interested in going to the mall with her new American friends or hanging out with your neighbor's teenage son. And finally, understand that she's not a housekeeper, nurse, professionally trained child-care worker, or servant.

someone else's home. Since the caregiver is usually looking after only two or three children (including yours), your baby will get the individual attention she needs as well as the opportunity to socialize with other children. And since the caregiver lives in his or her own house, personnel changes are unlikely; this gives your baby a greater sense of stability.

Be sure to ask potential family day-care providers what kind of backup system they have to deal with vacations and illness (the provider's). Will you suddenly find yourself without child care, or will your baby be cared for by another adult whom both you and your baby know?

GROUP DAY CARE

Many people—even those who can afford in-home child care—would rather use an out-of-home center. For one, a good day-care center is, as a rule, much better equipped than your home, or anyone else's for that matter, and will undoubtedly offer your child a wider range of stimulating activities. But remember, a toy-store-like atmosphere and a well-landscaped playground don't guarantee quality.

Many parents also prefer group day care because it usually offers kids more opportunities to play with one another. In the long run, most parenting experts agree that being able to play with a variety of other kids helps children become better socialized and more independent. The downside, of course, is that your child won't get as much individual attention from the adult caregivers; and since your six-month-old won't really be playing with other kids for a while longer, adult-baby contact is more important. In addition, interacting with other kids usually means interacting with their germs: children in group day care tend to get sick a lot more often than those cared for at home (whether yours or someone else's).

Where to Find Out-of-Home Caregivers

You're most likely to find out-of-home child-care facilities through word of mouth or by seeing an ad online or in a local parenting newspaper. Perhaps the easiest (and safest) alternative is through Child Care Aware, a nationwide campaign created to help parents identify quality child care in their communities. Contact information is in the Resources section.

However you find out about a potential child-care facility, there's no substitute for checking it out for yourself in person. Here are some of the things Child Care Aware suggests you keep in mind when comparing child-care facilities:

ABOUT THE CAREGIVERS
♦ Do they seem to really like children? And do the kids seem to like them?
♦ Do they get down on each child's level to speak to the child?
♦ Are the children greeted when they arrive?
♦ Are the children's needs quickly met even when things get busy?

♦ Are the caregivers trained in CPR, first aid, and early childhood development?

♦ Are they involved in continuing education programs?

♦ Does the program keep up with children's changing interests?

♦ Will the caregivers always be ready to answer your questions?

♦ Will they tell you what your child is doing every day?

♦ Are parents' ideas welcomed? Are there ways for you to get involved if you want to?

♦ Are there enough caregivers for the number of kids? Each state has different standards, ranging from 1:3 up to 1:6. Having taken care of two infants at the same time, I can tell you that while 1:3 is pretty tough, 1:6 is absolute insanity. The National Resource Center for Health and Safety in Child Care (see Resources section) has a great Web site that includes exact standards from each state.

Taxes and Government Regulations

If you hire an in-home caregiver or family day-care provider, here are some of the steps you have to take to meet IRS, INS, and Department of Labor requirements:

♦ Get a federal ID number (you may be able to use your social security number)

♦ Register with your state tax department

♦ Register with the Department of Labor

♦ Calculate payroll deductions (and, of course, deduct them)

♦ File quarterly reports to your state tax board

♦ Calculate unemployment tax

♦ Get a worker's compensation policy and compute the premium (usually a percentage of payroll rather than a flat fee for the year)

♦ Prepare W-2 and W-4 forms

♦ Demonstrate compliance with Immigration and Naturalization Service guidelines

If the prospect of doing all this doesn't make you want to quit your job to stay home with the baby, nothing will. Fortunately, there are some alternatives. In the Resources section at the end of this book I've listed several companies that, for a fee, will take care of all these matters and any other pesky details that may arise.

ABOUT THE FACILITY

♦ Is the atmosphere bright and pleasant?
♦ Is there a fenced-in outdoor play area with a variety of safe equipment?
♦ Can the caregivers see the entire playground at all times?
♦ Are there different areas for resting, quiet play, and active play?
♦ What precautions are taken to ensure that kids can be picked up only by the person you select? Do strangers have access to the center?
♦ Are there adequate safety measures to keep children away from windows, fences, and kitchen appliances and utensils (knives, ovens, stoves, household chemicals, and so forth)?

ABOUT THE PROGRAM

♦ Is there a daily balance of playtime, story time, and naptime?
♦ Are the activities right for each age group?
♦ Are there enough toys and learning materials for the number of children?
♦ Are the toys clean, safe, and within reach of the children?

ABOUT OTHER THINGS

♦ Do you agree with the discipline practices?
♦ Do you hear the sounds of happy children?
♦ Is the program licensed or regulated? By whom?
♦ Are surprise visits by parents encouraged?
♦ Will your child be happy there?

Try to visit each facility more than once, and after you've made your final decision, make a few unannounced visits—just to see what goes on when there aren't any parents around.

A FEW THINGS TO GET SUSPICIOUS ABOUT

♦ Parents are not allowed to drop in unannounced. You need to call before visiting or coming to pick up your child.
♦ Parents dropping off kids are not allowed into the care-giving areas.
♦ Your child is unhappy after several months.
♦ There seem to be new and unfamiliar caregivers almost every day.
♦ You don't get any serious response when you voice your concerns.

Finding a good child-care provider is a lengthy, agonizing process, and it's important not to give up until you're completely satisfied. Unfortunately, most parents get frustrated with the choices and end up settling for something less than optimal. The result? Most infants get mediocre care. A recent study by the Work and Families Institute found that only 8 percent of child-care facilities were considered "good quality," and 40 percent were rated "less than minimal." Worst of all, 10 to 20 percent of children "get care so poor that it risks damaging their development." So be careful.

Notes:

A Whole New Kind of Love

What's Going On with the Baby

Physically

- He's getting so good at sitting that he doesn't need his hands for balancing anymore. Instead, he can—and will—use them to reach for things.
- He can get himself to a sitting position from his stomach.
- He's starting to crawl, but don't be surprised if he goes backward at least some of the time or, instead of crawling, scoots around on his bottom, using one arm to pull, the other to push.
- If you hold him upright, supported under the arms, he can bear some weight on his feet and will stamp and bounce up and down.
- He now uses his opposable thumb almost like you do, and is able to pick up what he wants confidently and quickly. He still prefers objects he can bang together and, of course, put into his mouth.
- He's got some teeth, and if your partner is still breast-feeding, you're going to be hearing a lot about them.

Intellectually

- As his brain develops, so does his ability to make associations. He recognizes the sound of your approaching footsteps and starts getting excited even before you come into his room.
- If confronted with blocks of different sizes, he will pick each one up, manipulate them a bit, then line them up to compare them to one another.
- He's so thrilled with his newfound ability to pick up and hold objects, he

just can't get enough. He spends a lot of time examining objects upside down and from other angles. And if he's holding a block in one hand, he'll reach for a second one and eye a third—all at the same time.

♦ The idea that objects may exist even when he can't see them is just beginning to take shape. If he drops something, he no longer thinks it's gone forever. Instead, he'll grope around for it or stare intently at the place it disappeared, hoping to bring it back. But if it doesn't show up within 5 to 10 seconds, he'll forget about it.

Verbally

♦ A few months ago, your baby was capable (with practice) of producing any sound that a human can produce. But since he spends all his time trying to make the sounds *you* make, he's forgetting how to make the ones you don't (like rolled Rs or the clicks of the African bush people).

♦ In English, though, your baby's babbling is shifting from single-syllable to multisyllable (*babababa*, *mamamama*, *dadadada* . . .). He's able to modulate the tone, volume, and speed of his sounds and actively tries to converse with you, vocalizing after you stop speaking and waiting for you to respond to him.

♦ Your baby's passive language skills are also improving. He now turns when he hears his own name and understands several other words.

Emotionally/Socially

♦ Although he's fascinated with objects, your baby really prefers social interactions and one-on-one activities, such as chasing and fetching.

♦ He can now tell the difference between adults and children, and may be especially interested in playing with (actually, alongside) kids his own age.

♦ He recognizes, and reacts differently to, positive and negative tones of voice and happy or sad facial expressions. That means that the way you respond to your baby has a big influence on his behavior. If you seem angry or frightened by something he's done, he may cry, knowing he's upset you. At the same time, your smiles and encouraging words could be enough to end his frustration or soothe his tears.

♦ Shyness or anxiety around strangers continues, and he may fuss or even get really upset if you leave.

♦ Continuing on his mission to imitate everything you do, your baby now wants to finger-feed himself or hold his own bottle or cup.

What You're Going Through

A New and Different Kind of Love

Sooner or later, almost every writer takes a crack at trying to describe love. And for the most part, they fall short. The problem is that there are so many different kinds. The love I feel for my wife, for example, is completely different from the love I feel for my sisters, which is different from the love I feel for my parents. And none of those seems even remotely similar to the love I have for my children.

I usually describe my love for my children in fairly happy terms, but periodically I experience it in a completely different way—one that sometimes frightens me.

Here's how it happens: I'm watching one of my daughters (any one of the three will do) play in the park, her beautiful, innocent face filled with joy. All of a sudden, out of nowhere, I begin to imagine how I would feel if something terrible were to happen to her. What if she fell and broke her neck? What if she got hit by a truck? What if she got horribly sick and died? The loss is almost palpable, and just thinking about these things is enough to depress me for the rest of the day.

And there's more. Sometimes my imagination goes a step further, and I wonder what I would do if someone, anyone, tried to hurt or kidnap or kill one of my children. At the very instant that that thought pops into my head, my heart suddenly begins beating faster and so loudly I can almost hear it, my breathing quickens, and my teeth and fists clench. I haven't hit another person outside a martial arts class for about thirty years. But during those brief moments when my imagination runs loose, I realize that I would be perfectly capable of killing another human being with my bare hands and without a moment's hesitation.

Feeling Isolated

When my older daughter was still quite young, she and her babysitter spent several mornings a week at Totland, a nearby park that had become something of an oasis for caregivers and children. Most afternoons I'd come to pick up my daughter at the park, and I'd stay for an hour or so watching her play with the other kids.

The other caregivers—almost all of whom were women—would be gathered in groups of four or five, chatting, sharing information, and learning from each other. And newcomers—as long as they were female—were quickly welcomed into these groups. But despite the nodding relationships I had developed with a few of the women, I was never made completely welcome. "It's strange being a man in this woman's place," writes David Steinberg, describing a trip to the park with his baby. "There is an easy-going exchange among the women here, yet I am outside of it. . . . Maybe it's all in my head, just me being uncomfortable about integrating this lunch counter. Whatever it is, it leaves me feeling strange and alone."

Once in a while another father would come to the park with his child, and we'd nod, smile, or raise our eyebrows at each other. We probably had much in common as fathers, shared many of the same concerns, and could have learned a lot from each other. But we didn't. Instead, we sat ten yards apart; if we ever spoke, it was about football or something equally superficial. Each of us was afraid to approach the other for fear of seeming too needy, too ignorant, or not masculine enough. What a couple of idiots.

Over the past few years this has begun to change—a little. As fatherhood comes out of the closet and as stay-at-home dads are becoming more common, contemporary dads are making some tentative steps in each other's direction. But despite the progress, new fathers still tend to steer clear of each other. That approach, however, is often less than completely satisfying, and as a result, many new fathers feel isolated. They have all sorts of concerns, worries, and feelings they don't completely understand, and they think there's no one else they can share their experience with. Fatherhood, it seems, can be a lonely business at times.

Getting Together with Other Men

One of the best ways to overcome your feelings of isolation or loneliness as a father is to join or start a fathers' group. Even in California, where there are so many support groups that there are support groups for people who belong to too many support groups, the idea of being involved in a fathers' group still sounds a little risky. But it's a risk well worth taking.

I've led a number of groups for new dads, and they almost always start off the same way, with a discussion of sports or politics or almost anything that has nothing to do with parenting. Then, almost by accident, someone will say something about a child, and the floodgates open. Stories tumble out, advice comes in from all sides, and a lot of guys find out that they aren't as alone as they thought they were. The groups almost always go on for way longer than they were scheduled for.

Joining (or, gulp, starting) a support group for dads offers some wonderful benefits:

♦ **Secrets revealed.** Women get a ton of parenting (and other) advice from other women: where to buy the best used children's clothes, places to take

*"Gotta go, guys. I've had about all the male bonding
I can take for today."*

the kids on rainy days, surefire cures for illnesses, ways to soothe crying babies, finding and hiring babysitters. You'd be surprised how much you already know, and how much you'll be able to help other men.

♦ **A road map**. Although I'm tired of hearing the old cliché about how men don't ask for directions, when it comes to parenting, there's often some truth there. But in a group setting, you'll find out pretty quickly that you're not the only one who's feeling a little lost. Fortunately, every dad there has some directions that may help. And even if they don't, it's better to be lost with someone else than lost alone.

♦ **Safety**. I've found that dads' groups don't work nearly as well when there are women around. It's sometimes a lot easier to talk about sensitive issues with a bunch of guys who're going through (or have already been through or will be going through) what you are.

♦ **Entertainment**. Getting together with other men who've made fatherhood a priority in their lives can be a lot of fun. Could be in a park with the kids, or it could be an adults-only event at someone's house or in a bar.

Finding other fathers to join a group probably won't be easy. But if you put the word out, you're sure to get some responses. Here are some likely sources of new (or existing) fathers:

♦ Your church or synagogue
♦ The hospital where your baby was born

♦ Your partner's OB/GYN
♦ Your pediatrician
♦ Leaders of mothers' groups
♦ The Resources section on pages 297–304

If you aren't comfortable joining a group (and there are plenty of us who aren't), it's still important to make regular contact with other fathers—especially if you're a stay-at-home dad or you're raising your children without a partner. You can do this one-on-one with another father you know, or, if you've got a computer, by logging on to the Internet. There are discussion groups, lists, and Web pages dealing with just about every aspect of parenting: some for both mothers and fathers, some just for fathers. Almost all of these services are available for free. Check out the Resources section for a few suggestions. There's plenty of research indicating that fathers who join support groups are generally happier. So don't think you can handle by yourself every fatherhood-related matter that comes up. You can't. And trying to do so will only hurt your kids and yourself.

You and Your Baby

A (Very) Brief Introduction to Discipline

"Discipline is the second most important thing you do for a child," says pediatrician T. Berry Brazelton. "Love comes first." There's no question in my mind that Brazelton is absolutely right. But before we go any further, let's clarify one thing: Discipline does *not* mean "punishment"; it means "teaching" and "setting limits." And the goal is to help your child develop impulse control. At this age, though, that's almost impossible, for several reasons.

First, your baby can't make a distinction between a want and a need. Second, he's simply not capable of understanding that he's doing something wrong (or even what "right" and "wrong" mean). If he pokes you in the eye, head-butts you when you're leaning in to give him a kiss, or knocks over the fishbowl, he's not doing it to cause trouble. Finally, babies this age have very short memories. So by the time you've disciplined him, he's already forgotten what he did to get you so upset.

But now that your baby's getting more mobile, there's an increased chance that his accidental misbehavior could become dangerous. So it's time to start setting some limits. Nothing rigid—just some basic guidelines to get your baby used to the idea.

"Your father and I have come to believe that incarceration is sometimes the only appropriate punishment."

At this point, you have only two serious discipline and limit-setting options: minimize danger by baby-proofing the house (see pages 193–199 for more), and distract him; take advantage of his short memory while you still can. So if he's gotten hold of that priceless Van Gogh you accidentally left on the floor, give him a teddy bear; and if he's making a break for the nearest busy street, pick him up and turn him around the other way. Chances are, he won't even notice. And even if he does, he'll be disappointed for only a few seconds.

Talk to Me, Baby, Give Me a Sign

How many times have you wished your baby could tell you what he's thinking? Well, as it turns out, there's a pretty simple way to find out: teach him sign language.

A few decades ago, researchers began to notice that children whose parents were hearing impaired and who taught their children to sign were able to communicate before they were nine months old. Children with two hearing parents don't usually have much to say until after their first birthday. If you think about it, using the hands to communicate makes a lot of sense. After all, babies have a lot more control over their fingers and hands than they do over their tongue and mouth.

Besides giving them a way to communicate earlier, signing improves babies' motor skills, builds vocabulary and language abilities, reduces tantrums and frustration, and has even been linked with an increase in IQ. Signing with your baby is good for *you* too. When you understand what your baby wants, you'll have fewer tears to deal with, and you (and your partner) will be less frustrated. When you're feeling relaxed and in control, parenting is a lot easier and a lot more fun. And that in turn will bring you and your baby closer.

There are two major baby signing systems. They're similar but there are some important distinctions (there's more information on both in the Resources section):

♦ Joseph Garcia's *Sign with Your Baby* is based solidly on American Sign Language (ASL). Most of the signs your baby will learn are fairly intuitive, such as touching the fingers to the lips for *eat*, and hooking the thumbs together and flapping the hands for *butterfly*. Others are a little tougher to figure out (touching the thumb to the forehead for *dad* and to the chin for *mom*) or may be difficult for little hands (putting the thumb between the first and middle fingers of a fist for *toilet* or holding up your hand as if indicating *five* and lowering the middle and ring fingers for *airplane*). Garcia's philosophy is that if you're going to the trouble to teach your baby a language, you might as well go with a real one. A baby who knows some ASL will be able to communicate with other babies who sign (and deaf people of any age) anywhere. And if you're thinking long-term, ASL fulfills the language requirement for admission to a growing number of colleges.

♦ Linda Acredolo's and Susan Goodwyn's *Baby Signs* is also based on ASL but it's more flexible. Their theory is that since your baby isn't going to be using sign language all that long, it's best to make it as easy to learn as possible. So parents are encouraged to modify the ASL signs as they see fit and to invent their own. This could make communication with people outside the family a little tougher. However, most of the signs you and your baby are likely to come up with will be pretty easy to decipher.

Both systems are excellent, and both give you and your baby an incredible opportunity to communicate with each other. I like *Baby Signs* a little better, though, because the flexibility appeals to me. If you go this route, try to use as many of the ASL signs as you can and modify them only as necessary.

However, if you prefer a more systematic approach, or if there are any deaf people in your family, *Sign with Your Baby* is the way to go. And even though, as I mentioned above, some of the signs aren't completely obvious, if you practice them enough, you'll do fine.

When to Start Signing and How

Basically, if your baby is at least six months old, points to things on request (where's the kitty-cat?), and waves bye-bye, you're ready to go. Start off with a few (four or five at the most) of the most common signs. My wife and I taught our youngest *milk*, *food*, *more*, and *kitty*. Repetition is the key, so make the sign and say the word every chance you get. If you're feeding the baby, ask if he wants *more food*. If you're giving him a bottle, or your partner is still breast-feeding, tell the baby that he's about to get some *milk*.

Try to have everyone who has regular contact with the baby use the signs. The more people he sees using them—including babysitters, grandparents, and especially older siblings—the faster he'll learn them.

The big thing here is to be patient—and to keep it fun. You may not get any kind of response from your baby for as long as a month or two. But don't give up. And don't introduce any more signs until your baby starts either mimicking the ones you show him or initiating conversations of his own. As soon as that happens, add new ones as fast as your baby can absorb them.

Your Baby's Teeth

Although your baby's little chompers started forming when your partner was four months pregnant, they probably won't make their first appearance ("eruption," in dental lingo) until about six or seven months. However, plenty of babies start getting teeth as early as three months, and it's not at all uncommon for a child to be toothless until his first birthday. One thing you can count on, though: whenever your baby's teeth show up, they'll be followed immediately by plaque. Yes, the same stuff that your dentist has to chip off your teeth with a chisel a few times a year.

It's way too early to start taking your child to a dentist, but you should use a washcloth or a small piece of gauze to clean each of his teeth once a day. If you're feeling more adventurous, you might want to try using a *very* soft toothbrush. Either way, skip the toothpaste for at least another year and keep the tubes far away from your baby for even longer; toothpaste can be poisonous or even lethal in large doses. When he's a year old, use a toothbrush with a very soft bristle. Flossing won't be necessary for a while.

Pacifier Safety

Generally speaking, there's nothing wrong with giving your baby a pacifier. A lot of babies have a need to suck that can't be satisfied by breast-feeding or shoving their own (or even your) fingers into their mouths. And don't worry about damaging your baby's soon-to-be-dazzling smile; most dentists agree that sucking on a pacifier isn't a problem until about age four.

Thumbs, on the other hand, are a bit more problematic. First of all, because thumbs don't conform to the shape of your baby's mouth as well as pacifiers do, there's a greater chance that thumb sucking will damage your baby's teeth (although that won't be an issue until he's five or so). And if your baby is a constant thumb sucker, there's a small chance it will have an impact on the way he speaks. Finally, most illness-causing germs get into our bodies from our hands. Need I say more?

Here are some important guidelines for using pacifiers:

♦ Never, never, never tie the pacifier around your baby's neck or use string to attach the pacifier to your baby—it can pose a serious strangulation risk. But if you're tired of picking the pacifier up off the floor thirty-eight times a day, buy yourself a clip-on holder, one that detaches easily.

♦ Nipples should be made of a single piece of nontoxic material.

♦ The shield (the part that stays on the outside of the baby's mouth) should be nondetachable and have several holes for saliva.

♦ Check the nipple for holes, tears, or other signs of wear. If you find any, replace the pacifier immediately—you don't want your baby to chew off pieces and swallow them.

♦ Try to avoid using a pacifier at bedtime. If your baby gets too used to falling asleep with the pacifier, he may wake up if it falls out of his mouth.

TEETHING

There are two important things to know about teething. First, your baby's teeth start showing up in a fairly predictable order: first the two lower central incisors, then the two top central incisors, and then the ones on either side. Most kids will have all eight incisors by the end of their first year, and a total of 20 teeth by age two.

Second, teething isn't usually much fun for your baby or for anyone else nearby. Although some teeth come in without causing any trouble, most kids experience at least some discomfort for a few days before and after a tooth breaks through the gum. Your baby's gums may be sore or tender, he could be fussier and have trouble falling asleep, he'll start gnawing with a vengeance, and you'll need a bucket to mop up the extra drool. Despite what you may have heard, there's no evidence that symptoms such as headaches, diarrhea, or fever have anything to do with teething. The one exception is a rash that your baby may develop under the chin and on the upper chest. This is usually caused by drool that gets in between your baby's many chins and never has a chance to fully dry.

Fortunately, teething discomfort doesn't last long and is relatively easily dealt with. Most babies respond quite well to acetaminophen (ask your pediatrician how many drops to give and don't waste your time rubbing it on the baby's gums—it doesn't work. The gum massage itself may help, though). Teething rings are also helpful, especially the kind that are water-filled, and so are teething biscuits and frozen bagels (although if you go the bagel route, you'll be finding mushy crumbs all over your house for a month).

Childproofing Your House

Once your baby realizes that he's able to move around by himself, his mission in life will be to locate—and make you race to—the most dangerous, life-threatening things in your home. So if you haven't already begun the never-ending process of childproofing your house, you'd better start now.

Start by getting down on your hands and knees and looking at the world from your baby's perspective. Don't those lamp cords and speaker wires look like they'd be fun to yank or chew on? And don't those outlets seem to be waiting for you to stick something in them? Taking care of those enticing wires and covering up your outlets is only the beginning, so let's start with the basics.

ANYWHERE AND EVERYWHERE

◆ Move all your valuable items out of the baby's reach. It's not too early to try to teach him not to touch, but don't expect much compliance at this age.

◆ Bolt to the wall bookshelves and other freestanding cabinets (this is especially important if you live in earthquake country); pulling things down on top of themselves is a favorite baby suicide attempt.

◆ Don't hang heavy things on the stroller—it can tip over.

◆ Get special guards for your radiators and raise any space heaters and electric fans off the floor.

◆ Install a safety gate at the bottom and top of every flight of stairs. After a few months, you can move the bottom gate up a few steps to give the baby a low-risk way to practice climbing.

♦ Adjust your water heater temperature to 120 degrees. This will reduce the likelihood that your baby will scald himself.

♦ Get a fire extinguisher and put smoke alarms in every bedroom. If you want to be extra cautious, consider a carbon monoxide detector.

♦ If you have a two-story house (or higher), consider getting a rope escape ladder.

♦ Take first aid and CPR classes; they're usually offered by the local Red Cross, YMCA, or hospital.

♦ Put together a first aid kit (see page 197 for the ingredients).

♦ Empty your wastebaskets regularly, especially if you've just swept up some broken glass or anything else that might be dangerous.

♦ Keep the place clean. Coins, paper clips, cat litter (and what's in it), dog food, dust bunnies, and anything else that's reachable is fair game for the baby.

ESPECIALLY IN THE KITCHEN

♦ Install safety locks on all but one of your low cabinets and drawers. Most of these locks allow the door to be opened slightly—just enough to accommodate a baby's fingers—so make sure the kind you get keeps the door from closing completely as well.

Walkers

I had a walker when I was a baby, and my two older kids did too. But there's a lot of controversy about whether walkers are safe or not. Supposedly, 15,000 emergency room visits per year are attributed to them, and most pediatricians don't recommend them. However, this has less to do with the actual walker and more to do with falling down the stairs. So if you don't have any stairs or you keep them securely gated, walkers shouldn't be a problem.

Another common complaint about walkers is that babies can build up some real speed and fly around the house smacking into everything in sight—fun for them, not so fun for you. In addition, they can be a source of great frustration for the baby: he may have a hard time going over thresholds or making the transition from smooth floor to carpet; and because walkers are usually fairly wide, babies always seem to be getting stuck behind the furniture.

If you're worried, most of the potential problems can be resolved by buying an exersaucer, which is basically a wheel-less walker that's outfitted with a bunch of things to bang and squeak and twist and spin.

+ Stock the one unlocked cabinet with unbreakable pots and pans and encourage your baby to jump right in.
+ Your baby's high chair should be sturdy, with a tray that locks into place, and a crotch strap to keep the baby from slipping out.
+ Keep baby's high chair away from the walls. His strong little legs can push off the wall and knock the chair over. And never allow him to stand up while in the chair.
+ Watch out for irons and ironing boards. The cords are a hazard, and the boards themselves are very easy to knock over.
+ Get an oven lock and covers for your oven and stove knobs.
+ Use the back burners on the stove whenever possible and keep pot handles turned toward the back of the stove.
+ Try to keep the baby out of the kitchen when anyone is cooking. It's too easy to trip over him, drop or spill something on him, or accidentally smack him with something.
+ Never hold your baby while you're cooking. Teaching him what steam is or how water boils may seem like a good idea, but bubbling spaghetti sauce or hot oil hurts when it splashes.
+ Put mouse and insect traps in places where your baby can't get to them. Better yet, set them after he's asleep and take your kill to the taxidermist before he gets up.
+ Use plastic dishes and serving bowls whenever you can—glass breaks, and, at least in my house, the shards seem to show up for weeks, no matter how well I sweep.
+ Post the phone numbers of the nearest poison control agency and your pediatrician near your phone.

OUTSIDE IN THE SUN

Sunlight and fresh air are fantastic for you and your baby. But remember: no matter how cool you think it might look, when it comes to babies, there's no such thing as a good tan. Babies' skin is a lot thinner than ours and burns much faster—especially those with light complexion. And severe sunburns during childhood have been linked with skin cancers later in life. For that reason, here are some important thing to keep in mind if you're planning to be out of the house.

+ Don't be fooled by clouds or breeze. UV rays are still getting through and can burn your baby as badly as on a hot day. Be especially careful at high altitude and near water, snow, or sand, all of which can reflect and intensify the sun.

+ On sunny days, use the groundhog test: if your shadow is longer than you are tall, it's okay to come out (as long as you follow the other precautions in this section). If your shadow is shorter than you are, though, turn around and go right back into the house.
+ Cover up as much skin as possible. Have your baby wear a hat and sunglasses that offer UV protection, and dress him in pants and long sleeves. Tightly woven fabrics (ones that are hard to see through if you hold them up to the light), particularly cotton, are best.
+ Make sure any exposed skin is nicely lubed up. Apply sunscreen (SPF 15 or 30) half an hour before going out, and reapply every 60–90 minutes. Once you're outside, try to keep the baby in the shade as much as possible. Try out the sunscreen a few days in advance by applying a small amount to your baby's back or arm. If it gets red or irritated, he may be allergic, so try another brand.
+ Set a good example. Let your baby see you wearing a hat and putting sunscreen on yourself.
+ Do not use baby oil. It's worse than nothing at all.
+ If your baby does get sunburned, call your doctor immediately—sooner if there are blisters. He'll probably have you give the baby some acetaminophen (Tylenol) or ibuprofen (Advil) for the pain, and may recommend some ½-percent hydrocortisone cream. *Do not give your baby aspirin.* Sunburn can be dehydrating, so make sure the baby gets plenty of fluids. Apply a cool washcloth to the burned area and a water-based or aloe vera moisturizer. Stay away from petroleum-based products as well as anything that has benzocaine in it. And finally, stay out of the sun until the burn is completely healed.

ESPECIALLY IN THE LIVING ROOM
+ Put decals at baby height on all sliding glass doors and large windows.
+ Get your plants off the floor: more than seven hundred species can cause illness or death if eaten, including such common ones as lily of the valley, iris, and poinsettia.
+ Pad the corners and edges of low tables, chairs, and fireplace hearths.
+ Make sure your fireplace screen and tools can't be pulled down or knocked over.
+ Keep furniture away from windows. Babies will climb up whatever they can and may fall through the glass.

What Every Good First Aid Kit Needs

- Ace bandages
- acetaminophen (Tylenol) drops and tablets
- adhesive strips
- adhesive tape
- antibiotic ointment
- antiseptic ointment
- antibiotic wash
- butterfly bandages
- clean Popsicle sticks (for splints)
- cleansing agent to clean wounds
- cotton balls (sterile if possible)
- cotton cloth for slings
- disposable instant ice packs
- disposable hand wipes (individual packets)
- emergency telephone numbers
- gauze rolls or pads (sterile if possible)
- mild soap
- syrup of ipecac (to induce vomiting, if necessary)
- tweezers (for splinters and the like)
- pair of clean (surgical) gloves
- scissors with rounded tip
- sterile 4 2 4–inch bandages

It's also a good idea to have an emergency treatment manual around the house. Here are a few good ones:

- American Red Cross, *The American Red Cross First Aid and Safety Handbook* (Boston: Little, Brown Medical Division, 1992).
- Dr. Miriam Stoppard, *Baby First Aid* (London: DK Publishing, 2003).
- Stephen N. Vogel, *Emergency Medical Treatment: Infants, Children, and Adults: A Handbook on What to Do in an Emergency to Keep Someone Alive until Help Arrives.* (Wilmette, Illinois: Beechwood Healthbooks, 1996).
- Janet Zand et al., *A Parent's Guide to Medical Emergencies: First Aid for Your Child* (New York: Avery Penguin Putnam, 1997).
- National Safety Council, *Pediatric First Aid and CPR*, 4th ed (Boston: Jones and Bartlett, 2001).
- Gloria Blatti, ed., *The Pocket Guide to CPR for Infants and Children* (New York: Pocket Books, 1998).

ESPECIALLY IN THE BEDROOM/NURSERY

- No homemade or antique cribs. They almost never conform to today's safety standards. Cribs with protruding corner posts are especially dangerous.

♦ Remove from the crib all mobiles and hanging toys. By five months, most kids can push themselves up on their hands and knees and can get tangled up in (and even choke on) strings.

♦ Keep the crib at least two feet away from blinds, drapes, hanging cords, or wall decorations with ribbons.

♦ All toys should be washable, large enough so they can't fit in your baby's mouth, nose, or ears, and soft enough so they won't poke out an eye. No strings or detachable parts.

♦ Toy chest lids should stay up when opened (so they don't slam on tiny fingers). And don't feel that you need to fill the toy chest up. Three or four toys is plenty for now—more can overwhelm your baby. If you have more, rotate them in and out.

♦ Don't leave dresser drawers open. From the baby's perspective, they look a lot like stairs.

♦ Keep crib items to a minimum: a sheet, bumpers, and a few soft toys. Babies don't need pillows at this age and large toys or stuffed animals can be climbed on and used to escape from the crib.

♦ Don't leave your baby alone on the changing table even for a second.

ESPECIALLY IN THE BATHROOM

♦ If possible, use a gate to keep access restricted to the adults in the house.

♦ Install a toilet guard.

♦ Keep bath and shower doors closed.

♦ Never leave water standing in the bath, the sink, or even a bucket. Drowning is the third most common cause of accidental deaths among young children, and babies can drown in practically no water at all—even an inch or two.

♦ Keep medication and cosmetics high up.

♦ Make sure there's nothing your baby can climb up on to gain access to the medicine cabinet.

♦ Keep razors and hair dryers unplugged and out of reach.

♦ Never keep electrical appliances near the bathtub.

♦ Use a bath mat or stick-on safety strips to reduce the risk of slipping in the bathtub.

IN THE CAR

♦ Car seats should face backward until your baby's first birthday *and* until he weighs 20 pounds.

♦ Get a car seat safety check. Many highway patrols, fire departments, or police departments do them for free.

♦ Clean up the car. In an accident, anything that's just lying around becomes a dangerous projectile.

Notes:

Perpetual Motion

What's Going On with the Baby

Physically

- At this stage, your baby is in motion just about every waking minute. She's an excellent crawler and will follow you around for hours.
- Having mastered crawling, she's now working on getting herself upright.
- She'll start by pulling herself up to a half-standing crouch and letting herself drop back down. Sometime in the next few weeks, though, she'll pull herself up to a complete standing position.
- If she's really adventurous, she'll let go with one hand or even lean against something and release both hands. Either way, she'll be shocked to discover that she can't get down. Locking the knees is a skill that comes earlier than unlocking them.
- She now uses a "pincer grip" to pick things up and, because of her increased dexterity, becomes fascinated by tiny things.
- If she's holding a toy and sees something new, she'll drop what she's got and pick up the second. She may even retain the first toy and pick up the second with her other hand.
- Her self-feeding and bottle- or cup-handling skills are improving fast.
- All this activity is so exhausting, she may sleep as long as 10–12 hours at a stretch.

Intellectually

♦ Your baby's increased mobility has opened a new range of possibilities for exploration and discovery. She now gets into drawers and cabinets and can empty them amazingly quickly.

♦ Her mobility also lets her get better acquainted with some of the objects that, until now, she's seen only from afar. Crawling around on the floor, for example, your baby will stop underneath a chair and examine it from every possible angle. Then, writes child psychologist Selma Fraiberg, "Upon leaving the underside of the chair, he pauses to wrestle with one of the legs, gets the feel of its roundness and its slipperiness and sinks his two front teeth into it in order to sample flavor and texture. In a number of circle tours around the chair at various times in the days and weeks to come, he discovers that the various profiles he has been meeting are the several faces of one object, the object we call a chair."

♦ Slowly, slowly, she's learning that objects exist even when she can't see them, and she'll actively look for toys that she's seen you hide.

♦ She's been playing fetch with you for a while—dropping things and having you pick them up—and having seen so many things fall, she may start worrying what would happen if *she* fell. As a result, she may get very frightened at the tops of stairs or other high surfaces.

♦ Now able to pick up a different object in each hand, your baby will spend a lot of time comparing the capabilities of each side of her body.

Verbally

♦ She now babbles almost constantly, using your intonation and expression as much as she can.

♦ She can also use different sounds to express her changing emotions.

♦ She continues to concentrate on two-syllable "words"; *b*, *p*, and *m* are her favorite consonants. If you haven't yet, you'll be hearing *da-da* very soon.

♦ Her name is not the only sound she knows. She'll also turn her head in response to other familiar noises, such as a car approaching, the phone ringing, the television "speaking," and the refrigerator opening.

Emotionally/Socially

♦ With so much to keep her busy during the day, your baby may feel she doesn't have time for naps anymore. The lack of sleep, together with the frustration at not being able to do everything she wants with her body, may make her cranky.

*"Hey, would you kids mind holding down
the quality-time racket?"*

- When she's in a good mood, she really wants to be included in socializing; she may crawl into the middle of a conversation, sit up, and start chattering.
- She smiles at herself in the mirror, and raises her arms when she wants you to pick her up.
- She's smiley and happy with people she knows but wary and sometimes frightened around strangers. This may make her even clingier than before if she senses that you're going to leave her in an unfamiliar situation or with unfamiliar people.

What You're Going Through

Learning Flexibility and Patience

Before my older daughter was born, I was incredibly anal-retentive about time; I always showed up wherever I was supposed to be exactly when I was supposed to, and I demanded the same from others. But as you now know, going on a simple trip to the store with a baby in tow takes as much planning as an expedition to Mount Everest. And getting anywhere on time is just about impossible.

It took a while, but eventually I learned that trying to be a father and Mr. Prompt at the same time just wasn't going to work. And somehow, simply accepting that fact made me a lot more forgiving of other people's lateness as well. Interestingly, this new flexible attitude about time began to rub off on other areas of my life, and it'll probably have the same effect on you.

Besides learning to lighten up a little, most of the new dads in my research said that after six or seven months of fatherhood, they'd become much more accepting of other people's limitations, as well as their own. They'd learned the value of contingency planning, having a backup just in case plan A went awry. They thought that caring for a baby had made them more aware of other people's needs and points of view. And they felt more empathetic and "in tune" with other people's feelings and emotions.

Not everyone, of course, finds change quite as easy to accept. For some new dads, any sort of deviation from an orderly schedule, or any lack of continuity, can be very discombobulating.

Thinking about How Involved You Are— and What that Means

Being an "involved" dad means different things to different men. Among the most common definitions are:

- ♦ Being a teacher or moral guide for the children.
- ♦ Being there physically and being available for the children from the very first.
- ♦ Wanting to be an equal partner in parenting.
- ♦ Not wanting to be stuck in the role of the "wait-till-your-dad-comes-home" disciplinarian.
- ♦ Being a good provider.

I realize that throughout this book I may have given you the impression that being an involved dad is wonderful and fantastic and incredible every single minute. Well, it's not. While it *can* be the greatest thing you'll ever do, it can also be the most frustrating. It creates opportunities for growth and fun, but it also interferes with others. The following table summarizes many of the benefits and costs associated with being an involved dad. It's based in part on the work of fatherhood researcher Rob Palkovitz and on interviews I've done with hundreds of new dads.

Benefits

♦ Satisfaction of watching children grow and develop. You know that your teaching has made a difference in their lives, and you take joy in their accomplishments.

♦ Sense of pride—the feeling that what you're doing is right, that you've achieved something meaningful by making an investment in your children's development. This feeling comes whether or not you get compliments from others on how great a dad you are or on how great your kids are.

♦ Love received. In a sense this is your compensation for being an involved dad. You get to be needed, loved, admired, and appreciated and it feels great.

♦ Personal growth—maturity, self-discipline, role modeling, and more emotional expression. See this entire chapter for more.

♦ Perceptual shift/expanded self. You're less goal oriented, less driven, more interested in the family. Doing things for kids can be a tremendously satisfying experience.

♦ Extending the family line—passing on your name, your history. Your children are your legacy.

♦ Fun. Your kids give you all sorts of excuses to express joy, to experience life as a child again, to play and do things you'd never do without a child (go to a park or the zoo, collect baseball cards).

♦ Continued learning. You can learn and develop skills and interests you never had before just to keep up with your kids. You can also relearn some of the subjects you'd forgotten long ago or learn some of the ones you never got around to in the first place.

♦ Fathering gives life meaning. Having kids may give purpose and direction to an otherwise ordinary life.

♦ Enhanced marriage. Some men feel that having kids makes their marriage better, giving Mom and Dad a shared focus in life and in their children's accomplishments.

It's Hard to Make Up for Lost Time

There's nothing like a long day at the office to make you realize just how much you miss your baby. And when you get home, you might be tempted to try to make up for lost time by cramming as much active, physical father/baby con-

Costs

- Time. For some men time is a metaphor for freedom or the opportunity to focus on themselves. Having kids requires giving up the freedom to do what you want while you're with them. You may have to give up activities that brought you pleasure. (Although the opposite can be true: I rekindled an interest in martial arts when my middle daughter started taking karate.) You also may spend a lot of time thinking about them when you're not with them.

- Sacrifice. You may have to defer satisfying your own goals and dreams, or put off career advancement or continued education in order to be the good provider. This tends to be much more common among men who became fathers young.

- Finances. Again, a more common worry among younger dads. It costs a lot to raise a child these days. See later in this chapter for more.

- Marital closeness. You'll probably spend less private time with your partner. There'll be less time for physical and/or emotional intimacy or even to talk over important issues.

- Energy. There's the sleep loss of early fatherhood, then the physical exhaustion of chasing a baby around, then more sleep loss when you start worrying about a sick child or drugs and alcohol and sex and friends and grades.

- Potential. All that time and energy you put into being a father is time and energy you could have devoted to writing a book, directing a movie, painting a masterpiece, inventing a cure for cancer....

- Kids grow up and don't need you as much. A lot of the meaning in your life will come from your relationship with your kids. If that relationship changes or gets strained, as it is likely to do as your child grows up and seeks independence, you may mourn the loss of meaning.

- You get spread out. All the demands on your time and energy leave you feeling like there isn't enough of you left.

tact as you can into the few hours before bedtime (yours or the baby's). That's a pretty tall order, and just about the only way you'll be able to fill it is to be "overly controlling, intrusive, and hyper-stimulating," writes psychiatrist Stanley Greenspan. So before you start tickling and wrestling and playing with the baby, spend a few minutes reading or cuddling with her, quietly getting to know each other again—even at eight months, a day away from you is a looooong time for your baby. You'll both feel a lot better if you do.

Besides making you miss your baby, a long day at the office can also make you feel guilty about the amount of time you're away from her. A little guilt is probably a good thing, but far too many parents let their guilt get out of hand and end up backing away (emotionally) from their children.

Although there's no practical way for you to make up for lost time, it's important that you find some middle ground between being overly controlling and distancing yourself from your baby. The best way to do that is to make sure that whenever you're with your child, you're there 100 percent. Forget the phone, forget the newspapers or the TV, forget washing the dishes, and forget eating if you can. You can do all those things after the baby goes to sleep.

Circumstances may make it impossible for you to make any changes in the time you can spend with your family. But if you have any flexibility at all, take another look at the work/family options on pages 151–153. On his deathbed, no father ever wishes he'd spent more time at the office.

He Says, She Says

Remember the story about the five blind men and the elephant? Each of them approaches an elephant and bumps into a different part—the leg, the tail, the ear, the trunk, the side—and then authoritatively describes to the others what he thinks an elephant really looks like. The moral of the story, of course, is that two (or more) people looking at exactly the same object or situation may see very different things. The same moral applies when couples are asked to rate the husband's level of involvement in the home: men are more likely to be satisfied with their contribution and women are more likely to be disappointed.

The problem here is not one of blindness, however. Instead, it's that men and women, according to fatherhood researcher Jay Belsky, are using different yardsticks to measure. Women tend to compare what their partners do to what *they* do. Most dads come up short, which leaves the women feeling unhappy and overworked. But men tend to compare what they do to what their father did or what the guy down the street does. And when they add in being the main or sole breadwinner, men end up feeling pretty proud of themselves and how much they're doing.

You and Your Baby

Reading

At eight to nine months of age, children who have been read to regularly can predict and anticipate actions in a familiar book and will mimic gestures and noises. So at this age it's a good idea to involve your baby more actively in the reading process. Talk about the things on the page that aren't described in the text and ask your baby a lot of identification questions. If you can, show your baby real-life examples of the objects pictured in her books.

At around ten months, your baby may be perfectly content to sit with a book and turn pages—probably two or three at a time. Don't worry if she seems not to be paying any attention to what she's "reading"; she's learning a lot about books' structure and feel. If you put a book upside down in front of your baby she'll turn it the right way. And if you make a mistake in something you're reading to her, she'll correct you.

At eleven months, your baby may be able to follow a character from page to page. This is also the age at which she may start demanding that you read specific stories or that you reread the one you just finished. Board books, cloth books, and sturdy flap books are great for this age. And since your baby's most significant interaction with books is going to be to try to eat them, you might also want to pick up a few of the ones that come with teething rings or chewable corners.

By the time she's a year old, your baby may be able to turn the pages of her books one at a time. She will point to specific pictures you ask her to identify and may even make the correct animal sounds when you ask her, "What does a ___ say?" Be sure to respond positively every time your baby makes any attempt to speak—animal noises included.

As you've probably noticed already, reading provides you and your baby with a wonderful opportunity for close physical contact. The best position I've found (it's the one with maximum snuggle potential) is to put the baby on your lap and, with your arms around her, hold the book in front while you read over her shoulder.

When considering the next few months' reading, look for books with bright, big, well-defined illustrations, simple stories, and not too much text. Singing, finger plays, and photographs of babies and very young children are always popular. Keep in mind that what you read isn't as important as how you do it. Because babies prefer rhymed text to unrhymed, Mother Goose stories and other nursery rhymes are great. And don't feel obliged to finish every book you

"The weasel represents the forces of evil and the duck the forces of good,
a surrogate for American air and naval superiority."

start. Besides your baby's current favorites (which you should keep reading for as long as she's interested), you might want to check out a few of these books:

Baby Animals (and many others), Gyo Fujikawa
The Baby's Catalog, Janet and Allan Ahlberg
Baby's Bedtime Book, Kay Chorao
Baby Signs for Animals, Baby Signs for Bedtime (and others),
    Linda Acredolo and Susan Goodwyn
The Ball Bounced (and many others), Nancy Tafuri
Brown Bear, Brown Bear, What Do You See?, Bill Martin Jr.
But Not the Hippopotamus; Opposites (and others), Sandra Boynton
Chicka Chicka Boom Boom, Bill Martin Jr. and John Archambault
Daddy, Play with Me (and many others), Shigeo Watanabe
Dressing (and many, many others), Helen Oxenbury
Goodnight Moon, Margaret Wise Brown
"More, More, More," Said the Baby: Three Love Stories, Vera B. Williams

Peek-a-Who?, Nina Laden
Pretty Brown Face and *Watch Me Dance*, Andrea Pinkney
The Seals on the Bus, Lenny Hort
Sleepy Book, Charlotte Zolotow
Step by Step, Bruce McMillan
Spot Goes Splash (and many other Spot books), Eric Hill
Tickle; All Fall Down; Say Goodnight; Dad's Back (and many others),
    Jan Ormerod
Time for Bed (and others), Mem Fox
Tomie dePaola's Mother Goose, Tomie dePaola
What Sadie Sang; Sam Who Never Forgets (and others), Eve Rice
Wheels on the Bus and *Knick-Knack Paddywhack!*, by Paul O. Zelinsky
Who Said Meow?, Maria Polushkin

CONCEPTS
The ABC Bunny, Wanda Gag
Clap Hands (and many others), Helen Oxenbury
First Words for Babies and Toddlers, Jane Salt
Sparkly Day; Twinkly Night (and other Baby Dazzler books), Helen Stephens
Ten, Nine, Eight, Molly Bang

The list of good books for the under-a-year set gets bigger every year. I've included some information in the Resources section (pages 302–303) on how you can stay current.

Dealing with Stranger Anxiety

At about seven or eight months, you'll probably notice a marked change in your baby's behavior around strangers. Only a few weeks ago, you could have handed her to just about anyone, and she would have greeted the new person with a huge smile. But now, if a stranger—or even someone the baby has seen a few times before—comes anywhere near her, she'll cling tightly to you and cry.

Welcome to stranger anxiety, your baby's first fear. What's happening is that your baby is just beginning to figure out that she and you (and her other primary caretakers) are separate human beings. It's a scary idea, and she's simply afraid that some person she doesn't like very much might take you—and all the services you provide—away. Stranger anxiety affects 50–80 percent of babies. It usually kicks in at around seven or eight months, but sometimes not until a year. It can last anywhere from a few weeks to six months.

Your baby is more likely to experience stranger anxiety if she's withdrawing, slow-adapting, or has a low sensory threshold (see the "Temperament" section on pages 131–136). She'll be less likely to be affected if she's approaching or fast-adapting or if she's been exposed to a steady flow of new people since early infancy.

Here are a few things you can do to help your baby (and yourself) cope with stranger anxiety:

♦ If you're getting together with friends, try to do it at your own house instead of someplace else. The baby's reaction will be less dramatic in a familiar place.

♦ Hold your baby closely whenever you enter a new environment or anyplace where there are likely to be other people.

♦ When you enter a new place, don't just hand the baby off to someone she doesn't know. Let her cling to you for a while and use you as a safe haven.

♦ Warn friends, relatives, and strangers not to be offended by the baby's shyness, crying, screaming, or overall reluctance to have anything to do with them. Tell them to approach the baby as they might any other wild animal: slowly, cautiously, with a big smile, talking quietly, and perhaps even offering a toy.

♦ Be patient with your baby. Don't pressure her to go to strangers or even to be nice to them. And don't criticize her if she cries or clings to you.

♦ If you're leaving the baby with a new sitter, have her or him get to your house at least twenty minutes before you have to leave. This will (hopefully) give baby and sitter a few minutes—with you nearby—to get to know each other.

♦ If your partner stays at home with the baby while you're at work, you need to understand that your baby might lump you in with the people she considers strangers. Don't take it personally. Just follow the steps above on how strangers should approach the baby, and be patient.

Family Matters

Money

Without a doubt, money is the number-one issue couples fight about. And financial squabbles are especially common during the early parenthood years, while both parents are getting settled. Many factors contribute to quarrels over money. Here are some of the most common:

♦ **Lack of communication**. Honestly, did you and your partner have a plan for how long she would take off work after the baby came, or how the family's finances were going to be taken care of? Far too many couples put off these discussions (or never have them at all) because they're afraid that it would lead to fights. If you haven't figured these things out yet, it's not too late. Better to have a little fight now than a huge resentment-dripping explosion later.

♦ **Frustration**. Women who have put their careers on hold to take a more active role at home may resent having their income (and the associated power) reduced. This goes double for men because of the still-lingering "good provider" pressures.

♦ **Your childhood**. The way you were raised can have a big impact—positive or negative—on the way you raise your own kids. If you grew up in a poor family, you may feel weird spending money on anything more than the bare necessities. Or you may feel obliged to give your child all the things you never got—at least the ones that money can buy. And if your parents were big spenders, you may be inclined to bury your baby in gifts, or you may be afraid of spoiling your child and cut way back. Whatever your overall attitude toward money, if your partner's differs considerably from yours, look out.

♦ **Differences in spending habits**. You like Cheerios and eating lunch out; your partner wants you to buy the generic brand and bring lunch from home. She makes tons of cell phone calls in the middle of the day and uses up all your any-time minutes; you want her to wait until the weekend.

♦ **Differences in definitions**. My wife loves to get things "half off"; the way I figure it, half off of something that costs three times more than it should is still no deal.

♦ **Gender differences**. Generally speaking, fathers and mothers have different ideas about money and what should be done with it. Fathers tend to be more concerned than mothers with savings and the family's long-range financial outlook. Mothers tend to be more concerned with the way the children look, partly because they understand that a lot of people see the way a woman's children dress as a reflection of her abilities as a mother. The big problem here is that your partner may interpret your not wanting to spend money on clothes as a sign that you don't love your baby (and, by extension, that you don't love her either).

♦ **Lack of flexibility**. As you may have noticed, becoming a mother does funny things to women. Before our youngest was born, my wife and I agreed that she would take a four-and-a-half month maternity leave, go back to work part-time for five more months, and then transition to full-time. But a few weeks after the baby arrived, my wife decided that she wanted to work part-time until the baby was one. We ran the numbers and decided that could work. A month or so later, she told me that she really didn't want to go back to a full-time schedule until the baby was in preschool. The moral of the story is that even if you do have a plan, try to allow for some wiggle room. Things—and people—change.

Avoiding Money Problems, or at Least Learning to Live with Them

If you and your partner are fighting about money, or if you anticipate that you might, some or all of the following will help:

- **Be realistic.** Having a baby can have a major impact on your financial life. Food, clothing, medical expenses, and day-care or preschool tuition all add up pretty quickly. If you have a child with disabilities or are caring for an aging parent, you'll have to be even more conscientious.
- **Make a budget** (there are plenty of good budgeting software packages, Quicken being among the best). Keep track of everything coming in and going out—especially your cash expenditures, which tend to slip through the cracks but can really add up.
- **Hold regular meetings to discuss your financial situation.** Listen to each other's concerns and remember that whatever your differences, you both have the best interests of your family at heart. No blaming or yelling, and stay away from discussion-killing phrases like "You always" and "You never."
- **Rearrange your priorities.** Take care of the absolute necessities—food, clothing, shelter—first. If there's anything left over, start saving it for ice cream cones, vacations, private school education.
- **Do plenty of comparison shopping.** Stores in our area were selling breast pumps for over $200. I spent half an hour on the Internet and found the same pump from a place in Canada for 25 percent less.
- **Negotiate and compromise.** You give up Cheerios and take a brown bag to lunch; she uses the cell phone on the weekends. And remember, there are many ways to cut back without having to skimp. Why pay full price for a pair of pants your child is going to outgrow in a few months when you can get a perfectly good used pair for just a few bucks?
- **Make a plan.** Set realistic and achievable savings goals, and make sure you're adequately insured.

And while we're talking about money, I strongly suggest that you do the following as well:

- **Max out your 401k or other retirement plan.** There's a good chance that Social Security won't be able to cover all of your retirement expenses, especially if your baby moves back home in 25 years.

♦ **Max out your flexible spending account**. If your (or your partner's) employer offers one, you may be able to use pretax dollars to pay for a lot of your child care and medical expenses; exactly how much depends on the plan.

♦ **Start saving for college**. Some states offer prepaid tuition plans, which let you pay off your child's tuition at today's rates. Better yet, open a 529 account. Money you put into the account grows tax-free, so long as you use it for college tuition, books, room and board, and other expenses. The money can be used at nearly any post-high-school institution anywhere in the country, including state and private colleges, community colleges, and even vocational schools. You can find out more about 529s from the College Savings Plan Network at http://www.collegesavings.org/yourstate.htm.

♦ **Get your baby a social security number**. Without one you can't open up a 529 savings account, and perhaps more important, you won't be able to take your child as a deduction or claim a Child Tax Credit.

Notes:

The Building Blocks of Development

What's Going On with the Baby

Physically

- As if recovering from the frantic developmental pace of the past two months, your baby will probably not add many new skills this month. Instead, he'll spend his time perfecting the old ones.
- By the end of this month he'll be such a confident crawler that he'll be able to buzz around the house grasping a block or other toy in one hand. He'll be able to crawl backward and may even make it up a flight of stairs. When sitting, he can turn his body all the way around without falling over.
- He easily pulls himself to an upright position and can stand for a few seconds while holding your hand. He can cruise (sidestep) along furniture and walls, and when he's done, he no longer has any trouble unlocking his knees and sitting down.
- Now able to move his digits separately, he has discovered that the house is filled with holes and cracks that are just big enough to accommodate his index finger.
- The biggest development this month (and this is pretty important) is that your baby is now coordinated enough to build a "tower" of two or three blocks (which he'll knock down immediately).

Intellectually

- In previous months your baby would learn a new skill and then repeat it endlessly. At this point, though, he'll begin to experiment with new ways of doing things he already knows how to do. For example, instead of repeatedly dropping his spoon off his high-chair tray, he may start with the spoon, then drop his bowl off the other side, and finish up by tossing his cup over his shoulder. The purpose of the experiment, of course, is to see how many times he can get you to pick things up before you stop.

♦ He's just beginning to come to terms with the idea that he is not the power behind everything that happens. He may, for example, bring you a wind-up toy to wind up.

♦ He's also beginning to shake his if-I-can't-see-it-it-doesn't-exist attitude, but just barely. Now if he watches you hide a toy, he will look for it. But if you hide the same toy in a second hiding place, he will continue looking in the first hiding place. In his mind, something out of his sight can exist, but only in one specific place.

♦ He's also learning about actions and their consequences. If he sees you putting on a coat, he'll know you're going outside, and he may cry.

♦ As his memory gets better, you'll be able to interrupt him in the middle of an activity and he'll go back to it a few minutes later.

Verbally

♦ He's developing a distinctive "voice" in his babbling and may identify certain objects by the sound they make (*choo-choo* for train, *moo* for cow).

♦ Besides recognizing his name, your baby now understands and responds to other words and phrases, such as "No" and "Where's the baby?" He also understands and might even obey simple commands such as "Bring me my pipe."

♦ Although he's several months away from saying anything truly under-standable, your baby already has a good grasp of the rhythm and sound of his native language. A German researcher found that even at this young age, babies are sensitive to the structure of words in their own language and can listen to a string of speech and break it down into wordlike units.

Emotionally/Socially

♦ This baby loves to play. He'll shout if he thinks you should be paying more attention to him. He loves to make you smile and laugh and will do every-thing he can to get a positive reaction from you. He's also a wonderful mimic and will repeat phrases like "uh-oh" and imitate your facial expressions and such acts as blowing out candles, coughing, sneezing, and pretending to eat with a spoon or drink from a cup.

♦ He may be able to get you to understand—by pointing, grunting, squealing, or bouncing up and down—that he needs something specific.

♦ Preferences are becoming more distinct, and he'll push away things (and people) he doesn't want.

♦ Perhaps a little scared of the new world he's discovering, he clings to you more than ever and cries if you leave him alone; it's the beginning of separation anxiety (different from the stranger anxiety of the past few months). He may also develop fears of things that never used to bother him, such as the vacuum cleaner, dogs, or baths. When my oldest was eight months old, she loved driving over speed bumps in the car and potholes made her ecstatic. But only a few weeks later, even the slightest change in the surface of the road made her cry hysterically.

What You're Going Through

Feeling More Attached to Your Baby

As your baby gets older and becomes more and more responsive and interactive, your attachment and feelings of connection to him will deepen. But the big question is, When will your baby start feeling that way about *you*?

The answer is somewhere between six and nine months. By that time, he's developed the mental capacity to associate you with satisfying his needs and wants and can summon up a mental image of you to keep him company when you're not there.

Don't think that this means you needn't bother trying to establish an attachment to your baby from the beginning. On the contrary. Attachment doesn't just happen overnight; it's a gradual process that takes months to develop, and the sooner you get started, the better. And if you and your baby haven't been able to form a solid attachment to one another (if, for example, you're in the military and have just come home), it is *by no means* too late.

As you might imagine, the single most successful strategy for forming lasting, secure attachments with your children is to spend time with them one-on-one, doing everything you possibly can together, from the mundane to the exciting. "The earlier the father can feel involved with the infant," says psychologist Henry Biller, "the more likely will a strong father-child attachment develop." And the way you react and respond to your baby will have a great influence on the kind of attachment you and he eventually establish.

Attachment theories were first developed in the 1950s by researchers John Bowlby and Mary Ainsworth, who conducted detailed studies of the interactions between several hundred parents and their children. Bowlby and Ainsworth concluded that there are two basic types of attachment: *secure*, meaning that the child feels confident that the parent will respond appropriately to his needs; and *insecure* meaning that the child is constantly afraid his needs won't be met by the parent. They further divided the insecure category into two subcategories: *avoidant* and *ambivalent*. (See the chart on pages 218–219 for a more detailed explanation.)

Based on the information they gathered by observing babies in their first months of life, Bowlby and Ainsworth were able to predict accurately the specific behavior patterns those same babies would exhibit as they grew. Bowlby's and Aisworth's theories are just as valid today as they were when articulated over fifty years ago.

Like it or not, the type of attachment you establish with your baby will be influenced (not set in stone, just influenced) by your own attachment experience with your parents. So as you read this section, spend some time thinking about your childhood. Doing so may help you understand a few things about yourself and your parents. More important, it may help you avoid making some of the same mistakes with your own children that your parents made with you.

Attachment Basics

ATTACHMENT	TWELVE-MONTH-OLDS
Secure (about two out of three are securely attached, but that doesn't guarantee that they won't have any problems when they grow up)	♦ Are confident that their parents will be there when needed. ♦ Know they can depend on their parents to respond to their pain, hunger, and attempts at interaction. ♦ Readily explore their environment using parents as bases. ♦ Don't cry much and are easy to put down after being held.
Avoidant (one out of six)	♦ May avoid physical contact with parents. ♦ Don't depend on parents as a secure base. ♦ Don't expect to be responded to caringly. ♦ Learn not to act needy no matter how much they may want to be held or loved.
Ambivalent (one out of six)	♦ Cry a lot but don't know whether their cries will get a response. ♦ Are afraid of being abandoned physically or emotionally. ♦ Are worried, anxious, and easily upset. ♦ Cling to parents, teachers, and other adults. ♦ Tend to be immature and mentally scattered.

Your attachment to your child may also be influenced by your relationship with your partner. Dozens of studies confirm that the better the couple relationship, the more secure the parent-child relationship (see pages 281–282 for more on couple relationships). Other research indicates that having achieved a workable work/family balance promotes father-child attachment.

TODDLERS	PARENTS
◆ Are independent and trusting.	◆ Respond to children sensitively and consistently.
◆ Learn early how people treat other people.	◆ Pick up the baby when he cries, feed him when he's hungry, hold him when he wants to be held.
◆ Are open to having their behavior redirected.	
◆ Mix well with all age groups.	
◆ Become social leaders.	
◆ Are curious and eager to learn.	
◆ Are less curious.	◆ Deny their (and others') feelings and needs.
◆ Are frequently distrustful.	◆ Believe children should be independent early.
◆ Can be selfish, aggressive, and manipulative.	
◆ May have few friends.	◆ Don't like to cuddle with the baby or pick him up when he cries.
	◆ Can be emotionally cold.
◆ Lack self-confidence.	◆ Are wildly inconsistent and unpredictable in their parenting.
◆ May experience uncontrolled anger.	◆ Are frequently self-involved.
◆ May either overreact emotionally or repress feelings.	◆ Hope to get from the baby the love that they never had from their own parents and that they may not be able to get from each other.
◆ Are frequently less adaptable.	

The Father-Child Connection

Although the vast majority of research on attachment has focused on mothers and children, some researchers are now beginning to study father-child attachment. Their findings confirm what active, involved fathers have known in their hearts for years—that the father-child bond is no less important than the mother-child bond. In fact, over 80 percent of studies that have examined father-child relationships have concluded that there's a strong connection between a father's involvement and his infant's well-being. Here's what the experts say happens to babies who have a strong attachment to their fathers and are "well fathered" as they grow:

- They score higher on intelligence and motor development tests.
- They're more secure, more confident, and more interested in exploring the world around them.
- They're more independent, extroverted, self-confident, and interested in trying new things.
- They can handle brief periods of separation from Dad or Mom without getting too upset.
- They're more persistent and better at solving problems.
- Premature infants whose dads are highly involved have higher IQs at age three than those with less involved dads.
- They're exposed to a wider variety of experiences and will be more well-rounded.
- They're more socially responsible.
- They have higher verbal and math skills.
- They get better grades in school, participate in more extracurricular activities, are less likely to drop out, and are more likely to graduate from college.
- They're less likely to get pigeonholed by traditional gender stereotypes (things like "Girls aren't good at math").
- They're more affectionate and empathetic.

"My wife works, and I sit on the eggs.
Want to make something of it?"

♦ Girls enter puberty later and are less likely to become sexually active early or become teen mothers.

♦ They are more popular with their peers and have fewer behavior problems.

At the same time, there are a number of factors that may interfere with father-child attachments. Researcher Glen Palm and I have both investigated this issue, and here's a combined list of the top barriers:

♦ Fathers who are at work most of the week find that "reattaching" with the kids on the weekends takes a lot of time and energy.

♦ A small but significant percentage of fathers feel that their in-laws are overprotective of their adult daughters and get in the way too much.

♦ Some new dads buy into traditional gender differences and feel that women are naturally better parents than men are.

♦ Many fathers experience some tension in their relationships with their children because they feel excluded by the mother-infant bond, or because they feel that they have to compete with their partners to form a relationship with the child.

♦ A father's ability to form strong attachments with his children is influenced by the quality of his marriage, and his partner's confidence in his parenting abilities. In cases of divorce, the quality of the relationship between the former spouses is the biggest predictor of the kind of relationship the father and his children will have.

♦ Some fathers say it's hard to form a close relationship because they feel they are unable to comfort their children adequately. A lot of these fathers were able to form close attachments only after their children were weaned.

♦ Age. Because younger dads are generally less settled in their careers and relationships, they often spend less time with their children than older (over 35) dads.

♦ Temperament. No matter how much you love your child, you'll find it easier to attach to an "easy" child than to a "difficult" one. (See pages 131–136 for more on temperament.)

♦ Income. Unwed or unemployed fathers sometimes feel such shame at not being able to live up to society's "good father" image that they back away.

You and Your Baby

Playing Around . . . Again

For the first seven or eight months of your baby's life, he had to be content with

In Case You Thought You Were Alone . . .

There isn't a single animal species in which the female doesn't produce the eggs. But eggs aren't worth much without the male's sperm to fertilize them. In most cases, once the eggs are laid, neither parent sticks around to watch them hatch or to meet their babies. Sometimes, though, eggs need more specialized care, or they'll all perish. In these cases, one or both parents are required to pitch in. Here are just a few examples of some of the dozens of species of animals in which the father plays an important role in carrying, raising, protecting, and educating his young.

Long before the male three-spined stickleback has even met his mate, he sets to work building an attractive little house out of algae. When he's finished, he hangs out in front and makes a pass at the first female who happens by. If she's interested, the male invites her in, but, not being much of a romantic, he asks her to leave after she's laid her eggs, which he quickly fertilizes as soon as she's gone. For the next few weeks, the father guards his nest, keeping it well ventilated and repairing any damage. Until his babies hatch, the father never leaves the nest, even to eat.

Like the stickleback, the male giant water bug does everything he possibly can to attract females. If one shows any interest, he fertilizes her eggs. The female then climbs onto her lover's back and lays nearly a hundred eggs, securing each to his back with a special glue. For the next two weeks the father is completely responsible for the eggs' safety and well-being. When they finally hatch, the babies stick close to Dad until they feel confident enough to swim away.

Unlike the stickleback, a cichlid (pronounced SIK-lid) doesn't need a nest. As soon as the female lays the eggs, the male scoops them up into his mouth. Because his mouth is so full, the father can't eat until the babies hatch—sometimes up to two weeks. And after they're born and can swim by themselves, Dad still protects his children by carrying them in his mouth. He spits them out when it's time to eat, get some air, or just have a little fun. And when playtime is over (or if danger is lurking), he sucks them back in again.

Frogs are famous for being involved fathers. After the eggs of the two-toned poison-arrow frog hatch, the tadpoles crawl onto their father's back, where they hang on with their suckerlike mouths as Dad carries them through the jungle. Darwin's frogs take things one step further. Just as his tiny, jelly-covered eggs are about to hatch, the future father snaps them up with his tongue and slides them into a special pouch inside his body. The eggs hatch, and the tiny tadpoles stay inside the pouch until they lose their tails and jump out of their father's mouth.

Among birds and mammals, there is a high rate of coparenting. For example, male and female geese, gulls, pigeons, woodpeckers, and many other birds work as a team to build their homes, brood (sit on the eggs to keep them warm), and feed and protect the young after they're born. In a similar fashion, the male California mouse is responsible for bringing food into the nest and for huddling with the young to keep them warm (the babies aren't born with the ability to regulate their own body temperatures). These mice have at least two things in common with human parents. First, they are both generally monogamous. Second, the presence of an involved father has a major impact on the babies: pups weigh more, their ears and eyes open earlier, and they have a greater survival rate than pups who are separated from their fathers.

Animal dads, just like their human brothers, make some pretty incredible sacrifices to protect and provide for their families. The male killdeer (a tiny bird named for its "kill-dee" cry and not its big-game hunting skills) protects its eggs and hatchlings from predators by pretending to have a broken wing. The "wounded" bird then flops around on the ground, squawking as if he's about to die, distracting the predator and luring it away from the nest. And several species of desert-dwelling birds, including the sand grouse, fly dozens of miles in a day to soak themselves in water, which they bring back for their parched babies to drink.

The emperor penguin is perhaps the most impressive animal father of all. While the missus is out looking for food, Mr. Penguin incubates their single egg, keeping it off the frozen ground by balancing it on the tops of his feet. For two months, he doesn't eat—he just stands there protecting the egg. When the egg hatches, the Dad feeds the babies with a milky liquid he secretes from his esophagus. When Mom gets back, Dad—now about 25 pounds lighter—can go grab a bite to eat and take a short Arctic vacation.

"Really, Howard! You're just like your father."

staring at things from across the room and waiting for you to bring them to him. But now that he's mobile, he's going to try to make up for lost time. He's incredibly curious about his world, and no obstacle can stand between him and something to touch, squeeze, gum, or grab. (If your baby doesn't seem terribly curious, let your pediatrician know. But don't be alarmed if you catch the baby staring off into space once in a while. Babies this age spend about 20 percent of their waking time soaking up information visually, according to pediatrician Burton White.)

Although our society doesn't value play nearly as highly as some other parent-child pastimes such as feeding and diaper changing, it is nevertheless critical to your baby's development. "Many children who do not have much chance to play and who are only infrequently played with suffer severe intellectual arrest or setbacks," writes developmental psychologist Bruno Bettelheim.

One of your major goals should be to expose your baby to the most varied, enriching play environment possible. But perhaps even more important is your basic philosophy about play. "Parents' inner attitudes always have a strong impact on their children," says Bettelheim. "So the way parents feel about play, the importance they give it or their lack of interest in it, is never lost on their child. Only when parents give play not just respect and tolerance but also their personal interest, will the child's play experience provide a solid basis upon which he can develop his relation to them and further to the world."

Brain Builders

These games and exercises can stimulate your baby's capacity to use different skills at the same time (seeing, hearing, thinking, and remembering, for example).

♦ Get two toys that are nearly identical except that they react in different ways (one might need to be squeezed to make noise, the other shaken). Let the baby play with one of them for a few minutes, then switch. Did he get confused? In the bathtub you could also demonstrate that an empty cup floats, but when you fill the same cup with water, it sinks.

♦ Ring a bell, squeeze a toy, or shake a rattle. When the baby looks to see what made the sound, put the toy into a group of things he's familiar with. Will he go for the one that made the noise, or will he get sidetracked by the other toys?

♦ More hiding games. A few months ago you discovered that if you hid a toy under a pillow or towel, your baby would push the obstacle out of the way to "find" the toy. Now that he's a little older and more sophisticated, you can up the ante a little by hiding an interesting toy under three or four towels. The look on his face when he pulls the first towel off and doesn't see what he was expecting will be priceless. Until he's about a year old, he'll probably get confused by the extra obstacles and forget what he was looking for in the first place.

♦ Imitating and pretend games. When babies imitate us, they're trying to figure out who we are and what we're doing. "When they imitate an older sibling or friend, they're not only trying to understand them, but they're figuring out what it's like to be older," writes Bettelheim. When playing with blocks, for example, be sure to include some non-block things such as people, cars, trucks, and animals.

♦ Show him that objects can have more than one function. Envelopes, for example, can be shredded or used to contain other things.

♦ Encourage him to use tools. For example, tie a string around a toy that is well out of reach. Will he crawl to get the toy, or will he pull the string to bring it closer? What happens if you demonstrate what to do? A word of caution: once your baby has mastered the idea that there are new and exciting ways to get hold of things, watch out for low-hanging tablecloths and other dangling stuff.

♦ Encourage exploration. Babies who are curious and get lots of time and opportunities to explore end up doing better in school.

Vive la Différence!

As we've discussed earlier, fathers and mothers have distinctive but complementary styles of playing with their children: fathers tend to be more physical; mothers, less. But besides the physical nature of play, there are some other male-female differences you should be able to see now.

Fathers tend to encourage their children to do things for themselves, take more risks, and experience the consequences of their actions. Mothers, in contrast, tend to want to spare their children disappointment, are more protective and discourage risk-taking. (Keep in mind that I'm talking about *tendencies*. There are plenty of people who don't fit the mold.)

To see how these differences might play out, imagine that your baby is building a tower that is just about to collapse. You'll probably let the tower fall, hoping your baby will learn from his mistakes. Your partner, though, will probably steady the tower as it teeters. And if your baby were a little older and started climbing a tree, your partner would probably tell him to be careful and not to fall, while you'd encourage him to see how high he could go.

Many researchers have found that the differences in father-child and mother-child parenting styles can have a significant impact on the child. "There were indications that children's intellectual functioning was stimulated more in families with high father involvement," writes researcher Norma Radin. "We attribute this effect to the fact that fathers appear to have a different way of interacting with children; they tend to be more physical, more provocative, and less stereotyped in their play behavior than mothers."

Mothers and fathers also differ in the way they treat boys and girls. Fathers tend to vocalize more with infant sons than daughters; they're more rough-and-tumble with sons than with daughters; and they're a little less likely to hug or snuggle a son than a daughter. They also are more likely to encourage and support sons' quest for independence than daughters'. This plays out in responding a little more quickly to a fussy girl than a fussy boy, or by picking up an infant daughter who's fallen down sooner than an infant boy. Mothers do a better job of treating their boys and girls the same, but they, too, make some distinctions.

Interestingly, when it comes to gender roles, mothers and fathers are equally inflexible: both will dress a girl in blue or pink and will encourage her to play with dolls or trucks. But they'd never put a boy in pink, and they give more positive feedback to boys who play with boy toys than to boys who play with girl toys.

> ## Crawling
>
> Although you may be in a hurry to see your baby walk, be patient. Crawling (which includes just about any type of forward movement, such as slithering, hopping along on the butt, or "rowing" forward with one leg) is a major developmental stage, and you should encourage your baby to do it as much as possible. There's some evidence that makes a connection between crawling and later proficiency in math and sciences. Kids who don't crawl apparently don't do as well in those fields.

Exercises for the Major Muscle Groups

It's taken a while, but your baby is finally discovering that he has control over his feet. And over the next few months, he'll be making more and more use of them by learning to walk. He'll do this all by himself, of course, but helping him build up his muscles and coordination can be great fun for both of you:

♦ Put some toys near his feet and see if he'll kick them.

♦ Roll a ball far enough out of your baby's reach so he has to crawl to get it.

♦ Supervised stair climbing is great. But stay nearby and be extremely careful. This is a good time to start teaching your baby to come down stairs backward. But be prepared to demonstrate yourself and to physically turn your baby around a few dozen times a day.

♦ Play alternating chasing games: you chase him; he chases you. At the end, "reward" him with a big hug and—if he doesn't protest—a little wrestling. Besides being fun, these kinds of games teach your baby a valuable lesson: when you go away, you always come back. The more that idea is reinforced, the less he'll be impacted by separation anxiety (see page 216). Plus, as it turns out, kids who wrestle with their dads grow up with more highly developed social skills than kids who don't get as much physical play.

♦ Do some (gentle) baby bouncing. Get one of those big exercise balls and lay your baby on his back across it. Then press him into the ball and let him bounce. If you're feeling adventurous, hold the baby's legs and roll him around a little. Pay close attention to the baby's reaction—he can switch from ecstatic laughter to crying in a heartbeat. And be very careful not to do anything that could snap the baby's neck.

Getting Those Little Hands and Eyes to Work Together

There are many activities you and your baby can do that stimulate hand-eye coordination:

- Puzzles. The best ones for this age are made of wood and have a separate hole for each piece and a peg for easy lifting.
- Nesting and stacking toys. These help improve gentle placement skills.
- Things to crush, tear, or crinkle—the noisier, the better.
- Weave some string between baby's fingers or tape two of his fingers together. Can he "free" himself?
- Stock your bathtub with toys that squirt or spin.
- Get toys that can be used in the bathtub or a sandbox to pour stuff back and forth. Measuring cups and spoons are also good.
- When you're shopping, have the baby help you put things in the cart.
- If you're brave, let the baby change channels on your TV or load CDs into your stereo.
- Play hand-clapping games.

More Experiments from the Land of Consequences

The idea that different actions produce different effects is one that can't be reinforced often enough. Here are a few ways that are especially appropriate for your nine-to-twelve-month-old:

- Jack-in-the-boxes—especially the kind with four or five doors, each opened by a push, twist, poke, or some other action. These are also good for hand-eye coordination. Be cautious the first few times, though; some babies may be frightened.
- Balls are a big hit. They roll, they bounce off things, they can knock over other things. For your baby's protection (and to reduce the chance of breaking your good dishes), make sure the balls you use are soft.
- Pots, pans, xylophones, or anything else the baby can bang on. He'll learn that different things make different noises when smacked and that hitting something hard sounds different from hitting something soft.
- Doors (and anything else with a hinge)—provided you're there to make sure no one gets pinched. Books operate on the same basic principle.

Success and Failure

Whatever your baby is doing, be sure to praise his efforts as well as his accomplishments. Kids need to learn that *trying* to do something can often be just as important as actually doing it. Confining your praise and happiness only to the successful completion of a project can make your baby less likely to take risks or try new things for fear of failing.

The Building Blocks of Development

There are literally dozens of cutting-edge, high-tech (and expensive) toys and games that claim to be essential to your baby's physical and mental development. Some are worthwhile, others aren't. But there's one toy—just about the least-cutting-edge, lowest-tech, cheapest thing going—that truly is an essential part of every nursery: blocks. Here's why:

♦ They help your baby develop hand-eye coordination as well as grasping and releasing skills.

♦ They teach your baby all about patterns, sizes, categories (big ones with the big ones, little ones with the little ones); gravity, balance, and structure. These brief lessons in math and physics lay the foundation for your baby's later understanding of how the world works.

♦ They teach good thinking skills. "Taken from a psychological viewpoint," wrote Albert Einstein, "this combinatory play seems to be the essential feature in productive thought—before there is any connection with logical construction in words or other kinds of signs which can be communicated to others."

♦ They can help your baby grasp the difference between things he has control over, such as which blocks he wants to use and how high he wants to go, and things he doesn't, such as the law of gravity, which keeps pulling down his towers.

♦ They teach perseverance. Building a tower—or anything else—out of blocks can be an excruciatingly frustrating experience for a baby. But along the way, he'll learn that if he keeps working on something long enough, he'll eventually succeed.

The bigger your baby's world gets, the more interested he'll become in objects and the less interested in you. And why not? After all, you always seem to be around, but one of those exciting new toys might disappear before he gets a chance to grab it.

Giving up the number-one position in your baby's heart and mind can be tough on the ego, especially if you're being replaced by a stuffed animal or a toy car. But instead of pouting, take a more aggressive, if-you-can't-beat-'em-join-'em attitude: if you're having trouble keeping your baby interested in playing with you, use a toy to get his attention. But don't be in a hurry; wait until the baby has begun to lose interest in whatever (or whomever) he's playing with before replacing it with something new. And, above all, remember that you don't need to engage your baby every second he's awake. He needs some down-time too, to play on his own or just to think. Really.

Family Matters

The Division of Labor

About 90 percent of new parents experience an increase in stress after their babies are born. And the number-one stressor—by a pretty good margin—is the division of labor in the home. Money, which we talked about in the last chapter, is number two.

Oh, How Much Work Could a Baby Really Be?

Before your baby was born, you and your partner probably anticipated that having a baby would increase the amount of household work you'd both have to do. But I'll bet you were *way* off on your estimates.

Psychologist Jay Belsky found that for most new parents, dishwashing increased from once or twice a day to four times, laundry from one load a week to four or five, shopping from one trip per week to three, meal preparation from two times a day to four, and household cleaning from once a week to once a day.

And that's just the nonbaby areas of your life. When you factor in all the baby-related stuff, things really start to get out of control. "On average, a baby needs to be diapered six or seven times and bathed two or three times per day, soothed two or three times per night and often as many as five times per day," writes Belsky. In addition, the baby's helplessness makes just about every task, from going to the bank to getting dressed in the morning, take five times longer than it used to.

One woman in Belsky's studies summed up the discrepancy between her prebirth workload estimate and the postbirth reality as essentially the difference between "watching a tornado on TV and having one actually blow the roof off your house."

And Who's Going to Do It?

Another thing you and your partner may have agreed upon before your baby was born was that you'd both be sharing responsibility for all the extra work the baby would require. If so, you're among the estimated 95 percent of people who say that men and women should share equally in child care. And why not? The more equitably domestic tasks are divided up, the happier couples are with their marriages. Unfortunately, though, you (and everyone else) were probably wrong about this one too. The reality is that despite all the grand plans, most couples slip into "traditional" gender roles. "Women ended up doing more of the housework than before they were mothers," write University of California, Berkeley, researchers Phil and Carolyn Cowan. "And men did less of the baby care than they or their wives predicted."

Everyone Knows that Women Do More around the House, Right?

It used to be that every few months or so there was a new study reporting that although women were dramatically increasing the hours they worked outside the home, men's hours *inside* the home had hardly changed.

As it turns out, those studies were based on flawed or absurd data. First, calculations of men's hours usually didn't include weekends, which is when dads are more likely to be involved with their children. Second, they didn't include hours men spent playing with their children as "child care," which meant that the time Mom spent cooking dinner counted while the time Dad spent entertaining the baby and keeping him away from the stove didn't. Finally, they didn't make a distinction between accessibility (being on duty and available) and engagement (active involvement with a child). Most kids don't need or want to be entertained every second of the day, but an adult still needs to be around. When those errors were corrected, it turned out that men's and women's hours spent on child care were far closer, though admittedly, women still do more.

It's important to remember that in most cases this inequity is not a function of men's lack of interest in their families. Phil and Carolyn Cowan and several other researchers have identified a number of significant barriers that prevent men from taking on a completely equal role in the home:

◆ Both men and women can't seem to shake the age-old idea that child-rearing is women's work and that breadwinning is men's work. According to a recent study by the Families and Work Institute, 42 percent of men and 37 percent of women felt that men should earn the money and women should take care of the kids. Those numbers have come down quite a bit over the past few decades, but they're still surprisingly high.

◆ Mothers step in quickly to take over when either the father or the baby looks a little uneasy. At the same time, men—who hate feeling incompetent and who expect their wives to be competent with babies right from the start—are all too glad to hand over the baby to the "expert." Men whose partners criticize their parenting and express doubt about their abilities to handle the job often end up withdrawing.

◆ The roles available to men are considered second-rate and discourage male involvement. Feeding the baby—something women generally have a lock on—is considered the most important task, whereas soothing the baby and changing his diapers—tasks that are available to men—don't seem nearly as important.

◆ The more men attempt to take an active role in the care of their children, the more mixed or negative feedback they receive from their own parents. During my first few years as a father, my own parents, for example, would wonder—just loud enough for me to hear—when I'd be going back to work, or whether taking so much time off would have a negative effect on my career.

◆ The lack of quality child care encourages fathers to work and mothers to stay home while the children are young.

♦ Employers aren't as supportive of father involvement as they should be. As a result, many men are afraid they'll be committing career suicide if they openly express a desire to take time off for family and spend less at work.
♦ There's a glaring lack of role models, information, and social supports for fathers who want to be involved.

Despite these obstacles, men are slowly but surely starting to buck the traditional roles and do whatever it takes to get more involved. But it's not easy. Far too often both parents give up and adopt a more traditional division of labor. That, in turn, can lead to a decline in marital satisfaction.

Another big problem with the who-does-what-around-the-house studies is that they generally count only unpaid work, which skews the results in favor of moms. Guy things like fixing the car, balancing the checkbook, and mowing the lawn slip through the cracks. A far more honest calculation would be to count *all* the hours—paid and unpaid—that parents work in the service of their family. The "total productive time" calculation shows that men and women make almost exactly equal contributions. Yes, dads typically don't spend as many hours as moms cooking and cleaning and doing child care. But they put in longer days than moms at the office: 51 hours a week for men who work full-time, 43 hours a week for women who work full-time. That's an extra day a week at work—more if you factor in men's typically longer commute times.

Notes:

Forming an Identity

What's Going On with the Baby

Physically

- Unless your baby is extremely active, she won't make many big advances in motor skills this month. But not to worry, she's just taking a break before taking her first real steps towards independence.
- She moves easily from crawling to sitting and may even be able to pull herself upright. Once there, she can stand with very little support and may even try a few seconds without a net at all.
- She can "cruise" (sidestep while holding on to something) just about everywhere, and if you hold both her hands, she'll walk and walk and walk.
- She's getting to be a fairly confident climber as well, getting up and down from couches and chairs almost without fear. Going up stairs is no problem, but coming down is still a challenge.
- She's also much better at manipulating her hands now. She can grasp two objects in one hand, and most of the food she tries to feed herself actually gets into her mouth. Her hand-eye coordination is getting more impressive by the day, and she'll stop to pick up and examine every speck of dirt she crawls or cruises by.
- She is beginning to discover that each side of her body can be used differently. And she may even be exhibiting an early "handedness" preference. She can, for example, use one hand for picking up and manipulating toys, the other for holding.

♦ If both hands are full, she may put down one object in order to pick up a third.

♦ Although she's quite graceful in her grasping, her releasing is still fairly clumsy.

Intellectually

♦ Although she still isn't completely convinced that things she can't see do exist, she's starting to suspect as much. Being able to retain an image of you even when you're not in the room will make her a little less upset if you leave her with someone else for a few minutes. This month, she'll look for a toy she sees you hide. If she's seen you move the toy to a second hiding place, she'll look for it there as well.

♦ She now understands that objects of different sizes need to be treated differently. She'll approach small objects with her fingers, but large ones with both hands.

♦ She's also intrigued by the idea that objects can exist for several reasons at the same time (they have properties as well as functions). Paper, for example, can be chewed, crumpled, and torn. And crayons can be held, eaten, and, best of all, used to scribble on things. This ability enables your baby to organize things into two categories ("things I can chew on" and "things that are too big to get into my mouth") —a realization that gives her a bit of control and predictability in her life.

♦ As her memory improves, she's getting more persistent. It's harder to distract her from whatever she's doing, and if you manage to turn her attention to something else, she'll go right back to her original activity as soon as you quit bugging her.

♦ She's now capable of *symbolic thinking* (associating something she can see with something she can't). For example, a few months ago, your baby would probably cry when seeing the nurses at her pediatrician's office. She associated nurses with shots. But now she may recognize the doctor's office from the street and will start crying as soon as you pull into the parking lot.

Verbally

♦ Although she's been saying "dada" and "mama" for a while, she really didn't know what those words meant. But now "dada," "mama," "bye-bye," "no," and possibly a few others have a definite meaning that she uses deliberately. She may even pick a word and repeat it over and over, all day long. (If she's not using words yet, don't worry. Some kids don't start until well after their first birthday.) She's also figured out that she can use certain noises to attract your attention and may deliberately cough, sneeze, yelp, and gasp just to get a rise out of you.

♦ She now understands a lot of what she hears and may actually cooperate (but probably not in front of friends you're trying to impress) in a brisk game of Identify the Baby's Body Part ("Where's your belly button?").

♦ She's also able to combine words and gestures: a head shake with "no," a hand wave with "bye-bye."

♦ She listens actively to adult conversation and will frequently butt in with a few "words" of her own.

Emotionally/Socially

♦ After a long day of crawling, cruising, babbling, and exploring, your baby really enjoys a nighttime snuggle. Her attention span is much longer than it used to be, and she may want even more stories than before.

♦ Your baby's mimicking skills are growing by leaps and bounds, and she'll now try to imitate just about everything you do: rubbing her hands together under running water, saying "brr" and shivering after getting out of the bath, and talking on the phone.

♦ When she cries (which she does much less frequently than a few months ago), it's less to get you to come running and more out of fear—of unfamiliar places or things, or of separation from you.

♦ She's becoming more sensitive to your emotions and is better able to express her own. If you're happy, she will be too. But if you scold her, she'll pout; if you do something she doesn't like, she's capable of genuine anger; and if you leave her alone for too long (only she knows how long that is), she may "punish" you by clinging and crying at the same time.

What You're Going Through

Feeling Irreplaceable

You've been a father for most of a year now, and as we briefly discussed a few months ago (pages 166–168), you should be feeling pretty good about your fathering skills. If you're lucky, your partner, your friends, and your relatives have been telling you what a great dad you are. But there's one person whose opinion of your abilities probably means more to you than anyone else's: the baby.

As a grown man, you'd think you wouldn't need to have your ego stroked by a baby. But the fact is that there is absolutely nothing in the world that will

*"I've never once demanded respect from you simply because
I'm your father. You should respect me for that."*

ever make you feel better, more powerful, or more loved than the feeling of
being needed by your own child. Those feelings—that you're irreplaceable and
that your life has meaning because of your role as a parent—can do wonders
for your self-esteem.

A Sense of Fulfillment

If feeling needed and appreciated by your boss and coworkers can give you a
sense of self-worth and security at the office, feeling needed and appreciated
as a father has the same result at home. In fact, nearly half the men in Bruce
Drobeck's studies, and a similar percentage of men I've interviewed, described
fatherhood "as giving them more of a sense of fulfillment and/or purpose in
their lives."

For some, becoming a father was the achievement of their fondest dreams
and long-term goals. One man said, "I finally feel like I'm where I want to be
and doing what I want to be doing." After less than a year of fatherhood, most
new dads can hardly remember what it was like to have been childless. Fatherhood seems to have seeped into every aspect of their being.

A New Kind of Feeling Left Out, or Mr. Baby's Father

Becoming a father can wreak havoc on your identity in a lot ways. There's nothing quite like having a kid to make you realize that you're a grown-up. It also makes you realize that besides being a son, you're also a father. Now that may sound like a painfully obvious thing to say, but you'd be surprised at how many men have a hard time with the concept. After all, we've spent our whole lives looking at our fathers as fathers and at ourselves as sons.

At the same time, there's nothing like being a dad to put you back in touch with your own childhood and to release some of that childlike behavior you've been suppressing for most of your adult life. Having a child gives you that perfect excuse to coo and giggle and make faces and crawl around on the floor say things like "poop" and "pee." In a way it's liberating.

Strangely, not everyone you come across is going to include "father" in the list of nouns they'd use to describe you. I can't count the number of times that I've been out with my kids in the middle of the day, and someone says something like, "Hey! You babysitting today?" (I've always wanted to shout back, "No, bozo, I'm not babysitting, I'm taking care of my children!") I've never met a father who hasn't had a similar experience. Too many people see only "man" and not "father."

Sometimes they won't even see "man"—you'll just be Mr. Baby's Father, the invisible guy who's holding the baby. People love to come over and "talk" to babies who aren't nearly old enough to understand what they're hearing, let alone respond. They look the baby right in the eye and ask questions like "And how old are you?" "What's your name, you little cutie?" "Where did you get that darling little outfit you're wearing?" and on and on, in the same way that they might ask a cat whether it's hungry. And if you answer, they seem genuinely startled, as if they hadn't seen you at all.

Still other people—mostly single women—may see "father," but they also see "sensitive guy/potential mate." There's apparently something about a man playing happily with a child that a lot of women find very attractive. A man with a child and a dog is even better. If you're a single dad, this may be kind of fun. If you're married and want to stay that way, watch out.

You and Your Baby

Exposing Your Child to Music

By the time your baby started babbling verbally, she had already been babbling musically for several months—cooing happily, adjusting her pitch up or down to match yours. You'd sing or coo back, and the two of you would have a little "duet."

For your baby, there is little if any difference between musical and verbal babbling. But for most parents, the difference is enormous. And the minute parents get even the slightest hint that their babies are beginning to understand language, the cooing and singing stops, and they focus their attention on developing the baby's verbal skills. "Consequently," says Ken Guilmartin, president of the Center for Music and Young Children, "the singing form is not reinforced and becomes developmentally delayed, or even atrophies completely."

Even if you and your partner don't have any particular musical talent, there's no reason why you can't stimulate your baby's musical potential. Now, before you protest that you can't carry a tune to save your life, keep in mind that "potential" and "achievement" are not the same thing. Unfortunately, this is a distinction that far too many parents fail to make.

According to music education researcher Edwin Gordon, every child is born with at least some musical aptitude: 68 percent have perfectly average aptitude; 16 percent well above; and 16 percent well below. "Just as there are no children without intelligence," he says, "there are no children without musical aptitude."

Good, bad, or indifferent, your baby's musical aptitude is greatly affected by the environment you provide. Even if you're so tone-deaf that you're embarrassed to sing in the shower, you can easily provide your baby with a rich musical atmosphere—and you'll probably enjoy yourself in the process. Here's how:

♦ As you started when your baby was three months old (see page 116), continue exposing her to a wide variety of musical styles. But now try to choose recordings that have frequent changes in rhythm, tempo, and dynamics (loudness/softness). At ten months your baby's attention span is still quite short, and these contrasts will hold her interest longer and more easily, says Guilmartin.

♦ Never force your baby to listen to music. Your goal here is not to teach her (just like you won't be teaching her how to speak, crawl, or walk); rather, it is to guide and encourage her and let her develop at a natural pace.

♦ Don't turn off the music if the baby doesn't seem to be paying any attention. "There is little doubt that young children derive as much from listening to music when they appear not to be paying attention as when they appear to be paying attention," says Dr. Gordon.

♦ Try to avoid songs with words. Because your baby is rapidly developing her language skills, she may pay more attention to the words than to the music.

♦ Sing. Whenever and wherever you can. And don't worry about being in tune—
your baby doesn't care. As above, use nonsense syllables—*dum-dee-dum*
kinds of things—instead of real words.

♦ Listen to music you like. Your baby will be paying close attention to the way
you react to the music and will know if you've selected some "good-for-you"
piece that you really hate.

♦ Watch your baby's reaction to the music. She's moving much more actively
than a few months ago. Her arm and leg movements may seem (to adults,
anyway) to have no connection to the music, but they are actually internally
rhythmic.

♦ Be patient. "The process of learning music is much the same as the process
of learning language," write Gordon and his associates Richard Grunow and
Christopher Azzara. Here are the steps they've identified:

  ♦ Listening. From birth (and before), you absorbed the rhythm and
  inflections of your language—without any expectation of response.

  ♦ Imitating. You weren't too successful at first, but you were encouraged
  to babble even though no one understood a single "word" you said.

  ♦ Thinking (understanding). As you got more proficient with language,
  you were gradually able to decipher the muddle of sounds coming out
  of people's mouths into meaningful words and phrases.

  ♦ Improvising. You made up your own words and phrases, and
  sometimes other people actually understood them.

  ♦ Reading and writing. But not until you'd been listening, imitating,
  improvising, and thinking for more than five years.

Don't try to mess with the order—it's set in stone. If your parents had
insisted on trying to teach you to read before you could speak, you might never
have learned to do either.

Talking the Talk

Just because your baby isn't really able to hold up her end of a conversation,
that doesn't mean you should stop talking to her. In fact, the more you talk to
her, the more she'll learn.

♦ **Encourage and expand**. If your baby says "ba-ba," don't just leave it at
that. Instead, respond with a full sentence, something like, "Do you want
your bottle?" or "Yes, that's a sheep," depending on what you think she
means.

♦ **Identify.** Ask, "Where's your tummy?" If she points to it or pats it, praise
her and ask another question. If she doesn't answer, point it out for her

("Here's your tummy!") and ask another. Also identify the things your baby is interested in and talk about them.

♦ **Talk about differences**. Point to her fingers and then to yours, to her nose and then to an elephant's trunk. Tell her about how hers are smaller, and yours and the elephant's are bigger.

♦ **Explain everything**. If you're feeding her, talk about the food, the color, the taste, how messy her face is. If you're outside, talk about the traffic, weather, trees, construction sites. Remember, most of the things you come in contact with during any given day are familiar to you. But to her, it's all brand-new.

♦ **Don't lecture**. Just speak in a casual, conversational way, using full sentences and a vocabulary that's a little above where you think your baby is.

♦ **Keep "No" and "Don't" to a minimum**. It's incredibly hard, but try. First of all, they're very broad. If you say "No" or "Don't" to your baby, she may not understand exactly what you don't want her to do. All she really knows is that you're not happy with her. Too many *Nos* and *Don'ts* will discourage creativity and exploration. Instead, give her some details: "Knives are sharp, and they aren't for babies," or "It's not safe to try to put

*"I gotta go play with my doll now, so that I'll be a
really great Dad someday."*

Mommy's hairpins in the electrical outlets." Of course all your outlets are safely covered up, but you know what I mean.

♦ **Read**. Make stories and books part of your baby's daily routine.

♦ **Keep signing**. If you started doing this a few months ago, don't stop now. And if you haven't started yet, it's not too late. Working on spoken language and sign language are not at all contradictory. In fact, babies who've learned to sign usually have larger vocabularies than babies who don't.

Your Role in Molding Your Kids' Sexual Identity

Everyone knows that little girls are sugar and spice and all that's nice, while little boys are frogs and snails and puppy-dogs' tails, right? Well, as with most stereotypes, there is, at the core, a kernel of truth there: girls and boys are diferent, and the differences go way beyond anatomy. In fact, they may be present in children's brains before they're born. And after birth, those structural differences become the basis for behavioral differences. Here's what we know:

♦ Boys tend to be a little more irritable in their first weeks outside the womb, crying a little more and sleeping a little less than girls. One reason for this may be that mothers spend almost 100 minutes longer in labor with a son than a daughter—perhaps because boys tend to be physically heavier and longer. This extra time being born leads to increased birth trauma and maternal drug-taking, which may account for the difference in behavior.

♦ Within hours of birth, girls are much more interested than boys in people and faces. In fact, at only four months, baby girls can tell the difference between photographs of people they know and those of strangers; boys can't.

♦ Boys are a little less discriminating when it comes to food, and less sensitive to touch and pain. They also have a dominant ear, which means that they hear less in one ear than the other and can't pick up background noises as well as girls can. Some researchers speculate that this may account for parents' perceptions that boys are less responsive to verbal requests than girls.

Despite their number, the actual biological differences between boys and girls during the first 18 months of life are so slight that when babies are dressed in nothing but diapers, most adults can't tell a boy from a girl. But that doesn't stop us from treating them quite differently. That raises a very provocative question: Are the differences we see in boys' and girls' behavior—however they got there—real, or are we just imagining them?

Cornell University researchers John and Sandra Condry showed 200 adults a videotape of a nine-month-old baby playing with various toys. Half were told

"We're calling her Fred, after her father."

that they were watching a boy, half that they were watching a girl. Although everyone was viewing the exact same tape, the descriptions the two groups gave of the baby's behavior were startlingly different. The "boy" group overwhelmingly perceived the child's startled reaction to a jack-in-the-box as anger. The "girl" group saw the reaction as fear.

So do these imagined differences affect the way adults interact with children? Could be. Mothers, for example, respond more quickly to crying girls than to crying boys and breast-feed them longer. And when girls have a difficult disposition, mothers tend to increase their level of affection, holding and comforting the child. But when a boy is similarly fussy, they back off a little. This kind of behavior can have some serious long-term consequences. In one study, for example, boys who received more cuddling were found to have higher IQs than boys who didn't.

By treating boys and girls differently, adults may inadvertently reinforce sex stereotypes. For example, parents tend to react more positively to their daughters' attempts to communicate and more negatively to similar attempts by their sons, thus "confirming" that girls are more verbal than boys. Parents also react more positively when their sons engage in physical play and more negatively when their daughters do, thus "confirming" that boys are more physical than

It's a Boy Thing

Interestingly, many of our perceptions and prejudices about gender start even before our children are born. "Parents say they don't care what gender their child is as long as it's healthy," says sex researcher Carole Beal. "But the truth is that couples have a definite preference for the sex of their child." That preference is usually for a boy, and it's expressed by both men and women.

Fathers may prefer boys because they feel more comfortable with them or because they feel that a boy would carry on the family name. Mothers may prefer boys because they know—instinctively or otherwise—how much it means to their husbands. "Boy infants tend to bring fathers into the family more," says Beal. "Fathers of newborn boys visit the nursery more often and stay there longer than fathers of girls."

Preferences like these can have a major impact on everyone in the family. Couples who have girls first often have more children, trying to have a boy. But couples who have boys first often end up with smaller families. Some experts speculate that this is at least in part due to the perception that boys are more "difficult." And two researchers in Stockholm, Sweden found that men are generally more satisfied with their role as fathers when their babies—boys or girls—are the gender they'd hoped for.

At the same time, there's evidence that children who did not turn out to be the gender their parents preferred had worse relationships with their parents in childhood than preferred-gender kids. That was especially true for kids whose parents had wanted a boy but got a girl. And most interesting—and most horrifying—Carole Beal found that divorce rates are lower for couples who have only boys, while couples with only girls have the highest divorce rates of all.

girls. So do boys play with trucks and girls with dolls because they want to or because that's what their parents want them to? Think about that the next time you're looking for a gift for your baby.

So here's the big question: *Why* do we treat boys and girls differently? Some researchers say that parents are simply repeating the socialization they got when they were children. Others say that the differences are rooted in biology. "Boys and girls actually elicit different responses from us," says psychotherapist Michael Gurian. "Primal, visceral, instinctive responses that tell us how to treat them. Because boys are a little bigger and stronger, we tend to play with them more roughly. And because girls are quieter and enjoy eye-to-eye contact, we spend more time talking to them."

Whether it's socialization or biology, the bottom line is the same: boys and girls are different. But be very careful: biology does not have to be destiny. Acknowledging that boys and girls are not the same does *not* imply that one gender is somehow better or worse or smarter or dumber than the other.

The whole point of this section is to get you to see how easy it is to fall into sex-stereotype traps. Sure, you'll still probably treat girls a little differently from boys; that's normal. But hopefully, now that you're a bit more aware of the dynamics, you'll be able to avoid the larger problems and give your kids a richer childhood experience. If you limit your daughter's choices to the soft and cuddly and your son's to the rough and muddy, you could very well end up with a child whose biology has, in fact, become his or her destiny.

If you have a boy, encourage him to communicate as much as he can. Don't discourage him from crying or from playing with dolls, and teach him that asking for help isn't a bad (unmanly) thing. If you have a daughter, encourage her to play physically and teach her that assertiveness and independence aren't unfeminine.

But whether you have a boy or a girl, make sure you aren't forcing your child into a type of behavior that doesn't fit his or her character or temperament. The bottom line is that some boys, if you give them a Barbie to play with, will tear her head off and use her legs as a double-barreled shotgun; and some girls are going to want to wear lace everywhere they go.

You and Your partner

Communication

One of the most common traps new parents fall into is that they stop—or at least change—the way they communicate. Half the time these changes are permanent. I'll talk more about how this affects the overall couple relationship on pages 281–282. In the meantime, here are some factors that researcher Jay Belsky and others have identified as contributing to the problem:

♦ "A new child deprives a couple of many of the mechanisms they once used to manage differences," says Belsky. For example, when you used to have disagreements about who did what around the house, you might have solved the problem by getting a housekeeper. But with a new baby arrived, strained finances might not allow for a cleaning person, which means you'll have to deal with the once-painless who-does-what disagreements.

♦ The lack of spontaneity. Before your baby was born, if you wanted to go see a movie or even just sit around and talk, you could just do it. But now, as parents, you don't have that luxury. If you want to go out, you have to get a sitter a day or so in advance, make sure the baby is fed, and be back at a certain time.

♦ Physical exhaustion. Even if you stay home together with your partner, there's a better than even chance that you'll be too tired to stay awake for an entire conversation.

♦ There's a general decline in intimacy-promoting activities such as sex, hanging out with friends, and so on.

♦ With so much time, money, and energy focused on your baby, you and your partner don't have as many opportunities to pursue individual interests and activities outside the home. You won't have nearly as many new things to talk about, and you may lose (partially, at least) the ability to hear and understand each other.

♦ Expectations have changed. The time your partner spends with your baby is time she can't spend with you. She may be feeling pressured to be a fantastic mom, and you may be putting even more pressure on her by reminding her that she's not satisfying your emotional needs as much as she used to.

Notes:

Planes, Trains, and Automobiles

What's Going On with the Baby

Physically
♦ Your baby can get himself to a standing position by straightening his legs and pushing off from his hands. He may even be able to stand up from a squatting position and squat back down to pick something up.
♦ He may also be able to stand without any support and will try to do two activities at the same time, such as standing and waving.
♦ He can climb up stairs using the railing and can walk holding on to only one of your hands.
♦ He adores rough play—wrestling, rolling around on the floor, being held upside down, and bouncing on your knees.
♦ He can clap and turn the pages of a book, but not as accurately as he'd probably like to.
♦ He can operate a spoon pretty well but prefers to use his hands.
♦ He can hold onto a crayon and will draw on any surface he can reach. He still has a little trouble releasing objects exactly when and how he wants to.

Intellectually
♦ One day this month, your newly upright baby will be leaning against a chair, and he'll accidentally make it move a little. He'll immediately understand that he's the one responsible and will do it again. And again. He may, in fact, spend the rest of the day (and the month, for that matter) pushing the chair around the house.

- Imitation reaches new heights this month. But rather than mimicking specific actions, he's now able to imitate concepts, or even a series of actions. He'll hide things and get you to look for them, feed you, and try to brush his own teeth and get himself dressed.
- He'll spend a lot of time this month dropping small objects into larger containers, learning the difference between big and small, container and contained, "in" and "out."
- He's also expanding his knowledge about symbols. He's fascinated by books but doesn't really know what to make of them. He'll poke at the pictures in a book, intrigued by the idea that he can see something but can't pick it up.
- Although still convinced that he's running the world, he's discovering that his body has limitations. If some precious object is out of reach, he'll push you toward it, trying to get you to reach it for him, thus using you as a tool.

Verbally

- Although his vocabulary is growing, he's nowhere near being able to put together full sentences. But he'll babble in long "paragraphs"—sometimes to himself—and toss in an occasional recognizable word.
- Interestingly, the sounds he uses in his babbling are specific to his native language, and he can no longer produce some of the ones he could even a few months ago.
- Whenever he learns a new word, he'll repeat it to himself dozens of times.
- He recognizes the symbolic use of words: he'll say "yum" if you're talking about ice cream, "meow" if you point out a cat.
- He's developed an incredible ability to hear what he wants to: he'll completely ignore a shouted "Get away from that stove!" just to test out your reaction, but will stop whatever he's doing and rush to your side if you whisper "ice cream" from another zip code.

Emotionally/Socially

- Besides happiness and sadness, your baby is now capable of other, more sophisticated emotions. If you play with another baby, for example, he'll become jealous and protest loudly. He's also getting much more demonstrative, and will show genuine tenderness and affection to you as well as to his stuffed animals.
- He also understands approval and disapproval. When he cleans his plate, he'll joyously shout for you to come look, and he'll beam with pride at having done something good. If he's done something he shouldn't have, though, he knows it and will bow his head sheepishly in anticipation of a

few sharp words. Generally, he wants to please you, but he also needs to displease you to learn how you'll react.

+ He may scream or throw a tantrum if he doesn't get what he wants.
+ He may also be afraid of growing up and may regress emotionally as well as physically to a time when he was a baby and you took care of him.
+ Strange as it sounds, your baby is already beginning to establish his or her own sexual identity. Girls begin to identify with their mother and other females and do what they do, while boys will identify with you and other men and want to do what you do.
+ He loves playing alongside other children but isn't ready to play *with* them.

What You're Going Through

More Worries about the Baby's Health

For the first few months of your baby's life, you depended on your doctor to keep you informed as to how the baby was doing. And had there been any major problem (neurological defects, Down syndrome, and so on), or anything amiss with your baby's growth or development, you would have heard about it by now.

But most problems that affect children aren't easy to spot. And now that your baby is older and his well-baby checkups are further apart, your pediatrician will rely more on you and your daily observations about your baby's behavior to make any diagnoses. Keeping track of the following and reporting them to your pediatrician will help him or her better assess your child's continuing development:

+ Is the baby having trouble manipulating objects or moving around? Delays in developing sensory/motor skills can cause delays in language development as well.
+ Is the baby using his body fairly symmetrically? Does he use one hand (or foot, or eye) more than the other?
+ Is the baby having trouble eating or swallowing food? Besides resulting in nutritional deficiencies and general health problems, these problems may interfere with your baby's using his jaw, lips, and tongue, and may have an impact on language and cognitive skills.
+ Has your baby lost previously attained skills? Did he used to babble and coo but suddenly stop? Does he no longer react when people come and go? This could be an indication of a hearing problem, which, again, can affect language development.
+ Is the baby not achieving, within a month or two, the milestones described in the "What's Going On with the Baby" sections in this book?

Fear of Sexual Feelings

This may very well be the most controversial section in this book. So before you continue, you've got to promise that you'll keep an open mind and read all the way to the end.

Imagine this: You're rolling around on the floor with your baby, having the time of your life, or you're standing by your sleeping child's bed, stroking his beautiful, perfect cheek. Then, without warning, you get, well, aroused.

Now before you throw this book down and report me to the police, keep in mind that the overwhelming majority of mental health professionals say that it is perfectly normal for a parent to experience brief sexual feelings toward his or her child. "Most parents feel physical pleasure toward their babies," writes psychiatrist Stanley Greenspan. "For some, these pleasures are translated into fleeting sexual feelings."

Normal or not, feeling sexually aroused—even briefly—by a child can be especially terrifying for men. You might be afraid that someone will accuse you of being a child molester, or that you actually are one and won't be able to control your unnatural "urges." Or that you might have to be locked up to protect your children. Or that you're completely insane.

Despite everything we hear about the "epidemic of sexual abuse," the

---

+ Does the baby seem uninterested in exploring his surroundings?
+ Has your baby undergone a major change in temperament? (See pages 131–136.) But remember: difficult temperament by itself is not an indication of any kind of disability.

In most cases, the "problem" behaviors you identify will turn out to be perfectly normal. But that doesn't mean you should stop paying attention. Here are some things you can do to reassure yourself:
+ Spend some time studying the "What's Going On with the Baby" sections of this book. The more you know about what your baby is and isn't capable of, the less you'll worry.
+ Don't worry that your doctor—or your partner—will think you're asking too many questions or becoming overly concerned. You (or your insurance company) are paying your doctor more than enough for him or her to listen respectfully to any questions you might have.

truth is that well over 99 percent of parents never abuse anybody. So the odds are pretty slim that you'll do anything even remotely improper. Nevertheless, many men (and women as well) are so afraid and feel so guilty about their feelings that they withdraw from their children and stop playing with them, picking them up, or cuddling with them.

If you find yourself reacting in this way, stop it right now. "If you withdraw your physical displays of affection," says clinical psychologist Aaron Hass, "your child may believe there is something wrong with being affectionate in that manner. And if you stop hugging your child, you will miss the opportunity to enhance, in a very primal way, the bond between the two of you."

By reading this section, you have, without even being aware of it, taken a very important step toward understanding and dealing with your momentary sexual feelings. Simply being aware of how normal they are may be enough to keep you from doing anything untoward.

Of course, if you're seriously worried that your feelings toward your child are inappropriate, and/or if you're having trouble managing them, get some professional help quickly. And don't worry; telling your therapist about your feelings will not get you arrested.

♦ If, after talking to your doctor, you're still not satisfied (or you think you're being ignored), get another opinion.
♦ Keep a detailed log of things your child does (or doesn't do) that concern you, when they happen, and under what circumstances.
♦ Men have a tendency to ignore their own health concerns either because they hope whatever's worrying them will go away or because they're afraid the doctor will confirm their worst suspicions. If you want to ignore something that's been bothering you, that's your own prerogative. But don't apply the same standard to your baby. You may not be the most experienced parent in the world, but your gut reactions about what ails your children are usually pretty good and should be acted on. Of course, this doesn't mean bringing the baby into the emergency room every day, but an occasional call to your doctor's advice nurse is fine. If there is something to worry about, you're better off knowing sooner than later, when the problem will be much harder to deal with.

"I did ask her and she said to ask you where I came from."

You and Your Baby

Planes, Trains, and Automobiles

When my older daughter was only six months old, my wife and I decided it was about time to take that honeymoon trip we'd been putting off since we'd gotten married. So we traded in a few years' worth of frequent-flier miles, and the three of us took off on a month-long trip to New York, France, Israel, and Phoenix. All in all, it was a great trip.

While your first trip with your baby is not likely to be as big an expedition as ours, sooner or later you're going to want to pack up the family and go somewhere.

Planning Your Trip

♦ **Spend some time planning your itinerary**. You can take babies under about seven months just about anywhere anytime. After your baby has learned to walk, however, it's best to limit your destinations. Seven cities in four days is hard for even the most seasoned adult traveler. If possible, check out local baby-friendly attractions (zoos, museums, parks, beaches, puppet shows) before you leave.

♦ **If possible, pick destinations that won't be terribly crowded**. Large groups of unfamiliar people may spook babies and toddlers alike.

♦ **Get your tickets in advance**. There's no sense standing in lines if you don't have to.

♦ **Travel during off-peak times**. Christmas Day, New Year's Day, and Thanksgiving Day (as opposed to the days before or after), for example, are good. If you're driving, there'll be less traffic on the road; if you're traveling some other way, you'll find a lot more empty seats, meaning more room to stretch out or run around.

♦ **Consider red-eye flights**. They may increase the chances your baby will sleep on the plane, and can also help get the jet-lag acclimation process under way.

♦ **Prepare for jet lag/time differences before you leave**. You can keep the baby up late, put him to bed early, and so forth. Also adjust meal times.

♦ **Prepare your child for the upcoming trip by talking about it regularly**. Make it sound like it's going to be the most fun anyone has ever had.

♦ **Schedule a doctor's appointment (for your child) for a few weeks before you leave**. Tell your pediatrician where you're going and ask for the names of a few good local doctors. Also ask her to suggest any medical supplies you should bring along. If your child is taking any medication and will come anywhere near running out while you're on the road, get an extra prescription.

What to Bring

No matter where you go, the trick to making things run smoothly on a trip away from home is to surround your baby with as many familiar things as possible. This will help minimize the shock of the new routine and scenery. Whatever your destination, then, you'll probably need most of the following:

♦ Eating utensils and bibs.

♦ Bottles and formula, if you're using it. If you're traveling overseas and will be using powdered formula, plan on bringing some bottled water.

♦ Car seat. Doubles nicely as a high chair if you really need to restrain your baby while she's eating.

♦ A good backpack. It'll free up both your arms so you can schlep the six tons of other baby-related stuff you'll be needing.

♦ Pacifiers, especially if your baby sucks on one a lot during the day or needs one to get to sleep.

♦ A portable crib. Or, if you'll be staying in a hotel, call ahead to reserve one.

♦ A first aid kit (see page 197 for the ingredients).

♦ Baby shampoo and diaper cream.
♦ The All-Purpose Travel Bag (see page 255).
♦ Lots of familiar toys, stuffed animals, favorite foods, and a nightlight. These will help the baby adjust more quickly to the new surroundings.
♦ Try not to overpack. If you aren't going trekking in the Himalayas, for example, there's really no sense taking along three weeks' worth of disposable diapers—they're available just about anywhere. The first thing my wife and I did when we arrived in New York was get a huge cardboard crate and ship home about half of the stuff we'd brought.

Once You Get There

♦ Keep up the routines you've established at home. Read, sing, and play at the same times if you can. This is especially important for predictable babies (see page 133).
♦ Don't overbook activities. One or two excursions a day is plenty.
♦ Keep a sharp eye on baby/relative contact. If friends and relatives haven't seen the baby for a while or are meeting him for the first time, they'll all want to hold, squeeze, cuddle, and entertain. This can freak out even the calmest of babies. Be especially sensitive if your baby is going through a period of stranger or separation anxiety.
♦ If you're planning to leave the baby with a sitter or a relative, have her come early so the two of them can get to know each other for a few minutes.
♦ Stay away from meats, fish, eggs, and dairy products. If you're going to get food poisoning on the road, it'll probably come from one of those food groups. And if you're traveling overseas, stay away from water, milk, juice, raw foods, and anything served by street vendors unless you know for sure it's safe. This is especially important if your partner is still nursing.

Traveling by Car

♦ For short trips, try to leave an hour or so before your baby's usual naptime and, once he falls asleep, drive as far as you can while his nap lasts.
♦ For longer trips, consider doing your driving from 4 P.M. to midnight. That way, you'll only have a few hours of entertainment and stops for feedings before baby goes to sleep for the night.
♦ If you need to drive during the day, you or your partner should ride in the back seat with the baby in hour or two-hour shifts to keep him amused and awake. Car travel tends to knock babies out and can really screw up their sleep schedules.
♦ Take lots of breaks and make sure everyone has plenty of opportunity to

stretch, unwind, and relax. Stop at interesting places, pet the cows, watch the road-repair crews, point out new sights (forests, cloud shapes, and so forth), sing songs, read stories. Going through an automatic car wash can be a thrill for some kids, but for others it can be terrifying. Whatever you do, have fun.

♦ Put the car seat in the middle of the back seat; it's safest there. The seat should be facing backward, and you should make absolutely sure it's installed properly. As I mentioned earlier, you can probably get this done for free by your local police department or highway patrol.

♦ Lock car doors from the inside.

♦ Never, never leave your child alone in a car. Babies can suffocate a lot faster than you might think.

♦ If your baby is nursing and gets hungry while you're on the road, stop the car and let your partner feed the baby. In 2003, a woman was actually arrested for breast-feeding while driving. It's simply not safe to do that while driving—for you, your partner, your baby, or the truckers who may be distracted by the sight of your partner's exposed breast.

GOOD THINGS TO BRING IN THE CAR

♦ Lots of food and drink.

♦ Lots and lots of books, toys, blankies, and stuffies.

♦ An older child, if you happen to have one. This will make entertaining the baby a lot easier.

♦ A battery-operated CD player (if you don't have one in the car) and a good selection of music. Make sure to bring some you like as well. One warning:

The All-Purpose Travel Bag

If there's ever any danger of getting separated from your luggage (even if most of it is just in the trunk of your car), you should have a well-stocked bag with the necessary "emergency" supplies:

♦ Diapers, lots of wipes, and a few extra outfits.

♦ New toys or books (one for each hour of travel time); mirrors and suction-cup rattles are big hits with babies.

♦ Food, including extra formula if needed.

♦ Something to suck on (pacifiers, teething rings, and so forth).

♦ A few books.

♦ Some favorite comfort items (blankets, teddy bears, and so on).

---

if you have to slam on your brakes at sixty miles an hour, every object you have in your car is a potential projectile. So before you bring anything along, think about whether you'd like to be hit in the head by it.

Traveling by Plane

♦ Get to the airport early. Going through security with a baby can be a real adventure. You'll have to fold up the stroller to put it through the X-ray machine, and in most cases you'll have to carry the baby through the metal detectors. And be prepared: if you set off any alarms, the security people may pat your baby down too.

♦ Use your stroller to haul your carry-ons, car seat, and other stuff and carry the baby in a frontpack or sling. Most airlines will let you check the stroller at the gate.

♦ Try to get bulkhead seats (usually the first row). They generally offer a little more room, and you won't have to worry that your child will kick the seat of the people in front of you. Also, ask to be seated next to an empty seat if possible. Be sure to hold your absolutely adorable baby in your arms while you're asking—this can improve your chances of getting what you want.

♦ Don't board early. Instead, send your partner on with the carry-on stuff while you stay out in the lounge, letting the kids run themselves ragged until the last minute. Why spend any more time cooped up in the airplane than you absolutely have to?

♦ If you're going on a long trip, and your child is particularly restless or active, schedule a stopover or two to give you all a chance to get off the plane, stretch, and run around.

♦ Every child under two years old should suck on something —breast, bottle, or pacifier—on the way up and the way down. This will counteract the pressurization and reduce the chances of painful earaches. It may also make your baby a little drowsier.

♦ Make sure your child drinks a lot on board and try to keep his nasal passages moist. Airplane travel can dry out your baby's (and your) mucous membranes, making him more susceptible to colds or sinus infections.

♦ Buy your baby his own seat. Yes, it's more expensive, but holding a baby on your lap for a few hours, especially in a packed plane, can be a real pain. It's also not nearly as safe as having the baby neatly secured in a carseat.

♦ Check as many bags as you can, but carry on the All-Purpose Travel Bag (see page 255).

Eating Out with Your Baby

One day, when you and your partner are feeling very brave, you may decide to take your baby to a restaurant. If so, keep the following in mind:

♦ Call ahead to see whether babies are welcome and to make sure they have enough high chairs.

♦ Don't stay out past your baby's bedtime. Being in a new place can be stressful enough.

♦ Stay away from crowded, noisy places unless you know your baby loves that kind of environment.

♦ Keep it casual. White tablecloths and crystal wineglasses are to babies what red flags are to bulls.

♦ Sit near an exit. You may need to take an upset baby out of the restaurant.

♦ If the baby will be eating with you, don't forget his food and a few extra spoons, just in case one (or two) ends up on the floor.

♦ If your baby is walking, don't let him visit other tables unless you're absolutely sure that the people there really want to be visited. It may be cute to you but annoying to others. Also, wandering (and crawling) babies are tripping hazards to waiters.

♦ If you're holding the baby on your lap, be very, very careful. Babies are born with a sixth sense about restaurants, and they will lunge for whatever's hottest and sharpest and will make the biggest mess when it's spilled.

♦ Don't expect the restaurant staff to entertain your baby.

♦ Don't be embarrassed if you have to leave suddenly. Babies melt down, have blowups, get sick.

WHAT TO BRING

♦ Same as for cars (see pages 254–255).

♦ Some extra food—for the adults and the baby. The meals you ordered might not show up, or if you're taking a short flight, there might not be any food at all.

♦ A rear-facing car seat. Check with the manufacturer to make sure that it's approved for airline use and that it will actually fit in the seat.

♦ Pacifiers. This is *not* the time to break your child of his sucking habit. Your fellow passengers will thank you.

♦ If your partner is nursing, bring a light blanket that she can throw over her shoulder for privacy.

DEALING WITH JET LAG

♦ If you're traveling for only a few days, keep the baby doing things at the time he would be doing them at home. This will make it easier to return to your regular schedule when you get back home.

♦ Spend time outside. Natural light helps acclimate people to new time zones more quickly.

Family Matters

Insurance

Becoming a parent does some interesting things to your mind and to your outlook on life. On the one hand, having a child makes you want to live forever and not miss a single second with your child. On the other hand, watching your child grow older is like a hard slap in the face; it makes you realize that no matter how much you want to, you're not going to live forever.

Unfortunately, there really aren't any hard-and-fast rules or secret formulas to help you determine how much insurance you and/or your partner need. But

"Greetings, stockholders."

spending some time thinking about the following questions will help you clarify your needs.

♦ How much income would you need to maintain your current lifestyle? Could you or your partner take care of all the family's expenses alone if the other were to die? Life insurance is *not* a get-rich-quick scheme, and it's *not* a forced savings plan; it's a way to make sure expenses are covered so that you or your partner wouldn't have to sell your house or change jobs if, God forbid, the other should die unexpectedly.

♦ Do you need or want to pay off your mortgage, car, credit cards, or other debts?

♦ Do you need or want to leave an estate large enough to pay fully for your kids' college education?

♦ How many years of your income do you want your insurance to replace?

♦ What other expenses need to be covered? For example, if one parent dies, the surviving one would probably need additional child care.

♦ What do you expect your tax situation to be? If you have a huge estate, your heirs will have to come up with a tidy sum to cover inheritance taxes.

♦ How much coverage do you already have? You may already be covered under a policy provided by your employer, the military, or some organization you belong to.

♦ Do you or your partner have children from a previous relationship? Have either of you adopted the other's children? If not, and one of you dies, will the children live with the stepparent or with the other biological parent? How much of the children's expenses is the stepparent legally (and morally) required to pay?

♦ How much does Social Security provide? Most insurance salespeople never bring this up to their clients. But here's the deal: If you and/or your partner have been working for any length of time, your survivors are eligible for certain Social Security benefits. The Social Security Administration (SSA) estimates that about 98 percent of children with working parents would get some benefits if one of them died. If a 30-year-old who makes $50,000 per year died, his or her surviving spouse and child would *each* receive $1,170 per month until the child(ren) was sixteen. The total maximum for the family would be $2,730 per month. The benefits paid to a surviving spouse with one child would be more than $400,000, which is nothing to sneeze at. Social Security benefits may be taxable, and since they're paid monthly, they can't be counted on to help with estate taxes. The SSA has two Web sites that can help you sort through this: www.ssa.gov/pubs/10084.html or www.ssa.gov/pubs/10024.html#survivorchart.

There are two basic ways to make sure your insurance needs are properly taken care of:

+ Read a few good personal finance guides (or at least sections of them). Despite what you might think, it's not all that complicated.
+ Get yourself a financial planner (see pages 262–263 for some helpful tips).

Either way, you should at least be aware of your insurance options. Basically, there are two types of life insurance on the market: term and cash value; each is further divided into several subcategories. Here's a brief overview:

TERM

There are three types of term insurance, and they all share these features:

+ Fairly low cost, especially in the early years.
+ Premiums increase over time as your odds of dying go up.
+ Policies are in effect only for a specified period of time.
+ No cash value accumulation.
+ Benefits may be taxed.

Here are your basic term insurance choices:

+ **Renewable term**. If you keep your death benefit the same, the premiums will rise. But if you develop a health problem, you may get canceled altogether.
+ **Level premium**. The death benefit and the premium remain the same for a specified period of time, sometimes for as long as 30 years.
+ **Decreasing premium**. The death benefit decreases each year, but premiums remain the same. In other words, each year you get less insurance for the same premium.

CASH VALUE

There are an increasing number of cash value insurance products available. Despite their differences, they all share the following features:

+ These policies are essentially a combination of term insurance and a savings plan. A portion of your premium pays for pure term insurance, while the rest goes into some kind of side fund. Depending on the plan, you'll have more or less control over how the fund is invested.
+ These policies tend to offer—initially—very competitive interest rates. The rate is usually guaranteed for a year, but then drops to whatever the market is paying.

♦ You can pay pretty much whatever you want to. But because the cost of the underlying term insurance is rising every year, you may reach a point where your payment isn't enough to cover the cost of the insurance. If that happens, the shortfall will be taken out of your investment fund, which will reduce your cash value.

♦ The cash benefit accumulates tax-free, and you can borrow against it—usually at pretty competitive rates—or withdraw from it during your lifetime. Unless they're repaid, withdrawals and loans reduce the face amount of the policy.

♦ If properly placed in trust, the entire cash and accumulated savings can go to your heirs free of income tax.

♦ The fees can kill you, so to speak. Commissions—which are built into your costs—routinely run as much as 100 percent of the first year's premium. For that reason, if you cancel your policy within ten years or so, you could lose most or all of the value you've accumulated. In addition, management fees for the investment funds are often much higher than the industry average.

Here are your cash value choices:

♦ **Whole life**. Locks in a death benefit, cash values, and premium. The side fund is invested by the insurance company.

♦ **Universal life**. Similar to Whole life, except that you can change the premium payment and death benefits anytime. And since the side fund is invested in fixed-income home securities (bonds and so forth), your cash values can fluctuate.

♦ **Variable life**. Similar to Universal, except that you have a bit more input into how your side fund is invested. Your choices usually include money markets, government securities, corporate bonds, growth, fixed-income, or total-return portfolios.

Making the Choice

If you've decided that you need or want life insurance, the big question is whether to go with term or cash value. I've had long discussions with a number of insurance people and financial advisers, and here's what I think: Get yourself a guaranteed renewable policy with level premiums for at least 10 years. That way your policy can't be canceled if you get sick, and you won't need a physical exam every year. Then set up a good savings, investment, and retirement plan for your family. If you've got enough knowledge and expertise to do it on your own, great. If not, get an expert to help you (see pages 262–263).

There is one exception to this rule: if you expect your estate to be worth

Picking a Financial Planner

Most financial planners are paid on a commission basis, based on your insurance purchases, stock trades, and/or the total value of your portfolio. So whether or not your investments do well, the financial planner gets his commission. Others are paid on a fee basis and typically charge from $50 to $250 per hour.

This doesn't mean, of course, that fee-based planners are inherently better than their commission-based colleagues (although many experts believe that you'll be happier, and possibly richer, with someone who charges a fee). Your goal is to find someone you like and who you believe will have your best interests at heart. Here are a few things you can do to help you weed out the losers:

♦ Get references from friends, business associates, and so forth. Alternatively, the Financial Planning Association, (800) 282-7526 or www.fpa.org, will give you references to some local certified financial planners. The National Association of Personal Financial Advisors, (800) 366-2732, makes referrals to fee-only (as opposed to commission-based) planners.

♦ Select at least three potential candidates and set up initial consultations (which shouldn't cost you anything). Then conduct tough interviews. Here's what you want to know:

   ♦ Educational background. Not to be snobby here, but the more formal the education—especially in financial management—the better. Certified Financial Planners (CFPs) go through a rigorous training program, and the CFP certification can help you differentiate between someone who's really a planner from someone who just sells stocks and insurance.

more than the current estate-tax exemption, a cash value policy is a good way to leave your heirs something to pay off federal estate taxes. Estates below the exemption level pass tax-free.

Where to Get It

If you or your partner work for a big company or belong to a union, you probably already have at least some life and/or disability insurance. And you may even be able to get additional coverage for great rates and without having to have a physical examination.

- Licenses. Is he or she legally able to buy and sell financial products such as stocks, bonds, mutual funds, and insurance?
- Level of experience. Unless you've got money to burn, let your niece break in her MBA on someone else. Stick to experienced professionals with at least three years in the business.
- Profile of the typical client. What you're looking for is a planner who has experience working with people whose income level and family situation are similar to yours.
- Compensation. If fee-based, how is the fee calculated? If commission, what are the percentages on each product offered? Any hesitation to show you a commission schedule is a red flag.
- Sample financial plan. You want to see what you're going to be getting for your money. Be careful, though: fancy graphics, incomprehensible boilerplate language, and expensive leather binders are often used to distract you from the report's lack of substance.
- References. How long have customers been with the planner? Are they happy? Better off? Any complaints or weaknesses?
- Check your prospective planner's record with state and federal regulators. The North American Securities Administration Association has a list of each state's security regulators at www.nasaa.org/nasaa/abtnasaa/find_regulator.html. On a national level, you can also contact the NASD at www.nasd.org or 800-289-9999 to check on disciplinary action and consumer complaints, and to see whether your candidates have ever been sued.

Even if you are covered, you might want to consider getting some additional, independent insurance. If you ever leave your job, you'll probably be leaving your life insurance policy behind.

If you have a broker you work with, start there. But don't be shy about shopping around. Costs for the very same policy can vary by as much as 200 to 300 percent. There are a number of online services that can help you compare policies and get the one that's best for you.

Whether you opt for term or cash value, be sure to go with a carrier you can count on being around when the time comes to pay up. The best way to do this is to go with a company that's top rated by *Consumer Reports* magazine, AM Best, or Standard & Poors. You can find these ratings online (www.consumerreports.org, www.ambest.com, www.standardandpoors.com) or at your local library.

Disability

As long as you've got insurance on your mind, I'd suggest that you take a long, hard look at disability coverage. If your employer offers a long-term disability policy, sign up now. If not, or if you are self-employed, talk to your broker about getting one. A long-term disability can sometimes be more devastating to your family's finances than death.

Notes:

There Now, That Wasn't So Bad, Was It?

What's Going On with the Baby

Physically

- Still building toward walking, your baby can now get to a standing position from a squat and can lower herself gracefully from standing to sitting.
- She's also getting more confident about combining standing and walking. She can turn 90 degrees, stoop to pick things up, and walk holding on to you with one hand while clutching a favorite toy (or two or three) in the other. She might even experiment with taking a few backward steps or do a little dance if there's music on.
- Even if your baby does take a few unassisted steps this month, she'll still use crawling or creeping as her main means of transportation, mostly because it's faster.
- However, she's so excited by the prospect of finally being able to walk on her own that she may not want to sleep or eat. Expect her to bounce up and down in her crib instead of napping and to refuse any kind of new food. And since she may be able to climb out of her crib, make sure there's something soft on the floor for her to land on.
- She can take simple covers off containers (but probably not screw-tops), lift latches, and open doors. And she'll help you dress and undress her (well, at least she thinks she's helping . . .). What she really likes to do, though, is yank off hats, socks, mittens, and anything else she can get hold of.
- She's finally mastered her opposable thumb and can now pick up tiny

objects between her thumb and pointing finger. More important, she can release them whenever she feels like it.

♦ She's also expressing a strong preference for "handedness," using one hand for grasping, the other for manipulating. If you put an object in her "passive" hand, she'll transfer it to the "active" one.

♦ She's now learned to store objects. If she's holding one thing in each hand and you offer her a third, she wants to get control of all three; she'll transfer the contents of one hand to her mouth or armpit and then pick up the third object with the free hand.

Intellectually

♦ One of the most important intellectual accomplishments of your baby's first year is her ability to retain a visual image of an object she has seen before but that is currently out of sight. By the end of this month, she'll be able to demonstrate this ability by searching —in more than one place—for objects she has seen but that she didn't actually see you hide.

♦ In another major intellectual leap, your baby will begin to use trial and error to solve her problems and overcome obstacles.

♦ She loves putting objects inside other objects and imitating anything anyone does: sweeping the floor, typing on the computer, talking on the phone, or howling in pain if you hurt yourself.

♦ As annoying as it may get, it's important to recognize that your baby's constant banging, building and knocking over, and putting things in and dumping them out are important learning activities that are teaching her more about the multiple properties of the objects in her world. Adding water to sand changes the way the sand feels (and tastes); dropping marbles into a metal can produces a much different sound than dropping them into a plastic box; and dumping them onto the living room rug isn't nearly as much fun as watching them bounce and roll around after dumping them on the vinyl kitchen floor.

Verbally

♦ She probably has a vocabulary of six to eight real words, as well as five or six more sound words, such as *moo*, *woof*, or *boom*, which she'll practice over and over and over.

♦ Her passive vocabulary is significantly larger, and she'll gleefully identify quite a few of her body parts, as well as such familiar objects as you and your partner, her bottle, and her crib.

♦ She loves to try to imitate what you say, so watch your mouth. She's developing an amazing capacity to pick out the one swear word you use in a five-minute conversation, and she'll repeat it back to you twenty or thirty times a minute for the next few days.

♦ She'll also babble in phrases that have the same rhythm and intonation as her native language, and may make up words for people or objects.

♦ She still hasn't mastered the symbolic use of words. If you point to a book at a friend's house and say, "Look at the book," your baby may be confused. In her world, the word *book* applies only to the ones at home.

♦ She knows exactly what "No" means but she doesn't always pay attention. And she's discovered that it can be fun to make you repeat "No" again and again.

Emotionally/Socially

♦ She actively tries to avoid doing things she knows you don't like, and loves your applause, laughter, and approval.

♦ She's not always cooperative and will regularly test your limits (and your patience). She also is developing a basic sense of right and wrong and shows guilt when she does something she knows she shouldn't.

♦ She's developing a sense of humor and finds incongruities most entertaining. If you tell her a dog says "moo," or if you crawl or pretend to cry, she'll laugh hysterically.

♦ In her home, where she feels most secure, your baby will play with other kids and may share some of her toys with them. In less secure environments, however, she's not nearly as sociable and will not stray far from you.

♦ She's got some pretty firm ideas of what she wants and will do what she can (cry, have a tantrum, smile sweetly) to influence your decisions.

♦ All in all, she's a real person now, with a distinct personality all her own.

What You're Going Through

Anger

While my wife was pregnant with our first child, I spent a lot of time thinking about the things I would never do once I became a father. First on my list was No Hitting the Kids. Then I thought about all those parents (including my own) I'd seen over the years scream at their children in the grocery store or the post office. "How weak," I remember thinking to myself. "If people can't control themselves any better than that, they really shouldn't be parents." I quickly and rather smugly added No Yelling at the Kids to my list.

One afternoon my oldest daughter woke up from her nap crying like she never had before. I knew she wasn't tired, so I checked to see if her diaper was full (it wasn't), whether her clothes were binding her (they weren't), and even took her temperature (normal). She didn't respond to my comforting words or my requests to stop crying and tell me what was wrong (at six months, why should she?), and she continued howling. I was alone in the house, and after half an hour I'd had enough. I was frustrated and angry.

For months I'd been telling everyone in sight how perfect and well-behaved my baby was and how I love her so much that I'd throw myself in front of a steamroller for her. But at that moment I felt tempted to throw *her* under the steamroller.

Almost immediately, I was nearly overcome with feelings of embarrassment and guilt and shame. I also felt like a complete failure as a father. After all, what kind of father would have such horrible thoughts about his own baby? Well, the truth is that sooner or later, every parent feels some kind of intense anger toward his or her child.

COPING WITH ANGER

Besides the baby's actual behavior, things like job pressures, financial difficulties, health problems, sleep deprivation, or even car trouble can be redirected toward our kids and make us lash out at them. Whatever you're angry about, remember that there's nothing wrong with *feeling* it—even when it's directed at your kids. It's what you *do* with your anger, however, that can be a problem. Trying to deny it or imagine that it never happened doesn't work. Here are some suggestions that will help you understand, and better deal with, your anger.

♦ **Change your perspective**. Although your child may periodically do something deliberately to annoy you, many of her actions are really beyond her control. In fact, being able to make you angry is actually a normal part of your child's development—she's learning about actions and reactions.

♦ **Be your own shrink**. Do you find yourself getting angry at your child for the same thing over and over? Do you get angry at certain times of day or while you're doing certain kinds of activities? Some of your anger could be triggered by your baby reminding you of particularly painful memories of when you were a child. So try to figure out what your baby is doing and why it makes you so angry. At the very least, knowing what triggers your anger may help you to avoid those situations as much as possible.

♦ **Laugh**. It may be a pain to clean up, but drawing on the walls with lipstick can be funny—if you let it.

♦ **Take regular breaks**. This can help keep minor annoyances from accumulating and boiling over. Make sure your partner gets plenty of time off too.

"If you ask me, this kid isn't lost. His parents just made a run for it."

◆ **Have a plan**. It's a given that you're going to get angry at some point. So think now, when you're calm, about a few techniques you can use to diffuse some of your anger. You could clench and unclench your fists, close your eyes, count to ten, take deep breaths, remove yourself from the situation, or anything else that can distract you long enough that you won't do something you'll regret for a long, long time.

◆ **Watch what you say**. Don't insult or humiliate your child. If you must criticize her, do it in private. Contrary to the old adage "Sticks and stones may break my bones, but names will never hurt me," calling your baby names can, in fact, have a greater long-term negative impact than hitting.

　　◆ Use "I" messages: "I don't like it when you scratch me—it hurts" is a much more effective message than "You're a bad girl because you scratched me."

　　◆ Saying things like "You always . . ." or "You never . . ." can fill a child with a sense of futility, a conviction that she'll fail no matter what she does or how hard she tries.

♦ Avoid mixed messages. Yelling at your child to stop yelling will probably not do you a lot of good.

♦ **Watch what you do.** Children learn more about how to express anger from watching how you do it than from punishment. So don't let your baby see you vent steam in a physical way; she won't be able to understand your anger and might even be afraid that you'll turn on her. She could also try to imitate you, and might hurt herself, someone else, or someone's property.

♦ **Get physical.** Taking a long jog, swimming, jumping rope, punching a pillow, and taking a boxing class are good ways to let off some steam. If there are any batting cages nearby, try them out—if you squint, slow-moving softballs can look an awful lot like a human head . . .

If You Lose Control . . .

Because anger can completely take over your mind and body in a heart-beat, it's easy to understand how even parents with the best intentions accidentally lose control. If you do:

♦ Apologize. Explain to your child that you lost your temper. Make sure she knows that it was her behavior you didn't like, not her as a person, that you love her, and that you'll never hit her again.

♦ Don't go overboard, though. Resist the urge to punish yourself for your mistakes by being extra lenient with your child. You're only human, so lighten up.

Remember, anger can be just the first step in a vicious circle: something angers you enough that you lose control; feeling out of control makes you angrier; and feeling angry makes you feel even more out of control.

Unchecked, this process can escalate into physical and emotional abuse (which, besides screaming, can include insulting, humiliating, or withholding love). If you're worried that you might lose control again, get some help immediately: call a friend, a therapist, your child's pediatrician, or even a local parental-stress hotline (see also some of the suggestions for dealing with crying on pages 69–71). And if you're worried that your partner might prove to be violent, suggest she do the same.

You and Your Baby

Discipline Update

When I was a kid, one of my dad's favorite sayings was, "You're free to swing your arms around any way you want. But that freedom ends right where someone else's nose begins." In a nutshell, teaching your child this lesson—to be respectful of other people's noses—is the primary goal of discipline.

A few months ago this was a concept your baby couldn't possibly have grasped. And the only way for you to control her evil impulses was to distract her with a toy and hope she'd forget about whatever it was she shouldn't have been doing in the first place. But your baby's memory has been improving every day, and by the time she's a year old, one toy just won't do the trick anymore; now you'll need two or three. And pretty soon, toys won't work at all.

At this point, expect your baby to move things up a notch or two, behaving in

Dealing with Temper Tantrums

As you've seen, the end of the first year is packed with developmental milestones. Some, like walking and talking, are wonderful to see. Others, like temper tantrums, are a little less pleasant.

In some cases, your baby's tantrums may be the result of frustration at not being able to get you to understand something. More likely, though, her tantrums will be triggered by your not letting her have or do something she wanted to have or do. It's slowly dawning on her that she's not in control of as much of the world as she thought, and she's not happy about it. Here are a few ways you can deal with the inevitable:

1. If you know what she wants and you don't want to give it to her, try redirecting her or offering an option.
2. If you don't know what she wants, make a real effort to find out. Asking direct questions may help you straighten things out. Hunger and exhaustion are responsible for a lot of tantrums.
3. If she can't or won't tell you, do a quick check to make sure there's nothing physically wrong—no cuts, bruises, or assorted owies, no fever, no clothing that's too tight, and so on.
4. Now, here's the tough part: If she's not hungry, tired, sick, or in pain and the tantrum continues, make sure she's in a place where she can't hurt herself or anyone else and ignore her. Yes, ignore her. Nothing makes a tantrum disappear faster than the realization that it isn't having the desired effect.
5. If the tantrum happens in a public place—every parent's worst nightmare—quickly go through 1 through 3 above. If that doesn't work, immediately get her and yourself out of there. Just pick her up and carry her away. If you have to leave an almost-full shopping cart behind or walk out of a restaurant, do it.
6. Do not spank or yell at your child. Yes, this may be the most embarrassing moment of your life, and you may be worried that people are staring at you (some of them may be) thinking you're a horrible parent, but the sooner you get out, the sooner they'll stop staring at you. And hitting or screaming at your child will only make even more people stare at you.
7. Don't give in, no matter what. If you do, you'll be proving to your baby that she's discovered a great way to get Mom and Dad to do what she wants.

ways she knows she shouldn't just to trigger a reaction. For example, she'll wait until you're looking right at her before making a move for the stairs or taking a swipe at your fine crystal. As annoying and frustrating as your baby's parent-baiting will seem, try to remember that it's actually a healthy part of her development. In order to feel secure, she needs to have limits. And the only way to grasp where the limits are is to see how far she can push before they kick in.

The big question now—one that will come up again and again as your baby gets older—is, How much independence do you allow before drawing the line? For me, it gets back to my dad's line about swinging arms. Let her have plenty of room to explore, but stop her before she hurts anyone or anything, including herself. Here's how:

+ **Limit potential risks and give her a safe place to explore**. Basically, this means childproofing the hell out of your house and keeping anything you really want to stay in one piece as far away from the baby as possible. (To minimize problems elsewhere, ask your parents and in-laws to take similar preventive measures.)
+ **Put her in situations where you won't have to correct her as much.**
+ **Have plenty of substitutes available.** Old phones and remote controls, spare computer keyboards, and so on. But be prepared: some kids can tell instinctively that what you're giving them isn't the real thing, and they won't be amused.
+ **Stop dangerous behavior immediately, but subtly.** If your baby is pounding on a plateglass window with her toy hammer and you scream, drop your coffee, and leap across the room to wrestle her to the ground, she'll find your reaction so much fun that she'll be sure to repeat exactly the behavior that provoked it the first time. Instead, tell her to stop. If that doesn't work, calmly walk over and disarm her.
+ **Be consistent**. Don't allow certain kinds of behavior some days and forbid it on others. That just confuses babies.
+ **Don't have too many rules.** Saying something like, "You can tear up any section of the newspaper you want except for the comics," is too complicated for your baby to understand.
+ **Limit the number of warnings**. If you tell your baby no five times, give two "If you do that one more time" warnings and three final warnings, you're telling your baby that it's fine to ignore you at least 9 times.
+ **Give plenty of positive feedback when your baby does something right**. Children receive far more negative comments from their parents than positive ones (estimates vary from 1:3 to 1:48!).

♦ **Be realistic**. Babies are hardwired to explore. And sometimes even though your baby really wants to listen to you, her urges to touch, grab, toss, squish, or drop are too strong.

♦ **Be tolerant of your baby's "negativity."** Your baby's "no"s are an important part of her developing identity. Giving your baby some decision-making control will help her accept the limits you set.

♦ **Spend some serious time trying to figure out what the baby needs**. Research shows that early obedience (in nine-to-twelve-month-olds) is related to the sensitivity of responsiveness to infant signals, not to the frequency of commands or forcible interventions.

♦ **Be a good model**. While setting limits is important, it's really only half the battle. Your baby is learning a huge amount from watching and imitating you. So don't do anything you don't want the baby to do.

Biting, Pinching, and Hitting

For some strange reason, right around their first birthdays, almost all babies go through a phase when they bite and/or hit and/or pinch people—strangers, loved ones, and even animals. (This may be old news to your partner, who may have felt your baby's teeth on her nipples months ago.) If (when) your baby starts, the first thing you need to do is find out why. Your baby may be acting this way because she's:

♦ Trying to express affection (you probably nibble gently on her, and she may simply be trying to imitate you).

♦ Trying to communicate a particular need.

♦ Frustrated that she can't express herself verbally.

♦ Teething and trying to relieve her discomfort.

♦ Simply conducting an experiment to see how others will react.

♦ Tired, overstimulated, or frustrated.

♦ Trying to defend herself or her property.

♦ Imitating an older friend or sibling.

Fortunately, the hitting-and-pinching-and-biting phase usually lasts no longer than a few months (although, when you're getting bitten a few times a day, that can seem like a very long time). Here, however, are a few dos and don'ts that may make this painful period a little shorter:

♦ Don't get angry; it will only make her defensive.

♦ Don't slap or spank.

♦ Don't bite back or have the baby bite herself "to show her what it feels like"; this sets a rotten example and will only reinforce the behavior by implying that it's really okay.

♦ Do remove the baby promptly. If she's sitting on your lap and bites you, put her down for a minute (no longer); if she's hit or bitten someone else, take her away from that person for a minute.

♦ Don't say, "You're bad," or any variation on that theme. Instead say, "*Biting* is bad."

♦ Don't insist on an apology. There's almost no chance that your baby has any idea what regret is or that biting really hurts (babies this age are completely incapable of imagining anything from any other perspective than their own).

♦ Don't overreact. The baby might find your reaction so amusing that she'll bite or hit again just to get your attention.

♦ Do spend some time trying to figure out why your baby is biting or hitting. Is it happening at certain times of the day (right before naptime, for example)? Does she do it only to certain people?

♦ Do rethink your discipline policies. You may be setting so many limits that your baby may be trying to bite her way to freedom.

♦ Do model good behavior. Take your baby's hand and pet the dog (or human) gently while saying, "Nice dog. This is the way we pet a dog. Nice dog."

Weaning Your Baby from Breast or Bottle

Most pediatricians today agree that mothers should breast-feed their babies for as long as possible—generally between six months and a year. What to do after that, however, is the source of far less agreement.

So should your partner stop breast-feeding completely now or gradually phase it out? Should you transition your baby from breast to bottle, or skip the bottle and go directly to cups? And if you've been bottle-feeding from the start, when should you stop? The answers, of course, are up to you, your partner, and your baby.

We're assuming here that your baby is eating at least *some* solid foods in addition to her breast- or bottle-feeding. Eventually, she'll get all her food via cup and utensils, but the process of weaning her completely can take months or even years.

WHY TO WEAN YOUR BABY FROM THE BREAST (OR AT LEAST CUT BACK SOME)

♦ By the time she turns one, your baby will have gotten most of the long-term health benefits from breast-feeding. She's also getting far more emotional nourishment than gastronomic nourishment from nursing. Your partner may decide to nurse for longer, which is fine as long as she realizes that breast milk alone can't satisfy all the baby's needs and may, in fact, suppress her appetite for solids.

♦ The baby may start (or may already be) using the breast as a comfort or sleep aid, thus delaying development of the ability to soothe herself or fall asleep on her own.

♦ A small number of dads feel that enough is enough: their partner's breasts may have been at least partially off-limits for a year, and they feel that it's time to unlatch that baby. They may see their partner's refusal to do so as a kind of slap in the face.

WHY TO WEAN THE BABY FROM THE BOTTLE (OR START CUTTING BACK)

♦ Your baby may fill herself up on liquids so much that she will lose interest in all those solid foods she needs for a well-balanced diet.

♦ Babies who feed from bottles are more susceptible to ear infections and/or tooth decay. Babies usually use bottles when on their backs. In addition, when coming from a bottle, the milk (or juice) can flow even when the baby isn't sucking. Those two factors can combine to leave a pool of liquid in the baby's mouth that could back up into the Eustachian tubes and cause an ear infection. And if the baby's teeth slosh around in that pool long enough, they could rot. Nursing babies are rarely on their backs. Plus, since milk flows into the baby's mouth only when she sucks, the mouth is usually emptied completely with each swallow, thereby reducing the chance of developing either an ear infection or a cavity.

♦ By about fifteen months your baby may begin forming an emotional attachment to her bottle (just as she might to a blanket, thumb, or favorite stuffed animal). Emotional attachments are nice, but breaking an attachment to a bottle will be a lot easier now than in a few months, when the baby starts getting stubborn and contrary.

♦ Some experts believe that overdependence on the bottle can interfere with physical and mental developmental milestones and advise giving it up entirely by eighteen months.

♦ A hint for easing the process of giving up the bottle: If the baby protests her missing bottle, offer her some solid food first. If she's full before starting the bottle, she probably won't be as interested in it and will miss it less when it's gone.

From the Baby's Point of View, the Whole Thing Just Sucks

Babies are born with an intense desire to suck. It's what enables them to get milk out of a breast or bottle when they're only hours or days old. Some babies outgrow their need to suck very early on and will do their sucking only when they're eating. These babies may not have much trouble with the whole weaning process. Others, though, also suck to calm themselves or when they're feeling tired, overwhelmed, lonely, stressed, unloved, or even bored. So if your baby seems to want to suck something, let her—especially if you're taking away the breast or the bottle that has been the source of so much comfort. And don't worry: as I discussed earlier, there's no danger that sucking a pacifier or thumb at this age will hurt your child's teeth in any way.

PERFECTLY GOOD REASONS TO CONTINUE LIMITED BREAST-FEEDING

- The baby likes it.
- Your partner likes it, likes the contact and connection with the baby, and doesn't want to give it up.
- It's more natural, cheaper, and more convenient than prepared food. Although remember, your baby should be moving toward getting most of her nutrition from sources other than your partner's breasts.
- Just because. Whether and how long to nurse can become a very political issue. But the decisions you make regarding your baby should be made with only her best interests in mind. You and your partner know your baby better than anyone, and if the two of you decide that you want the baby to nurse until she's three, go ahead and do it.

MAKING THE SWITCH

On one occasion while my wife was still nursing, she got held up in meetings and couldn't get home to feed the baby. If our daughter had been used to taking a bottle, this wouldn't have been a problem. But I'd only tried once or twice to get her to take a bottle and hadn't put up much of a fight when she'd spit it out. My punishment for having been so lax was that I had to drive twenty miles to my wife's office—with the baby screaming at the top of her lungs—so she could nurse. The moral of the story is: get the baby used to taking a bottle as

---

Temperament Tidbits

How well your baby makes the transition from breast-feeding to bottle-feeding or cups may depend more on her temperament than on any other factor. According to temperament researcher Jim Cameron:

♦ Extremely active toddlers with high frustration tolerance (they aren't easily frustrated) usually wean themselves. They prefer bottles to breast because of the convenience.

♦ Highly active, slow-to-adapt kids also like the independence and convenience of a bottle or cup during the day. But they'll still want to nurse in the morning and at night.

♦ Active kids who don't tolerate frustration as well, however, know that parents are quite helpful in overcoming frustration. To them, giving up nursing means giving up support and help from parents, and they won't be in any hurry to do it.

♦ Slow-adapting kids see the breast as security and won't want to give it up without a fight, especially at night. A gradual phaseout is particularly important for these kids.

♦ Moderately high-energy, high-adjustability kids wean themselves naturally.

♦ Kids who are moderately high in activity level and moderately low in frustration tolerance are fairly ambivalent about weaning. They'll generally take their direction from you and your partner.

---

early as possible (but not before she's completely comfortable with the breast). Here are some things you can do to get even the most committed breast feeder to give the bottle a try:

♦ Use smaller bottles and nipples. Keep experimenting until you find a size and style the baby likes. If she's got a pacifier, try a bottle nipple that is shaped like the one on her pacifier.

♦ When introducing the bottle, hold the baby in the position she's in for breast-feeding.

♦ Ease the transition by filling bottles or cups with expressed breast milk. Some women find pumping very painful, so leave this one up to your partner.

♦ Go slow. Introduce the bottle for a few minutes at first, then add a minute or two every day.

♦ Phase the breasts out gradually. Kids tend to be more attached to the morning and evening nursings, so start by eliminating your baby's midday feed-

ing(s) first and replace it with a bottle, some solid food, or both. If that goes
well for a few days, drop the morning feeding next. Of course, exceptions
can be made: we dropped the evening feeding first because our daughters
were getting up at five in the morning to eat anyway. But do what works best
for your partner and your baby. A lot of moms have trouble giving up the last
evening feeding because it's been a special time for her and the baby to

Introduction to Potty Training

Have you heard the one about the kid who was toilet-trained at eight
months? If you haven't, you will soon. But prepare yourself: it isn't a
joke—or at least, it isn't supposed to be one. People will tell you all sorts
of things about the babies they knew who were out of diapers before they
could walk. But no matter what anyone says, or how much you might want
to believe the stories, they're really just urban nursery legends.

First of all, there's really no such thing as potty training; your child
will learn to use the toilet on her own only when she's ready. And at eight
months or even a year, she's simply incapable of controlling her bowels
or bladder. Sure, she may grunt and groan while producing a bowel
movement, and everyone in the house (except her, of course) will be able
to smell it, but she has no idea there's any connection between the feeling she gets when she's filling a diaper and the actual contents. If
anybody's being "trained" at this age, it's the parents, who may have
learned to recognize their baby's signals and rush her to the toilet. But
rest assured, the baby can't do it on her own.

At about fifteen months your baby will begin associating what's in her
diaper with herself and may announce from time to time that she's pro-
duced something. But only after the fact. At eighteen months she may
occasionally announce that she is about to do something, but she still
hasn't learned how to hold it in long enough to get to a toilet. For the best
results, unless your child is extremely interested, wait until she's at least
two before seriously starting to "train" her.

In the meantime, however, you *can* help increase your child's awareness of what's going on in her diapers by talking about the process as it's
happening. As you're changing her, show the baby what she's done, but
don't emphasize the yuckiness of it. Instead, say something admiring,
like, "Hey, that's a pretty impressive load—someday you'll do this in the
toilet like me and Mommy."

Screening Your Baby's Entertainment

I've talked throughout this book about the fantastic benefits of reading to your child. But as your baby gets older, she'll get more and more of her information from other sources, in particular, television, videos, and computers. In principle, there's nothing wrong with any of those things. There are several great shows out there for very young children and some excellent videos as well, including *Baby Einstein*, which my younger daughter loved. But there are two enormous problems.

First, electronic screens too often become either a quick-and-easy babysitter or a substitute for love and nurturing. A number of studies report that children watch a huge amount of television. One done in 2003 at the Children's Hospital Medical Center of Cincinnati found that 40 percent of children under three watch at least three hours of television a day. Even worse, a third of children live in a home where the television is on all the time—even if no one's watching. And a quarter of children under two actually have a television in their own room.

Second, most of the time babies are exposed to television, they're not watching age-appropriate programming. Instead, they're watching something with their parents or an older sibling. A significant amount of recent research has shown that even babies as young as 10 to 12 months are influenced by the behavior of the characters they see on television. The solution? There are several:

♦ If there's a television in your baby's room, take it out.
♦ Make sure that whatever your baby watches is made specifically for babies. You may love Hitchcock films but watch them after your baby is down for the night.
♦ Watch with your baby. Use the time to cuddle and to talk about what's on the screen. The Parents Television Council (www.parentstv.org) has extensive listings and reviews.

bond. And if nursing has been part of the bedtime routine, your baby may not want to give up that last feeding quite yet.

♦ A tip: Make sure your partner is out of the house (or at least out of sight in another room) when you're trying to give the baby a bottle. If your partner (actually, her breasts) are within smelling distance, your baby may refuse the bottle.
♦ A warning: The American Academy of Pediatrics suggests not starting your baby on cow's milk until after the baby's first birthday. When you do finally

switch to milk, start with *whole* milk. Your baby needs the fat in it for healthy brain development.

♦ A final note: Don't try to wean your baby in one day—it could be traumatic to both your partner and the baby. So take your time and do it over the course of a few weeks or months.

When Not to Wean Your Baby

No matter how old your baby is or how long she's been breast- or bottle-feeding, there are a few really rotten times to try to wean her:

♦ When any impending or recent major transition might make the baby feel vulnerable, out of control, and in need of extra parental support. Moving to a new home, the birth of a younger sibling or the announcement of pregnancy, a new babysitter, and starting day care are good examples.

♦ If the baby has been sick.

♦ If you or your partner are under some kind of extreme pressure.

♦ If the baby is teething.

Family Matters

Ch-Ch-Ch-Changing Relationships

Considering how small and helpless babies are, it's sometimes surprising just how much of an impact they can have on the lives of the adults around them. Just think, for example, about how different things are for you now compared to your prefatherhood life.

Babies create new relationships in people's lives simply by being born: you and your partner have gone from being children to being parents, your parents are now grandparents, your brothers and sisters are uncles and aunts, and so on. And naturally, those relationships (as well as the rights and responsibilities that go with them) will take some getting used to.

But perhaps babies' greatest power is their ability to change profoundly relationships that had existed long before they were born. They can re-unite families and mend old wounds, or they can open new ones. They can even change the nature of your friendships. Here are a few ways this might play out.

Your Changing Relationship with Your Partner

"Most couples approach parenthood imagining the new baby will bring them closer together, giving them a new and deeper sense of 'us,'" writes researcher

Jay Belsky. For most families, things ultimately work out this way. But Belsky found that in the early stages of parenthood a new baby "tends to push his mother and father apart by revealing the hidden and half-hidden differences in their relationship."

In previous chapters I've talked a lot about some of the ways that having a baby might strain your relationship with your partner. So let's spend a little time focusing on some of the very positive ways the baby can affect your life and your relationship with your partner.

♦ You may feel a sense of gratitude to the baby for enabling you to feel what it's like to be loved and to love more deeply than you ever have before.

♦ For some men, having a baby is like having a great new toy and may give you a chance to relive certain parts of your childhood.

♦ The baby may bring you and your partner closer together and may make the two of you feel more deeply committed to the marriage and to making it work. You now also have someone to pass along new and old family traditions to.

♦ The baby may give you and your partner a sense of tremendous pride at having jointly created something absolutely amazing.

Parent/Grandparent Relationships

THE GOOD . . .

♦ After their first child is born, most men feel closer to their parents, especially their fathers. Even those who don't feel closer are usually at least willing to end, or put behind them, long-running family disputes.

♦ Seeing your parents in action with your child may bring back happy memories of your own childhood. You may also be pleasantly surprised at how your parents have changed since you were young. The father who may not have had much time for you, for example, may now spend hours with his grandchild. And the mother who limited your junk food intake to half a stick of sugarless gum a week may be a little more relaxed now.

♦ Now that you know exactly how much work it is to be a parent, you may be a bit more appreciative of what your own parents did—and sacrificed—for you.

♦ After all these years of being a child, you're in charge now; if they want to be with the baby, they'll have to do things your way.

♦ You'll develop a closer relationship with your in-laws.

"Do you remember any of those things people said we'd tell our grandkids someday?"

THE BAD . . .

♦ Seeing your parents in action with your child may bring back unhappy memories of your own childhood. And if your parents are treating the baby differently (i.e. better) than they treated you, you may be jealous, wondering where all that love was when you were a kid.

♦ Your parents may not be supportive or accepting of your increased role in your child's life.

♦ They may want to assume a role in your child's life—either too involved or not involved enough—that you aren't happy with. Grandparents are free to love their grandchildren without any of the restrictions of parenthood, says psychologist Brad Sachs.

♦ There may be some friction between your parenting style and that of your parents, between the way you react to the baby's needs and the way they do. It's not uncommon to hear from parents statements such as, "I did a pretty good job of raising my own kids, so don't tell me how to . . ." or "Don't you think it's time she (your partner) stopped nursing that child?"

♦ If you think they did a lousy job as parents, you may be afraid of repeating their mistakes.

♦ If your parents live nearby, they may always be "in the neighborhood," and you might be seeing them more than you really care to. At the same time, they might resent it if you're too dependent on them for child care.

♦ There may be disputes and power struggles between your parents and your partner's about their grandparental roles.

However your relationship with your parents and/or in-laws changes, remember this: "A loving and vigorous bond between the grandparent and grandchild," writes Sachs, "is not just related to, but essential to, the emotional health and stability of all three generations."

Other Relationships

You may not realize it at first, but you and your partner will gradually find that your relationships with friends and other non-immediate family members have changed.

♦ You may be interested (or at least more interested than you were before becoming a parent) in getting together with relatives your own age, especially those with kids, so that the next generation can get to know their cousins.

♦ Similarly, your circle of close friends will gradually change to include more couples, especially couples with kids.

♦ You and your partner aren't going to be nearly as available for last-minute movies or double dates, and you might not be quite as happy to have friends drop by unannounced.

♦ Your new, less spontaneous lifestyle may affect your relationships with your single male friends most of all. Having a new baby probably means fewer all-night poker games. Your buddies may stop calling you because they think you're too busy or not interested in hanging out with them anymore. Or you might stop calling them because seeing their relatively carefree and obligation-free lives may make you jealous.

♦ While your child is young, she'll be happy to play with whomever you introduce her to, and her first friends are most likely going to be your friends' kids. But as she gets older and starts showing an interest in other children and making friends of her own, she'll take on a more active role in the family social committee. And all of a sudden you'll find yourself socializing with her friends' parents.

♦ Relationships between you and other adults may continue longer than they otherwise might because the kids like playing together.

♦ Relationships can be subtly—or not so subtly—affected by competition. Let's face it: we all want our children to be the biggest, smartest, fastest, cutest, and funniest, and it's only natural (especially for guys) to get a little competitive.

♦ Friends or relatives with children who are older than yours might start getting on your nerves by insisting on telling you every single thing they think you're doing wrong as a parent.

♦ As with your parents and in-laws, some friends or relatives may be disdainful or unsupportive of your taking an active, involved role in your baby's life, falling back on the old stereotype that men should leave the parenting stuff up to their wives or that putting your family first could have a negative impact on your career.

Here are a few things you can do to smooth out some of the bumps in your changing relationships with friends and family:

♦ **Watch what you say.** No matter how much people without kids pretend, there's a limit to how much they really want to hear about all the exciting things (to you, anyway) that your baby can do or how many times she filled her diaper today.

♦ **Learn to accept change.** It may seem harsh, but the fact is that you may lose some friends (and they'll lose you) now that you're a parent. But you'll gain plenty of new ones in the process.

♦ **Don't listen to everything everyone else tells you.** Whatever they know about taking care of children they learned on the job. And that's how you're learning too.

♦ **Watch the competition.** If your friend's baby crawls, walks, talks, sings, says "da-da," or gets a modeling contract or an early-admissions preschool acceptance letter before your baby does, you may find yourself more than a little envious. But you know that your baby is the best one in the world. Go ahead and let them delude themselves into thinking that theirs is. Why burst their bubble?

Going Public with Fatherhood

In the concluding chapter of *The Expectant Father*, I painted a rather gloomy portrait of the ways men and women—both individually and collectively as a society—actively discourage men from getting involved with their children.

Baby's First Birthday Party

Let's get one thing straight: your baby's first birthday party is really more for you than for her. She won't help you put together the guest list, she's too little to play Pin the Tail on the Donkey or to bob for apples, and she'll probably be more interested in the wrapping paper than what's inside it. Still, it's a major event for the whole family. Here are a couple of first birthday dos and don'ts:

♦ Don't knock yourself out planning special activities. At this age your baby will prefer the familiar to the new almost every time. Save the piñatas for a few years on—the last thing you want is a bunch of kids running around your house swinging broom handles or baseball bats.

♦ Don't invite too many kids—two or three is plenty. And limit the adults to six or seven. Any more and you run the risk of overwhelming the baby. If you're inviting other adults with children, make sure they stay to take care of their own.

♦ Do a quick childproofing sweep of the area where the party will take place. The house may be perfectly safe for your baby, but not safe enough to stand up to the invasion of a horde of toddlers.

♦ Don't make a huge cake (unless the adults plan to eat it). And don't serve any choking foods—popcorn, peanuts, small candies, even carrot sticks.

♦ Save the clowns, magicians, and masks for next year or the year after. Kids under two or three are more often scared by masks and magic than entertained.

♦ Keep the party short (no more than an hour and a half) and try not to have it overlap with nap or sleep times or any other time when your baby tends to be cranky.

♦ Don't go overboard on gifts. And don't demand or even expect wild declarations of thanks or any other great performances for the cameras. It's just not going to happen.

♦ Give identical party favors to any other child guests. Make sure your baby gets one as well.

♦ If you have older children, include them as much as you can. Even

Sadly, very little has changed. Men still don't get enough of the support and encouragement they so sorely need to assume a greater nurturing role.

Fortunately, though, more and more men are expressing their dissatisfaction though your baby doesn't know what's going on, your other children do, and they can get very jealous. So have them help you design the birthday cake, put together the menu, and select the music. Also let each of them invite a special guest of their own.

♦ Get special presents for your older children. Their world has changed a lot over the past year, and you should acknowledge it.

♦ Keep a list (or have someone else do it) of who gave what so you can send thank-yous later.

After the party, try to devote some time to reminiscing—and taking notes—about your baby's first year. When you think about it, she's come a tremendously long way—so long that it's hard to remember the way things were twelve short months ago. To start with, she's about 50 percent longer and three times as heavy as she was at birth. She's gone from crying as her only means of communication to being able to make specific requests with words or gestures. She's progressed from being a collection of almost random twitches and jerks to being able to move around wherever she wants. All in all, she's just like a real person, only smaller.

Do you remember when your baby made her first noncrying noise and her first nongas smile? When did you first feel that she loved you? When did she first look at you with true recognition? When did she start using a spoon, crawling, taking her first steps, sleeping through the night? It's so easy to forget these milestones, so write down as many as you and your partner can think of, and try to collect some baby-related anecdotes from friends and family. You might want to put all of this in a scrapbook or a time capsule that you can open up when your baby is older.

Once all the guests have gone home, the mess is cleaned up, and the baby is down for the night, pop open a bottle of champagne with your partner and drink a toast to each other. You've got plenty to celebrate too! In a lot of ways you've grown and developed as much as your baby has. You've found child care and endured sleepless nights, sibling rivalries, and work-family conflicts. And you've gone from being tentative and worried that you wouldn't know what to do, to confident and competent.

with this Neanderthal status quo and are taking a far more active role in their children's lives. Of course, some of this may be happening because of economic necessity: more and more mothers are entering the workplace, and

*"My father wakes up the sun every morning.
What does your father do?"*

someone else has to step in to share the child-care burden. But in my view, the more significant reason for the nurturing-father revolution has to do with men themselves.

Most men, especially those whose fathers were physically or emotionally absent, instinctively know what they missed when they were young. And just as they know they were deprived of a relationship with their fathers, they know that their fathers were deprived of relationships with them. The real measure of a man's commitment to a new kind of relationship with his kids is how he feels about being a father and about the impact fatherhood is having on his life.

In one major study, researchers found that fathers generally see fathering as an important and satisfying experience. They disagree that only mothers should be responsible for discipline or for caring for a sick child; instead, they consider parenting a partnership experience to be shared equally with their wives.

Clearly, things are changing for fathers—perhaps not as quickly as we would like, but they are changing. At hospitals around the country, almost as many men as women are attending new-parent classes; the number of stay-at-home dads is growing; more and more dads' groups are starting; and seeing dads out in the middle of the day with their children or bringing them to the office is raising fewer and fewer eyebrows.

Still, far too many men continue to undervalue the importance of the role they play in their children's lives. Too many children have missed having a relationship with their fathers, and too many fathers have missed having relationships with their children.

As a new father, you are in a unique position to break this cycle and to make the word *fatherhood* as synonymous with child-rearing and nurturing as *motherhood*. And there's no better time to start than right now.

For most new fathers, the last few months of their first year as parents are a time of relative calm. They've dealt with the big emotional, professional, and personal hurdles of fatherhood and are now comfortably juggling their roles as husband, father, provider, and son. In short, they're finally feeling "like a family," and are entering what my colleague Bruce Linton calls the "community phase" of fatherhood.

This is a time when many new dads feel ready to socialize—along with their partners and children—with other families, and use their fatherhood as a way to participate more actively in the public domain. They typically take on a more active role in their churches or synagogues, and they experience a heightened sense of public responsibility. Issues such as the quality of schools, city planning and zoning, the environment, and public safety become much more pressing than before.

In the introduction to this book, I quoted author Michael Levine, who said that "having children makes you no more a parent than having a piano makes you a pianist." Well, at this point you may not be any closer to being a pianist than you were a year ago. But there's no doubt that you're a father. And a pretty good one, at that.

Notes:

Selected
Bibliography

Books

Acredolo, Linda, and Susan Goodwyn. *Baby Signs: How to Talk with Your Baby Before Your Baby Can Talk.* New York: McGraw-Hill, 2002.

Akhtar, Salman, and Selma Kramer, eds. *The Seasons of Life: Separation-Individuation Perspectives.* Northvale, N.J.: Jason Aronson, 1997.

Ames, Louise Bates, and Carol Chase Haber. *Your One Year Old: The Fun-Loving, Fussy 12- to 24-Month-Old.* New York: Delta, 1982.

Ambert, Anne-Marie. *The Effect of Children on Parents.* New York: Hayworth Press, 2001.

Austrian, Sonia G., ed. *Developmental Theories through the Life Cycle.* New York: Columbia University Press, 2002.

Barry, Dave. *Bad Habits.* New York: Henry Holt, 1985.

Batten, Mary. *Hey, Daddy: Animal Fathers and Their Babies.* Atlanta: Peachtree, 2002.

Belsky, Jay, and John Kelly. *The Transition to Parenthood: How a First Child Changes a Marriage: Why Some Couples Grow Closer and Others Apart.* New York: Delacorte, 1994.

Bettelheim, Bruno. *A Good Enough Parent: A Book on Child-Rearing.* New York: Vintage, 1987.

Biller, Henry B. *Fathers and Families: Paternal Factors in Child Development.* Westport, Conn.: Auburn House, 1993.

Biller, Henry B., and Robert J. Trotter. *The Father Factor: What You Need to Know to Make a Difference.* New York: Pocket, 1994.

Bluestine, Eric. *The Ways Children Learn Music: An Introduction and Practical Guide to Music Learning Theory.* Chicago: GIA, 1995.

Brazelton, T. Berry, and Bertrand Cramer. *The Earliest Relationship: Parents,*

Infants, and the Drama of Early Attachment. Reading, Mass.: Addison-Wesley, 1990.

Bronstein, Phyllis, and Carolyn Pape Cowan, eds. *Fatherhood Today: Men's Changing Role in the Family.* New York: John Wiley & Sons, 1988.

Britton, James. *Language and Learning: The Importance of Speech in Children's Development.* New York: Penguin, 1970.

Brott, Armin. *Father for Life: A Journey of Joy, Challenge, and Change.* New York: Abbeville Press, 2003.

Brott, Armin, and Jennifer Ash. *The Expectant Father: Facts, Tips, and Advice for Dads-to-Be,* 2d ed. New York: Abbeville Press, 2002.

Caplan, Frank, ed. *The First Twelve Months of Life.* New York: Grosset & Dunlap, 1973.

Carnoy, Martin, and David Carnoy. *Fathers of a Certain Age: The Joys and Problems of Middle-Aged Fatherhood.* Minneapolis: Fairview Press, 1997.

Cath, Stanley H. *Father and Child: Developmental and Clinical Perspectives.* Hillsdale, N.J.: Analytic Press, 1994.

Cowan, Carolyn Pape, and Philip A. Cowan. *When Partners Become Parents: The Big Life Change for Couples.* New York: HarperCollins, 1992.

Cullinan, Bernice E., and Lee Galda. *Cullinan and Galda's Literature and the Child With Infotrac.* College ed. Belmont, Calif.: Wadsworth Publishing, 2001.

Daniels, Marilyn. *Dancing with Words: Signing for Hearing Children's Literacy.* South Hadley, Mass.: Bergin & Garvey, 2001.

Drobeck, Bruce. "The Impact on Men of the Transition to Fatherhood: A Phenomenological Investigation." Ph.D. Diss., Texas Woman's University, 1990.

Finley, G. E. *Adoptive and Biological Fathers' Enjoyment of First-time Fathering.* Minneapolis, Minn.: National Council on Family Relations, 1999.

Flint Public Library. *Ring a Ring O'Roses: Finger Plays for Pre-School Children.* Flint, Mich.: Flint Public Library, n.d.

Fraiberg, Selma H. *The Magic Years: Understanding and Handling the Problems of Early Childhood.* New York: Scribner's, 1959.

Fox, Mem. *Reading Magic: Why Reading Aloud to Our Children Will Change Their Lives Forever.* San Diego: Harcourt, 2001.

Garcia, Joseph. *Sign With Your Baby: How to Communicate With Infants Before They Can Speak.* Seattle: Northlight, 2002.

Gordon, Edwin E. *A Music Learning Theory for Newborn and Young Children.* Chicago: GIA, 1990.

Greenspan, Stanley, and Nancy Thorndike Greenspan. *First Feelings: Milestones in the Emotional Development of Your Baby and Child.* New York: Penguin, 1985.

Hass, Aaron. *The Gift of Fatherhood: How Men's Lives Are Transformed by Their Children.* New York: Fireside, 1994.

Hoare, Carol Hren Erikson. *On Development in Adulthood: New Insights from the Unpublished Papers.* London: Oxford University Press, 2002.

Jacob, S. H. *Your Baby's Mind.* Holbrook, Mass.: Bob Adams, 1991.

Jordan, Pamela L. "The Mother's Role in Promoting Fathering Behavior." In *Becoming a Father: Contemporary Social, Developmental, and Clinical Perspectives,* edited by J. L. Shapiro et al., pp. 61–71. New York: Springer, 1995.

Karen, Robert. *Becoming Attached: Unfolding the Mystery of the Infant-Mother Bond and Impact on Later Life.* New York: Warner, 1994.

Kitzinger, S. *The Experience of Breastfeeding.* Middlesex, England: Penguin, 1987.

Lamb, Michael E., ed. *The Role of the Father in Child Development.* New York: John Wiley, 1996.

Leach, Penelope. *Your Baby and Child: From Birth to Age Five.* New York: Knopf, 1997.

Lehane, Stephen. *Help Your Baby Learn: 100 Piaget-Based Activities for the First Two Years of Life.* New York: Prentice Hall, 1976.

Linton, Bruce. "The Phases of Paternal Development: Pregnancy Through Twelve Months Post-Partum." Ph.D. diss., University of the Pacific–Stockton, Calif., 1991.

Marino, Jane, and Dorothy F. Houlihan. *Mother Goose Time: Library Programs for Babies and Their Caregivers.* New York: H. W. Wilson, 1992.

Meyer, Donald J. *Uncommon Fathers: Reflections on Raising a Child with a Disability.* Bethesda, Md.: Woodbine House, 1995.

Minnesota Fathering Alliance. *Working with Fathers: Methods and Perspectives.* Stillwater, Minn.: nu ink unlimited, 1992.

Needleman, Robert. *Dr. Spock's Baby Basics: Take Charge Parenting Guides.* New York: Pocket, 2003.

Newman, Barbara M., and Philip R. Newman. *Development Through Life: A Psychosocial Approach,* 6th ed. Pacific Grove, Calif.: Brooks/Cole, 1994.

Noller, Patricia, Judith A. Feeney, and Candida Peterson. *Personal Relationships across the Lifespan.* Philadelphia: Psychology Press/Taylor & Francis, 2001.

Odean, Kathleen. *Great Books for Babies and Toddlers.* New York: Ballantine, 2003.

Palkovitz, Rob. *Involved Fathering and Men's Adult Development: Provisional Balances.* Mahawah, N.J.: Lawrence Erlbaum, 2002.

Parke, Ross D. *Fatherhood.* Cambridge, Mass.: Harvard University Press, 1996.

Pleck, Joseph H. "Are 'Family Supportive' Employer Policies Relevant to Men?" In *Men, Work, and Family,* edited by Jane C. Hood, pp. 217–237. Newbury Park, Calif.: Sage, 1993.

Pruett, Kyle. *Fatherneed: Why Father Care Is as Essential as Mother Care for Your Child.* New York: Free Press, 2000.

Sachs, Brad E. *Things Just Haven't Been the Same: Making the Transition from Marriage to Parenthood.* New York: William Morrow, 1992.

Sheehy, Gail. *Understanding Men's Passages: Discovering the New Map of Men's Lives.* New York: Random House, 1998.

Snarey, John. *How Fathers Care for the Next Generation: A Four-Decade Study.* Cambridge, Mass.: Harvard University Press, 1993.

Spangler, Doug. *Fatherhood: An Owner's Manual.* Richmond, Calif.: Fabus, 1994.

Trelease, Jim. *The Read-Aloud Handbook,* 5th ed. New York: Penguin, 2001.

Ulene, Art, and Steven Shelov. *Discovery Play: Loving and Learning with Your Baby.* Berkeley, Calif.: Ulysses Press, 1994.

Unell, Barbara, and Jerry L. Wykoff. *The Eight Seasons of Parenthood: How the Stages of Parenting Constantly Reshape our Adult Identities.* New York: Random House, 2000.

Weissbluith, Mark. *Healthy Sleep Habits, Happy Child.* New York: Ballantine, 2003.

White, Burton L. *The New First Three Years of Life.* New York: Fireside, 1995.

Journal Articles

Bailey, William T. "Fathers' Involvement and Responding to Infants: 'More' May Not be 'Better.'" *Psychological Reports* 74 (1994): 92–94.

———. "Psychological Development in Men: Generativity and Involvement with Young Children." *Psychological Reports* 71 (1992): 929–30.

Baumrind, Diana. "Current Patterns of Parental Authority." *Developmental Psychology Monograph* 4, no. 1, part 1 (1971): 1–101.

Brookes, Helen, et al. "Three-Month-Old Infants Learn Arbitrary Auditory–Visual Pairings between Voices and Faces." *Infant and Child Development* 10 (2001): 75–82.

Children's Defense Fund. "Overview of Child Care, Early Education, and School-Age Care." *1999 Key Facts.* www.childrensdefense.org/pdf/99_overview.pdf.

Cohn, Deborah A., et al. "Working Models of Childhood Attachment and Couple Relationships." *Journal of Family Issues* 13, no. 4 (1992): 432–49.

Condry, John, and Sandra Condry. "Sex Differences: A Study of the Eye of the Beholder." *Child Development* 47 (1976): 812–19.

Condry, John, and David F. Ross. "Sex and Aggression: The Influence of Gender Label on the Perception of Aggression in Children." *Child Development* 56 (1985): 225–33.

DeLuccie, Mary F. "Mothers as Gatekeepers: A Model of Maternal Mediators of Father Involvement." *Journal of Genetic Psychology* 156, no. 1 (1994): 115–31.

Dickstein, Susan, and Ross D. Parke. "Social Referencing in Infancy: A Glance at Fathers and Marriage." *Child Development* 59 (1988): 506–11.

Draghi-Lorenz, Riccardo. "Jealousy in the First Year: Evidence of Early Interpersonal Awareness." Unpublished paper, presented at the conference of the British Psychological Society's Developmental Section, September 1997.

Fagot, Beverly, and Richard Hagan. "Observations of Parent Reactions to Sex-Stereotyped Behaviors: Age and Sex Effects." *Child Development* 62 (1991): 617–28.

Field, Tiffany, S. Schanberg, et al. "Tactile/Kinesthetic Stimulation Effects on Preterm Neonates." *Pediatrics* 77, no. 5 (1986): 654–58.

Fishman, Elizabeth A., and Steven A. Meyers. "Marital Satisfaction and Child Adjustment: Direct and Mediated Pathways." *Contemporary Family Therapy* 22, no. 4 (2000): 437–52.

Freiberg, Kate, Kim Tually, and Boris Crassini. "Use of an Auditory Looming Task to Test Infants' Sensitivity to Sound Pressure Level as an Auditory Distance Cue." *British Journal of Developmental Psychology* 19 (2001): 1–10.

Gambill, Lionel. "Can More Touching Lead to Less Violence in Our Society?" *Human Touch* 1, no. 3 (1985): 1–3.

Goldbloom, Richard B. "Behavior and Allergy: Myth or Reality?" *Pediatrics in Review* 13, no. 8 (1992): 312–13.

Hall, Wendy A. "New Fatherhood: Myths and Realities." *Public Health Nursing* 11, no. 4 (1994): 219–28.

Jewett, Don L., et al. "A Double-Blind Study of Symptom Provocation to Determine Food Sensitivity." *New England Journal of Medicine* 323, no. 7 (1990): 429–33.

Jordan, Pamela L. "Laboring for Relevance: Expectant and New Fatherhood." *Nursing Research* 39, no. 1 (1990): 11–16.

Jordan, Pamela L., et al. "Breastfeeding and Fathers: Illuminating the Darker Side." *Birth* 19, no. 4 (1990): 210–13.

———. "Supporting the Father When an Infant is Breastfed." *Journal of Human Lactation* 9, no. 1 (1993): 31–34.

Krupper, Jan C., and Ina C. Uzgiris. "Fathers' and Mothers' Speech to Young Infants." *Journal of Psycholinguistic Research* 16, no. 6 (1987): 597–614.

Lamme, Linda, and Athol B. Packer. "Bookreading Behaviors of Infants." *Reading Teacher* 39, no. 6 (1986): 504–9.

Lovestone, S., and R. Kumar. "Postnatal Psychiatric Illness: The Impact of Partners." British Journal of Psychiatry 163 (1993): 210–16.

McBride, B. A., and G. Mills. "A Comparison of Mother and Father Involvement with Their Preschool Age Children." *Early Childhood Research Quarterly* 8 (1993): 457–77.

MacDonald, Kevin, and Ross D. Parke. "Parent-Child Physical Play: The Effects of Sex and Age of Children and Parents." *Sex Roles* 15, nos. 7–8 (1986): 367–78.

McKenna, James J., and Sara Mosko. "Evolution and Infant Sleep: An Experimental Study of Infant-Parent Co-Sleeping and Its Implications for SIDS." *ACTA Paediatrica: An International Journal of Paediatrics* 82, supplement 389 (June 1993): 31–35.

Medoff, David, and Charles E. Schaefer. "Children Sharing the Parental Bed: A Review of the Advantages and Disadvantages of Cosleeping." *Psychology: A Journal of Human Behavior* 30, no. 1 (1993): 1–9.

Mumme, Donna, and Anne Fernald. "The Infant as Onlooker: Learning from Emotional Reactions Observed in a Television Scenario." *Child Development* 74, no. 1 (2003): 221–237.

Neville, B., R.D. Parke. "Waiting for Paternity: Interpersonal and Contextual Implications of the Timing of Fatherhood." *Sex Roles* 37, nos. 1–2 (1997): 45–61.

Nicolson, P. "A Brief Report of Women's Expectations of Men's Behaviour in the Transition to Parenthood: Contradictions and Conflicts for Counselling Psychology Practice." *Counselling Psychology Quarterly* 3, no. 4 (1990): 353–61.

Palkovitz, Rob, Marcella A. Copes, and Tara N. Woolfolk. "'It's Like . . . You Discover a New Sense of Being': Involved Fathering as an Evoker of Adult Development." *Men and Masculinities* 4, no. 1 (2001): 49–69.

Palm, G. "Involved Fatherhood: A Second Chance." *Journal of Men's Studies* 2 (1993): 139–54.

Palm, G., and Bill Joyce. "Attachment from a Father's Perspective." *Typescript*, 1994.

Papousek, Mechthild, et al. "Didactic Adjustments in Fathers' and Mothers' Speech to Their Three-Month-Old Infants." *Journal of Psycholinguistic Research* 16, no. 5 (1987): 491–516.

Power, Thomas G., et al. "Compliance and Self-Assertion: Young Children's Responses to Mothers versus Fathers." *Developmental Psychology* 30, no. 6 (1994): 980–89.

Rauscher, Frances, et al. "Music Training Causes Long-Term Enhancement of Preschool Children's Spatial-Temporal Reasoning." *Neurological Research* 19 (February 1997).

Sorce, James F., et al. "Maternal Emotional Signaling: Its Effect on the Visual Cliff Behavior of 1-Year-Olds." *Developmental Psychology* 21, no. 1 (1985): 195–200.

Whaley, Kimberlee K. "The Emergence of Social Play in Infancy: A Proposed Developmental Sequence of Infant-Adult Social Play." *Early Childhood Research Quarterly* 5, no. 3 (1990): 347–58.

Whitehurst, G. J., et al. "Accelerating Language Development Through Picture Book Reading." *Developmental Psychology* 24, no. 4 (1988): 552–59.

Wilson, Andrea C., et al. "Relation of Infant Diet to Childhood Health: Seven Year Follow-Up of Cohort of Children in Dundee Infant Feeding Study." *British Medical Journal*, no. 316 (1998): 21–25.

Resources

Adoption

NATIONAL ADOPTION CENTER offers a great list of questions to ask adoption agencies; addresses tax, single-parent, and legal issues; provides photos of kids waiting to be adopted, book reviews, lists of state and local contacts, and links to other adoption-related organizations.

Tel.: (800) TO-ADOPT
e-mail: nac@adopt.org
www.adopt.org

Advice, General

There are literally dozens of parenting resources out there for new parents. Among my favorites are:

BABYCENTER
www.babycenter.com
I do a chat the first Tuesday of every month at 9:30 p.m. EST.

PARENTSPLACE.COM has one of the largest clearinghouses of parenting advice on the Net.
www.parentsplace.com

iPARENTING.COM
www.iparenting.com

MR. DAD is my Web site.
www.mrdad.com

PREGNANCY AND BABY
www.pregnancyandbaby.com

At-Home Dads

SLOWLANE.COM is the most comprehensive resource for stay-at-home dads and primary caregiving dads. They have news, articles, advice, and a fantastic listing of dads' groups across the country.

www.slowlane.com

CINCINNATI AT-HOME-DADS is an active group of stay-at-home dads. Besides being a great resource for dads in the Cincinnati area, they have a nice listing of other groups in states east of the Mississippi.

www.cincinnatidads.com for the group itself

www.cincinnatidads.com/more_dads_groups.htm for the listing

Babies, Health Issues

AMERICAN ACADEMY OF PEDIATRICS has one of the biggest collections of resources for parents who need basic information fast on everything from colic and treating diaper rash to sleep problems and introducing solid foods.

www.aap.org

THE ASSOCIATION FOR CHILDREN WITH DOWN SYNDROME trains and educates children with Down syndrome.

www.acds.org

BIRTH DEFECT RESEARCH, INC. has information, books, and links on birth defects, and provides support and referrals for parents.

www.birthdefects.org

KIDS HEALTH has a full range of doctor-approved information.

www.kidshealth.org

THE NATIONAL FATHERS' NETWORK is devoted to supporting fathers (and families) who are raising children with special health-care needs and developmental disabilities.

Tel.: (206) 747-4004

www.fathersnetwork.org

See also Advice, General. Most of the Web sites listed there also have experts who can answer questions on any topic you can think of.

Babies, Premature

PREEMIEPARENTS.COM is a well-stocked collection of articles, books, links, and resources for parents of preemies.

www.preemieparents.com

WWW.PREEMIES.ORG is a community of parents of preemies, with chats, mailing lists, and other resources.

www.preemies.org

Child Care

CHILD CARE AWARE is a nationwide campaign created to help parents identify quality child care in their communities.

Tel.: (800) 424-2246

www.childcareaware.org

NANNYTAX, INC. will take care of all your payroll needs for nannies and sitters.

Tel.: (888) 626-6982

www.nannytax.com

BREEDLOVE AND ASSOCIATES is another payroll servce.

Tel.: (888) BREEDLOVE

www.breedlove-online.com

THE NATIONAL RESOURCE CENTER FOR HEALTH AND SAFETY IN CHILD CARE is a wonderful general resource. Plus, it has a listing of child-care regulations for all 50 states.

Tel.: (800) 598-KIDS

nrc.uchsc.edu

UNITED STATES DEPARTMENT OF STATE manages the au pair program.

exchanges.state.gov/education/jexchanges/private/aupair.htm

Death and Grief

AMERICAN SIDS INSTITUTE

Tel.: (800) 232-7437

e-mail: prevent@sids.org

www.sids.org

SIDS ALLIANCE

www.sidsalliance.org

Tel.: (800) 221-7437

SIDS NETWORK
  e-mail: sidsnet1@sids-network.org
  sids-network.org

All three organizations offer great resources, information, references, and support to help parents and other surviving family members deal with the tragedy of the death of a child.

Fatherhood, General

DADS AND DAUGHTERS is a nonprofit membership organization for fathers with daughters.
  www.dadsanddaughters.org

THE FAMILIES AND WORK INSTITUTE is a nonprofit research organization focusing on work-family issues.
  www.familiesandwork.org

THE FATHERHOOD PROJECT is a national research and education project that is examining the future of fatherhood and developing ways to support men's involvement in child-rearing. Books, films, and seminars.
  www.fatherhoodproject.org

FATHERSWORLD.COM offers a huge listing of resources on many aspects of fatherhood.
  www.fathersworld.com/resources/index.html

FATHERVILLE.COM has lots of articles by dads for dads about fatherhood
  www.fatherville.com

MR. DAD has many of my articles and columns on all aspects of fatherhood.
  www.mrdad.com

THE NATIONAL CENTER FOR FATHERING has resources designed to help men become more aware of their own fathering style and then work toward improving their skills.
  Tel.: (913) 384-4661
  e-mail: ncf@aol.com
  www.fathers.com

THE NATIONAL CENTER ON FATHERS AND FAMILIES is a great source of research and data on fathers, father involvement, and so forth.
Tel.: (215) 686-3910
www.ncoff.gse.upenn.edu
fatherfamilylink.gse.upenn.edu/ (links page)

THE NATIONAL FATHERHOOD INITIATIVE offers membership that includes the quarterly newsletter "Fatherhood Today"; updates on family issues and political/legislative developments; the Fatherhood Resource Catalog of books, videos, and audio tapes, offering a discount on all items; and updates on activities and events.
600 Eden Road, Building E
Lancaster, PA 17601
Tel.: (800) 790-DADS or (717) 581-8860
Fax: (717) 581-8862
www.fatherhood.org

Fathers, Divorced or Single

AMERICAN COALITION OF FATHERS AND CHILDREN is dedicated to promoting equal rights of all parties affected by divorce or the breakup of a family. Chapters nationwide.
Tel.: (800) 978-3237
e-mail: info@acfc.org
www.acfc.org

CHILDREN'S RIGHTS COUNCIL has a well-stocked catalog of resources, including a listing of great books on the subject for kids and their parents. Chapters in most states.
Tel.: (301) 559-3120
www.childrens-rights.org

MAKING LEMONADE is an online resource community for single parents. Find support, information, referrals to experts, and a good laugh.
www.makinglemonade.com

Fathers, Older

THE OLDER FATHERS WEB RING is made up of a number of sites created by and for older dads.
www.geocities.com/olderdads/

THE BABY CENTER'S BULLETIN BOARD FOR OLDER FATHERS is a great place to get—and give—advice.
    bbs.babycenter.com/board/baby/dadsbaby/6694

Healthy Living

GREENHOME offers a full range of healthy, eco-friendly products for home and nursery, from paints that don't give off toxic gases to nontoxic insecticides and cleaning products.
    www.greenhome.com

THE GREEN GUIDE is a wonderful newsletter (and Web site) filled with tips for healthy organic living.
    www.thegreenguide.com

Men, General

THE MEN'S HEALTH NETWORK is a national education organization that recognizes men's health as a specific social concern. They have a fantastic database of articles, resources, and links on every conceivable fatherhood issue.
    www.menshealthnetwork.org

MENSTUFF is a huge collection of resources on men, men's health, fatherhood, parenting, relationships, and more.
    www.menstuff.org/resources/resourcefiles/fathers.html

Music

MUSIC TOGETHER
    www.musictogether.com

KINDERMUSIK
    www.kindermusik.com

Both companies offer music and movement programs for infants and their parents. CDs and song books are available. Classes in each method are offered throughout the United States. Listings are available on the Web sites.

Reading

THE AMERICAN LIBRARY ASSOCIATION has reviews of children's books and lists of award winners.
    www.ala.org

CHILDREN'S LITERATURE provides a searchable database of reviews of the latest kids' books.

www.childrenslit.com

CHILDREN'S LITERATURE WEB GUIDE has a wealth of information on children's books, recommendations, and links to other good sites.

www.ucalgary.ca/~dkbrown/

CHINABERRY publishes a wonderful catalog of books for readers (or listeners) of all ages.

www.chinaberry.com

THE HORN BOOK has lists of children's classics, medal winners, and other resources for parents.

www.hbook.com

THE INFANT LEARNING COMPANY produces a set of videos (and DVDs) and books designed to help children of all ages—even infants—learn to read.

www.infantlearning.com

PLANET ESME.COM reviews, rates, and recommends books for kids of all ages.

www.planetesme.com

Sign Language

SIGN2ME offers videos and books based on the work of Joseph Garcia.

www.sign2me.com

BABYSIGNS offers videos and books based on the work of Linda Acredolo and Susan Goodwyn.

www.babysigns.com

Toys and Games

BABY SCHOLARS.COM offers a large selection of toys and games, from classic wooden blocks to the latest computer games.

www.babyscholars.com

DR. TOY provides information, articles, reviews, and recommendations of educational and non-educational (just plain fun) toys. She also has tips on buying toys and top-ten lists for various themes (holidays, travel, and so on).

www.drtoy.com

NATURAL PLAY.COM sells toys and games made from all-natural materials.

www.naturalplay.com

Travel

FAMILY FUN MAGAZINE
family.go.com/travel/

FAMILY TRAVEL FILES.COM
www.thefamilytravelfiles.com

TRAVEL WITH KIDS.COM
www.travelwithkids.com

All three offer tips and recommendations for family vacations, from where to go to what to do when you get there.

Twins and More

PREEMIETWINS.COM is a nice resource for parents of twins born prematurely.
www.preemietwins.com

TOBUYTWO.COM is an auction Web site that features new and used equipment and supplies. Sections for twins, triplets, and more.
www.tobuytwo.com

TWINS MAGAZINE has print and online versions. Both offer advice, anecdotes, facts, support, and resources for parents of twins.
www.twinsmagazine.com

THE TWINS FOUNDATION is a great source for research on twins.
www.twinsfoundation.com

TWINSTUFF.COM is a Web portal for parents of twins and more.
www.twinstuff.com

We're constantly revising and updating this book and are always looking for ways to improve it. So if you have any comments or suggestions, please send them to:
Armin Brott
P.O. Box 16064
Oakland, CA 94610
e-mail: armin@mrdad.com

Acknowledgments

I'd like to thank the following people (roughly in alphabetical order), whose help has made this book far better—and far more accurate—than it otherwise might have been. Some helped with the first edition, some with the second, some with both:

Bob Abrams for his confidence and support; Justin Anderson for everything having to do with teeth; Jim Cameron and the folks at Temperament Talk, whose work on temperament changed my life; Susan Costello for her support, encouragement, patience, and editing skills; Phil and Carolyn Cowan and Ross Parke for their inspiration, suggestions, and for having paved the road; Jackie Decter, for her wisdom, insight, patience, sense of humor, and, above all, her sharp eye; Bruce Drobeck, Bruce Linton, Rob Palkovitz, and Glen Palm, who, completely independently of each other, have made major contributions to the literature on fatherhood and freely shared their research with me; Celia Fuller and Misha Beletsky, for their design contributions; Ken Guilmartin and Edward Gordon for their valuable contributions to the sections on music; Amy Handy, for her constructive criticism and for smoothing out the rough edges; Seth Himmelhoch, who more than once magically pulled out from his files precisely what I needed; Pam Jordan, for her wisdom, guts, and encouragement; Louise Kurtz for supervising the production of this book; Jim Levine, for getting everyone together with a minimum of bloodshed; the wonderful, compassionate, and completely selfless folks at the SIDS Alliance; Dawn Swanson, the incredible children's librarian at the Berkeley Public Library, for her help selecting the best kids' books; my parents, for their hospitality, careful editing, and for not getting too upset when I griped about their parenting techniques—thirty years too late for them to do anything about it; Liz for her careful eye, constant support, and wonderful soul; and finally, to the hundreds of dads—new, expecting, and experienced—I've relied on over the years who bravely and openly shared their insights, thoughts, fears, worries, advice, and wisdom.

Index

ILLUSTRATION CREDITS

Height and Weight Charts

The charts on pp. 318–319 are very similar to the ones used by your child's pediatrician. Please remember that "normal" is something of a sliding scale. As a result, use these charts for reference only. Many factors, including your baby's birth weight, nutrition, and genetics (such as your height and weight) will influence your child's measurements. Don't focus on a single entry: squirming babies are hard to weigh and measure. What's most important is consistency over time. If you and your partner are short and thin and your 6-month-old has been in the 10th percentile since birth, that's probably perfectly normal. However, if your baby was in the 50th percentile in height and weight at one month and drops to the 10th or zooms up to the 90th at three months, there could be a problem. As always, if you're worried about your child's growth, be sure to discuss your concerns with your child's doctor.

Birth to 36 months: Boys

Length-for-age and Weight-for-age percentiles

Birth to 36 months: Girls

Length-for-age and Weight-for-age percentiles

About the Author

A nationally recognized parenting expert, Armin A. Brott is also the author of *The New Father: A Dad's Guide to the First Year, Fathering Your Toddler: A Dad's Guide to the Second and Third Years, Fathering Your School-Age Child: A Dad's Guide to the Wonder Years 3 to 9, The Single Father: A Dad's Guide to Parenting without a Partner,* and *Father for Life: A Journey of Joy, Challenge, and Change.* He has written on parenting and fatherhood for the *New York Times Magazine,* the *Washington Post, Newsweek,* and dozens of other periodicals. He also writes a nationally syndicated column, "Ask Mr. Dad," and hosts "Positive Parenting," a weekly talk show. Armin lives with his family in Oakland, California. To learn more, please visit his Web site, www.mrdad.com.